Computing Calamities

ISBN 0-13-082862-9

Other books by Robert L. Glass:

Prentice-Hall and Yourdon Press:
Software Runaways, 1998
An ISO 9000 Approach to Building Quality Software, 1996
Software Creativity, 1995
Building Quality Software, 1992*
Measuring and Motivating Maintenance Programmers, 1992*
Software Conflict: Essays on the Art and Science of Software Engineering,
    1991
Measuring Software Design Quality, 1990*
Software Communication Skills, 1988*
Real-Time Software, 1983*
Modern Programming Practices: A Report From Industry, 1982*
Software Maintenance Guidebook, 1981*
Software Reliability Guidebook, 1979*

Computing Trends:
Software 2020, 1998
Software Folklore, 1991
Computing Shakeout, 1987
Computing Catastrophes, 1983, 1991
Software Soliloquies, 1981
The Second Coming: More Computing Projects Which Failed, 1980*
The Power of Peonage, 1979*
Tales of Computing Folk: Hot Dogs and Mixed Nuts, 1978*
The Universal Elixir, and Other Computing Projects Which Failed, 1977,
    1979, 1981, 1992

IEEE Computer Society Press:
In the Beginning: Recollections of Software Pioneers, 1998

* Out of print

Computing Trends books are available from 1416 Sare Rd.,
    Bloomington, IN 47401

Computing Calamities

Lessons Learned from Products, Projects,
and Companies that Failed

Robert L. Glass

 Prentice Hall PTR, Upper Saddle River, New Jersey 07458

Library of Congress Cataloging-in-Publication Data

Glass, Robert L.., 1932–
    Computing calamities : lessons learned from products and companies
that failed / Robert L. Glass.
      p. cm.
    ISBN 0-13-082862-9 (pbk.)
    1. Computer industry--United States--Management--Case studies.
2. Computer software industry--United States--Management--Case
studies.   3. Corporate turnarounds--United States--Case studies.
I. Title.
HD9696.2.U62G55   1999
004'.068--dc21   98-40889

Editorial/Production Supervision: *Precision Graphics*
Acquisitions Editor: *Jeffrey Pepper*
Manufacturing Manager: *Alexis R. Heydt*
Marketing Manager: *Dan Rush*
Art Director: *Jerry Votta*
Cover Designer: *Design Source*

Contents

Foreword

In this book, Bob Glass has assembled a fascinating collection of stories about computing companies, projects, and products that failed. While the stories are interesting in their own right, the importance of learning from these failures is underscored by the fact that the world economy has become increasingly dependent on computer technology. Computer hardware and software have become an integral part of products ranging from automobiles to microwave ovens. To most observers, the computer hardware and software that is embedded in these products remains unnoticed—*except,* that is, when it fails. Such failures, when they do occur, can be catastrophic, especially in the context of medical devices. In the mid-1980s, for example, a software bug caused a medical device to deliver huge overdoses of radiation to six cancer patients, ultimately killing three of them. Since 1986, more than 450 reports have been filed with the U.S. Food and Drug Administration concerning software defects in medical devices (Anthes, 1997). The problems associated with computer failures extend beyond medical devices. Listed below are several examples of computer failures that have occurred in other product categories.

◆ During the Gulf War in 1991, a software bug in the targeting software of a Patriot defense missile allowed an Iraqi Scud missile to hit the barracks of American servicemen, killing 29 Americans (Anthes, 1997).

◆ In 1996, General Motors recalled nearly 300,000 automobiles because of a software problem that could cause an engine fire (Anthes, 1997).

◆ In 1998, a satellite that handles most of the pager traffic in the U.S. stopped working when both the primary and the backup computer failed (Thibodeau, 1998).

In addition to safety-related issues that can arise from computer hardware and software failures, computer projects themselves frequently fail and are notorious for going significantly over budget and behind schedule. Based on a survey conducted by the Standish Group, a Massachusetts-based consulting organization, it was revealed that companies in the US alone spend an estimated $81 billion per year on canceled software projects and an additional $59 billion per year in cost overruns for software projects that are eventually completed (Johnson, 1995). Whether these figures are accurate is not the point; the point is that we live in a world that has grown increasingly dependent on computers and that not all computer projects are as successful as we might like them to be. In some cases, mismanagement of software projects means that they escalate out of control, continuing to absorb valuable resources without ever delivering benefits to the organizations that undertake them (Keil, 1995). Consider the following example:

> In 1987, California's Department of Motor Vehicles (DMV) began developing a new information system that would combine the state's driver and vehicle registration databases. By 1990, after $14.8 million had already been spent, there were warning signs that the project was in serious trouble. Yet, according to the state auditor's report on the project, these problems were ignored. Despite two additional reports (in 1991 and 1992) showing further evidence of "serious problems with the project," DMV officials pushed on. Instead of terminating or redirecting the project, they "continued to pour money into the project . . . and, as a result spent an additional $34.6 million on a project that ultimately failed" (Cringely, 1994; Gibbs, 1994; Ellis, 1994).

Unfortunately, the California DMV case is not an isolated example, one need only turn through the pages of this book to find other examples. Indeed, a recent survey sponsored by the Information Systems Audit and Control Association (ISACA) found that 30–40 percent of all software projects experience some degree of project escalation (Keil and Mann, 1997). Why does such escalation occur? Poor project management practice is certainly a contributing factor, but research has also shown that managers have a tendency to become over-committed to failing courses of action. Sometimes, senior management doesn't understand the gravity of the situation until it is too late. In the case of the CONFIRM project undertaken by AMR (in partnership with

Hilton, Marriott, and Budget Rent-A-Car), for example, it seems that employees were aware of project problems but chose to "keep mum," leaving their superiors in the dark (Oz, 1993). In other cases, employees come forward with the bad news and senior management is made aware of the problems but turns a deaf ear to it all. What we see here is that there is no single failure pattern, but instead a complex array of forces that come together. In short, failure can take many forms.

While there are many reasons for taking an interest in computing failures, one of the most compelling in my mind is that failure is an excellent teacher. As Bob Dylan once said in a song lyric: "There's no success like failure and failure's no success at all." Failure analysis is routinely practiced in many disciplines. Students studying Civil Engineering are frequently shown the famous video that graphically illustrates the collapse of the Tacoma Narrows bridge. When aircraft disasters occur, government investigators comb the wreckage looking for clues that will help explain the failure and prevent it from re-occurring. In the computer industry, however, the tradition of learning from failure is not as well established.

In my own research, I have visited companies and encountered many projects in which failure seemed imminent, but nobody was willing to acknowledge this reality. Almost any outsider could walk into such a situation, and in the words of one of my colleagues, see the "moose on the table," but those inside the organization would continue as though the moose didn't exist. Given the growing popularity of such concepts as knowledge management and organizational learning, I find it particularly disturbing when companies ignore the warning signs associated with troubled projects. Then, when these projects fail, there is seldom any effort to systematically learn from that failure; instead the whole episode is swept under the rug. One of the best things about this book is that it encourages us to think about, confront, and learn from failure. As Glass suggests, these stories of failure are "fascinating and fun." The hard part is getting the companies and organizations we work for to embrace failure and to learn from their mistakes.

Mark Keil
Associate Professor, Department
of Computer Information Systems
Georgia State University
June 5, 1998

REFERENCES

Anthes, G. H., Killer apps, *Computerworld,* July 7 1997, 73–74.

Cringely, R. X., When disaster strikes IS, *Forbes ASAP,* August 29, 1994, 60–64.

Gibbs, W. W., Software's chronic crisis, *Scientific American,* (273) 3, 86–95, 1994.

Ellis, V., Audit says DMV ignored warning, *Los Angeles Times,* Los Angeles, August 18, 1994, A3–A24.

Johnson, J., Chaos: The dollar drain of IT project failures, *Application Development Trends,* (2) 1, 41–47, 1995.

Keil, M., Pulling the plug: software project management and the problem of project escalation, *MIS Quarterly,* (19) 4, 421–447, 1995.

Keil, M. and Mann, J., The nature and extent of IT project escalation: results from a survey of IS audit and control professionals, *IS Audit & Control Journal,* (1) 40–48, 1997.

Oz, E., When Professional Standards are Lax: The CONFIRM Failure and Its Lessons, *Communications of the ACM,* (37) 10, 29–36, 1994.

Thibodeau, P., Satellite glitch spawns big headaches, *Computerworld,* May 20, 1998.

About the Author

Robert L. Glass has meandered the halls of computing for over 40 years now, starting with a three-year gig in the aerospace industry (at North American Aviation) in 1954–1957, which makes him one of the true pioneers of the software field.

That stay at North American extended into several other aerospace appearances (at Aerojet-General Corp., 1957–1965) and the Boeing Company, 1965–1970 and 1972–1982). His role was largely that of building software tools used by applications specialists. It was an exciting time to be part of the aerospace business—those were the heady days of space exploration, after all—but it was an even headier time to be part of the computing field. Progress in both fields was rapid, and the vistas were extraterrestrial!

The primary lesson he learned during those aerospace years was that he loved the technology of software, but hated being a manager. He carefully cultivated the role of technical specialist, which had two major impacts on his career: (a) his technical knowledge remained fresh and useful, but (b) his knowledge of management—and his earning power (!)—were diminished commensurately.

When his upwards mobility had reached the inevitable technological Glass ceiling (tee-hee!), Glass took a lateral transition into academe. He taught in the Software Engineering graduate program at Seattle University (1982–1987) and spent a year at the (all-too-academic!) Software Engineering Institute (1987–1988). (He had earlier spent a couple of years (1970–1972) working on a tools-focused research grant at the University of Washington).

The primary lesson he learned during those academic years was that he loved having his Head in the academic side of software engineering, but his Heart remained in its practice. You can take the man out of industry, apparently, but you can't take the industry out of the man. With that new-found wisdom, he began to search for ways to bridge what he had long felt was the "Communication Chasm" between academic computing and its practice.

He found several ways of doing that. Many of his books (over 20) and professional papers (over 60) focus on trying to evaluate academic computing findings and on transitioning those with practical value to industry. (This is decidedly a non-trivial task, and is largely responsible for the contrarian nature of his beliefs and his writings). His lectures and seminars on software engineering focus on both theoretical and best-of-practice findings that are useful to practitioners. His two newsletters, *The Software Practitioner* and *PERC* (Practical Emerging Research Concepts in Information Technology), tread those same paths. So does the (more academic) *Journal of Systems and Software,* which he edits for Elsevier. And so do the columns he writes regularly for such publications as *Communications of the ACM, IEEE Software, Journal of Systems and Software, Managing System Development,* and ACM SIGMIS's *Data Base.* Although most of his work is serious and contrarian, a fair portion of it also contains (or even consists of!) computing humor.

With all of that in mind, what is his proudest moment in the computing field? The award, by Linkoping University of Sweden, of his honorary Ph.D. degree in 1995.

Introduction: What's So Great About Failure?

Do computing companies and projects fail more often than other companies and projects?

Sometimes it feels like it. There, on the nightly news, is yet another tale of woe, a story related to computing that shows some stupid computing system doing something that no sensible human being would ever have done. There, in the computing literature, are the findings of yet another survey saying that 57%, or 68%, or 95% of computing projects fail. There, on the Nightly Business Report, is the story of a computing company whose stock just did a nose-dive into obscurity.

But there is something, I want to say, badly wrong with that picture. For every stupid computer trick on the nightly news, there are a hundred interactions that all of us have with a variety of computing systems on a daily basis where nothing whatsoever goes wrong. For every survey finding showing that an enormous number of computing projects fail, there are systems up and running and doing precisely what they are supposed to do, in companies ranging from the Fortune 500 to the not-so-Fortunate 5,000,000. For every stock nose-dive on NBR, there are stratospheric rises of some other computing company's stock. Something is wrong with that picture, indeed!

To be honest, I don't quite understand what's going on. I read those surveys by quite reputable companies that say things like "84% of US IT projects fail to meet original expectations and 94% of those started have to be restarted" (the Standish Group, published in 1997), and 85% of UK companies "reported problems with systems projects that were either late, over budget, or that fail to deliver planned benefits" (Coopers & Lybrand's Computer Assurance Services risk management group, also published in 1997). And I see lots of other data points that come out telling a roughly similar story.

But the more of those stories I read, the more perplexed I get. For one thing, although lots of these stories quote high percentages of computing project failure, there's very little consistency in the numbers. For example, Standish, which gave us the 84% and 94% figures I quoted above, gave us another set of data in 1995 and 1996; they said (for 1995) that 31% of projects failed and 53% were "challenged," and (for 1996) 40% failed and 33% were "challenged." Other figures from other sources tell a similarly inconsistent story. I could find you data saying that the correct percentage of failed computer projects is 46%, or 62%, or 81%, or any number you'd care to name. And the dilemma here is, those figures simply can't all be right!

I'm a professional in the computing field. I've participated in a lot of projects over the years. Some of them failed. A lot more of them didn't. I very strongly believe that those failure numbers, the ones I've been quoting to you above, are very sincerely obtained—and very wrong!

Some of my best friends in college (ah, those days have long been gone!) were ministerial students. When they wanted to say something nice about the trial sermon that one of them had just given but there was little to compliment, they would say "Well, you were sincere!" That's the sense in which I use the word "sincere" to describe my computing colleagues who generate or quote those failure statistics! I don't think any of them are being insincere; I just think their numbers are relatively worthless.

Let me tell you a story about computing failure stories. Several years ago, it was popular for people who studied the field of computing to speak of a "software crisis." When they named that crisis, what they really meant was that software had the reputation of being "always behind schedule, over budget, and unreliable." To support their declaration of a crisis, they would often quote numbers from a study by a US Government watchdog agency, the Government Accounting Office (GAO), which showed that a very high percentage of government software projects they tracked had failed.

The use of these GAO numbers persisted for several years. Then a colleague of mine got curious about the GAO report, and read the original study. He discovered, much to his surprise (and what should have been the chagrin of many computing professionals), that the study was being misinterpreted. The GAO had found a high percentage of failed projects, but the projects it had tracked were already in trouble when the GAO began studying them! In other words, the simple and clear message of the GAO study was that a large percentage of software projects that got into trouble never rose above that trouble. And anyone who used that study to try to show anything else—for example, that a large percentage of *all* software projects failed—had misunderstood the data.

Call me crazy, but I think a lot of that computing project failure data, when the smoke all clears away, will be of this kind. Misused numbers. Failures to use agreed-upon definitions of terms. Gathering information from biased sources. Making up numbers to fit a preconceived notion.

So, given all of that, what the heck am I doing writing a book about computing calamities? Doesn't a book telling computing failure stories tend to reinforce the notion that computing failure is common? Shouldn't I be trying to write a book about computing successes, instead, to prove the point I apparently so deeply believe in?

There are several reasons why I have chosen to write this book on failure:

1. Failure is a far stronger learning experience than success. I hope that these stories of failure will contain some lessons learned of value to you.

2. Failure is just plain fun! I have no idea why we human beings laugh at pies in the face and pratfalls down a flight of stairs, but it seems—for better or worse—to be part of our humanity. I think you're going to enjoy reading the things I've written.

3. Success is transient. I once added a success story to an earlier book I wrote about failure. It told the story of the Intel 286 chip, and what a great design it was. Ten years or so have now passed since I put that book together. Every single one of the other stories in that book is still up-to-date—none of the failed projects I wrote about ever came back to life! But the 286 is ancient history. And that story dates the book like nothing else I said in it.

4. I'm a failure nut! This isn't, as I hinted above, the first book I've written about computing failure. I once wrote a column for *Computerworld,* way back in the 1960s, which consisted largely of computing failure stories. (The column used disguised names for the people and places whose stories I told, and I wrote it under an assumed name, Miles Benson!) I collected those columns into a couple of self-published books in the 1970s. I also gathered stories about early computing companies and projects that failed, both during the mainframe era and the early microcomputer era, and published those books during the 1980s. And, in fact, I wrote a predecessor to this book, *Software Runaways,* which Prentice-Hall published in 1998 (actually, the fall of 1997—like car companies, publishers label books that come out in the fall with the model year still to come!), and which has sold quite handsomely (perhaps that's why you're reading this one!)

The question that began this chapter of the book was "What's so great about failure?" I think I've given you at least an implicit answer to that question. Failure is a learning experience. Failure is fun. Success is transient, and failure usually isn't. Failure never quits happening.

Many of the failure stories I have published over the years were written by someone else. I take a hunter-gatherer approach to these stories, reading quite a bit of the computing literature and a slice of the more general literature, looking for in-depth reports by careful journalists who have pursued a computing failure story and come up with a well-told, fact-based, human-interest-focused tale. Nearly all of the stories in this book are from sources other than me, from publications ranging from *Computerworld* to the *Wall Street Journal.* (The source of each story is found at the beginning of the story.)

I love gathering and telling these failure stories. Not because they prove a point—as you have already seen, I don't believe they do—but because I personally find them fascinating and fun.

I hope you do, too!

Robert L. Glass
Summer, 1998

Overview: The Many Faces of Failure

Most of us feel that failure is a bad thing, something to be avoided at all costs. For the most part, we are right in that feeling. Failed projects can be detrimental to your professional health. Careers rarely get destroyed by too much success!

This book is a collection of stories about failure. In the chapters following this one, we will tell war stories about computing companies and projects and products that went down in (usually, figurative!) flames. Most of the people involved in those stories would rather not have been among the key players named. Do you want your name and professional reputation attached to a failed project and discussed on the nightly news?

Still, there is more than one facet to failure. In this section of the book, we'll do a little (rah-rah) "cheerleading" about failure. Perhaps surprisingly, there are some good things to say about being involved in companies or projects that turn bad. Let's get those things out of the way here. They need to be said, because there are things to be salvaged from failure, and it's wise to know what those things are and how one goes about it.

But, to be honest, there's a certain pie-in-the-face fun quality to failure stories. It may not be to our credit as human beings, but we enjoy watching other people's failures, especially when there is no hint in the failure story that it involves us in any way! That's why most of this book is about failure. It's simply a fun subject to read about.

For now, though, let's take a look at failure in a positive light.

2.1   WHEN FAILURE MEANS SUCCESS

One of my favorite books is *To Engineer Is Human*. Henry Petroski, in that book, takes the position that failure is an inevitable component of success. He makes the point that the more we fail, the more we learn from that failure. And the more we learn, the more likely we are to succeed in our next venture. In other words, failure begets success.

Petroski is right, of course. There are plenty of brilliant success stories that emerge from a terrible history of failure. Hershey of Hershey's chocolates, for example, had failed in many ventures before he came up with the candy bar that made him famous way back then—and to this day. President Harry Truman was a failed haberdasher early in his career, and his bankruptcy became grist for the presidential election campaign, which he won in spite of that history. There are plenty of people who have built their success on a foundation of failure. Fill in your own favorite examples here!

In this section, we present an article that advises us not to avoid failure, but to actively court it. For one thing, says its author, it is common to learn more from failure than success. He describes a company where "falling forward" is advocated. That means that the employees of the company are encouraged to take positive risks, and failure is seen as one honorable byproduct of risk-taking. (A more desirable byproduct, of course, is success, which is why the falling is seen as "forward"—the expectation is that the risk-taking will more often move the enterprise forward than backward.)

The author notes a study showing that "more than 80% of new IS initiatives fail to meet at least one predefined goal." This does not indicate that the initiative has failed, the author points out—there are normally many additional predefined goals that *are* achieved.

One CIO quoted in the story even attributes his bank's dominant competitive position to its "encouragement of risk taking and its acceptance of failure."

"If you're not failing, you're not serious about new ideas," another IT players says.

Are you beginning to get the feeling that failure isn't the worst thing that could happen to you? That stagnancy is far worse? If you are, then you get the point. Read on into the rah-rah world of failure as a means to success!

THE SWEET SMELL OF FAILURE

by Alan S. Horowitz

Wells Fargo Bank has a good market-share chunk of customers who use online banking—about 500,000 of the bank's 4 million users worldwide, says Barry Lynn, the bank's vice president and chief information officer.

Sounds like quite a success. It is now, but it wasn't always. "We developed our Internet site three times before it worked right," Lynn admits. An unfriendly graphical user interface and a confusing sign-up procedure were a couple of reasons the project failed initially.

Failure. It's often easier to avoid than accept. And many in information systems will do almost anything other than risk failure. Yet some people think failure is helpful, even desirable. Bill Walsh, former coach of the National Football League's San Francisco 49ers, wrote the following in *Forbes ASAP*: "The key to long-range success in sports—and in business—isn't how you deal with winning but how you deal with losing."

In fact, if you rank experiences, failure is among the most valuable because it's common to learn more from failure than from success.

If you're highly risk-averse, know that it's possible to fail and still survive. And that the benefits of taking risks often outweigh the consequences of blowing it. Here are some failure rules to live by:

Concretely Demonstrate Your Support of Failure

Many IS managers say they encourage failure, but then don't back that up. Not Lynn. To reflect his notion that failure is good, Lynn has a program he calls "falling forward," so named to demonstrate that falling can propel an individual—and an organization—to new successes. Each month, an internal publication at the bank has a falling forward story that gives kudos to those who failed with honor (robustly, as it were).

But Lynn does differentiate between types of failures. He breaks them down into two categories: stupid, uncaring failures, in which the individual who failed should be punished; and calculated risks or honest mistakes, which were risk-worthy and valuable learning experiences.

The latter is the type of failure Lynn tolerates, even promotes.

Forget Avoiding Failure

There's evidence that working to avoid failure can be a fool's game. Fred Magee, vice president and research director at Gartner Group, Inc., in Stamford, Conn., studied failure and found that more than 80% of all new IS initiatives failed to meet at least one predefined goal. Magee doesn't view this as bad; instead he considers it primarily a question of perception. "Best-in-class organizations recognize that no complex project succeeds in accomplishing all it was designed for. [It] recognizes that the modern IT infrastructure is a continuum of planned and unplanned change," he wrote in a July 1996 research report.

Someone once observed that tennis star Jimmy Connors never lost a match, he just ran out of time—a reflection of his never-give-up, never-fail attitude. Darwin A. John, managing director of information and communication systems at The Church of Jesus Christ of Latter-day Saints in Salt Lake City, holds the same view. "Lots of progress is made by what we might label as failure [that] you can also label as small progress or learning," John says.

Author and management guru Tom Peters berates IS folk, proclaiming, "[Failure] is normal, for God's sake! What I want to tell [IS managers] is that if they're not failing, then they're not serious about the new technologies. Because nobody knows how all this is going to sort itself out." A lot of time and energy can be wasted trying to avoid the inevitable—failure.

Failure Isn't Fatal—if You're Trusted

Eileen Strider, a principal at Strider and Cline consulting firm in Kansas City, Mo., until recently was CIO at Universal Underwriters Insurance Group. While there, she hired an outside vendor to develop a system. One year and about a million dollars later, she gave up and canceled the project.

Her head didn't roll, which she attributes to several things she did. Strider held weekly meetings with the business side to tell them how the project was going, was honest and open about the project's progress and established trust between her and the project's other important layers, including the CEO and the lead person on the business side.

"I think if the senior business person and my boss, the CEO, had not known me and known my intentions were good and I was trying very hard, I think they would have fired me," she says. Gain the trust and respect of those in your organization, and your chances of losing your head decline.

The Truth Helps

Be truthful. David Schmaltz, president of True North PGS, Inc., a project management consulting firm in Portland, Ore., recently worked on a project for a manufacturer in which management gave IS an "impossible" deadline. Previously, IS would have just gone ahead as if it could make deadline and then at a really inconvenient time, the truth would be disclosed, Schmaltz says. "This time they decided they would speak the truth," he says.

Top management didn't want to hear it, but eventually a compromise was reached: A series of milestones were set so any slip-ups would be revealed earlier rather than later. "They still have an impossible date, but they have a process where they can talk about more truth as their experience tells them what's really going to happen," Schmaltz says. The end result: No one got hurt as a result of failing to meet the original deadline.

Unprogram the Fear of Failure

Although failure is natural, we often take unnatural steps to avoid it. IS managers must reprogram their employees to accept failure. That was demonstrated to Magee when he spoke with a CIO who asked a team of employees to work with customers to learn how to best use various technologies. He didn't want success stories, he wanted war stories—things that worked and especially, things that didn't.

What didn't work was the project itself. The CIO wanted his team members to learn from their failures. But they were programmed to succeed and felt uncomfortable with failure. So they refused to fail. "The team was incapable—without extra training—of failing," Magee says. You will likely need to train your people to feel comfortable with failure.

A Technique to Turn Your People into Risk-takers

When Naomi Karten, now a management consultant in Randolph, Mass., was a CIO, she fostered risk-taking by giving each of her employees two small and one large peel-and-stick dots, along with a set of rules governing their use. "These allowed each person two small screw-ups and one outrageous screw-up during the course of a year," she says. Her employees incurred no negative consequences as long as they turned in the appropriate dot and told her what had happened. If she heard about a screw-up from someone else, the guilty party was in big trouble. "It created a culture of 'nobody's perfect.' We can be human and still survive," she says.

"You have to manage by example," Lynn says. If you want to promote risk-taking in your organization, you have to make it clear you're willing to live with failure. That's why he publicizes failures and rewards them.

Encourage your people to admit failure early, while the costs are still low, Karten recommends.

And create a risk-accepting culture. "Anyone can buy the same expertise we can. So we really have to [create] a culture and start taking more risks and experimenting more." Is there a payoff for risking failure? Lynn thinks there is. He attributes his bank's dominant position in the online banking industry in large part to his encouragement of risk-taking and accepting failure. Small failures can add up to major successes.

2.2   THE ROLE OF THE WHITE KNIGHT

Just because failure can lead to success (as we just finished reading in the previous section of this book), it doesn't mean we should accept failure when it hits us.

In fact, there are people who make a career out of fighting corporate failure. We call them "White Knights," and they ride to the rescue of companies in trouble, bringing a set of failure-fighting skills with them. They are the Red Adairs of the executive suite. (Adair is the man who is called in to extinguish those terrible and out-of-control oil field fires, such as the ones that continued burning in Kuwait long after the military fighting had stopped.)

In the article "Miracle Men" that follows, we look at the failure fighters of the computing world, the "turnaround managers" who leap into the fray to reverse the terminal course of the company that seeks their services. How great is the need for such people? One industry observer tells us that "at any one time, one in three companies in the high-tech industry is in trouble."

What kind of a job is this? It is, the author of "Miracle Men" tells us, "fraught with personal risk," and "requires a ruthless streak." Then why do people do it? Because it's a personal challenge of the highest order. Because the successful turnaround specialist will make an enormous amount of money.

What does the turnaround specialist do? There's no set formula, of course, since the actions must be very enterprise-dependent. But some things are a given—sell off non-core products, business units, and land or buildings; cut expenses, especially via massive layoffs; restructure the debt and funding; and initiate promising new, long-term projects. Quickly. Boldly. Decisively.

How much danger is present for this turnaround specialist? We see, in what follows, the story of one CEO who installed bullet-proof glass in his office windows. Obviously, leading a troubled company—or attempting to turn one around—is not a task for the faint hearted!

In learning about these computing turnaround specialists, we are exploring yet another of the many faces of failure. The number of turnaround successes—and the article that follows names specific and successful people and companies—is mightily encouraging. In this section of the book, we are still in the rah-rah phase of our computing failure stories!

MIRACLE MEN

by Kenny MacIver

Del Yocam was at home in Lake Tahoe, California reading the newspaper. It was 1992 and his 10 years at Apple Computer during the 1980s, where he had risen to be chief operating officer, had left him wealthy enough to retire at age 45.

That day he read: "The key years in an executive's working life are 45 to 50—that is when they make most money and when they make most impact." It set him thinking, and by coincidence, he got a call the next day from Apple's former general counsel who was working for hardware technology giant Tektronix.

The Wilsonville, Oregon-based company was in bad shape: Sales had been stagnant at $1.3 billion for four years and earnings were on a downward spiral. The crunch had now come: Tektronix's weakened financial state had attracted the attention of financial speculator George Soros, who had bought 14.9% of its stock with a view to taking control of the company, dissecting it and selling off its four major units. To make Soros go away, Tektronix needed to be turned around—fast.

Jerry Meyer, the company's CEO, flew down to see Yocam. He argued that the former Apple executive was one of the few people in the industry with sufficient operational metal to save Tektronix. Within a matter of days the initially reluctant Yocam was exchanging Lake Tahoe for Lake Oswego, Oregon, taking up the position of president and chief operating officer of Tektronix.

For Yocam, Tektronix was the first of a series of corporate encounters that have earnt him a reputation as a highly-effective turnaround manager. After his three years with the company, he retired again, taking up non-executive board positions with eight technology companies, several of which needed nursing back to health. Then in the fall of 1996, he got another irresistible call. This time the board of Borland were after a track-record turnaround executive to halt the implosion at the programming software maker.

Originally published in Global Technology Business, *February 1991. Used with permission.*

Sick Companies

Demand for executives such as Yocam has never been higher. In an industry where the life span of some technologies is a matter of months and where companies constantly vie to outdo each others' innovations, there are naturally going to be more companies like Borland and Tektronix than there are flawless success stories. In the past, failed companies may have been absorbed by acquisitive rivals, but the sheer numbers of companies either funded via stock markets or from venture capital sources means that many that hit trouble have to be salvaged in some other way.

Companies that a few years ago would have been sold, closed or asset stripped, are now being pulled back from the edge of disaster by turnaround teams. Sapiens, Borland, Seer, Dynasty, are all examples from the application development software sector alone, but there are plenty of others elsewhere in the industry including Wang, the computer services company, Object Design, the object database company, and QSP, the financial application specialist.

As often as not, the task is handed to a seasoned troubleshooter—an executive who may not be a turnaround veteran but who is a sharp-thinking, gutsy manager capable of boiling the company down to its bare bones and getting it re-started, says Igor Sill, general partner at investment and executive search company, the GenevaGroup.

The roll call here is extensive: Ray Lane, who was lured from consultancy Booz Allen & Hamilton in the early 1990s to put Oracle back on track; former 3Com star Bob Finocchio, currently charged with doing the same for Informix; David House, who has completed most of the fix at Bay networks; Lou Gerstner at IBM; and many others. But the real experts are an elite group of individuals who, by design or caprice, have set themselves apart as serial turnaround artists.

And there is certainly plenty of material for them to work with, says self-styled 're-positioning specialist', Peter Boni, currently working on a long haul turnaround at Cayenne Software. At any one time, he says, "One in three companies in the high-tech industry is in trouble."

Not that many executives want the job. The role of the turnaround manager is fraught with personal risk and requires a truly ruthless streak. Being associated with a failure is bad enough; showing you cannot stop the rot can bring a career to an abrupt halt. The CEO headhunters are hardly circling around Gil Amelio, for example, after his stint at Apple. But the upside for a successful turnaround executive is considerable: Not only is there the prestige that will take him or her to the next high profile job, but bringing a company back from a near-death experience brings huge financial rewards.

But who are these executives that have emerged as master turnaround artists and what do they undertake? What formula and skills do they possess that help them restore revenue growth, profitability and a re-elevated share price? And what motivates them to put their reputation on the line time and time again?

The Right Stuff

Not surprisingly, the job itself is at its least attractive early on. When a turnaround specialist arrives on the scene, employees—at least those that remain—are often disillusioned and shareholders are out of pocket.

Witness Tektronix circa 1992: "It was nasty there at the beginning," says Yocam. "George Soros' team had absolutely destroyed the CEO, Jerry Meyer, who even went as far as installing bullet proof glass in the windows of his new office. The atmosphere was bloody." It got a lot worse before it got better.

Yocam applied what is widely regarded as classic turnaround medicine—a cure few executives have the breadth of skills or the boldness to apply. To save the company, noncore products and business units were sold off; excess land and buildings were disposed of; expenses were cut by roughly a third through a massive headcount reduction; debt was restructured and new funding and a line of credit established; and at the same time, a series of new product projects were initiated to foster a basis for future revenue growth should the company survive.

According to Yocam and his peers, the measure of a turnaround manager is to act like this—boldly and decisively. "It takes courage and inspiration. You've got to do it hard and fast," agrees Peter Boni.

Other key skills include being financially astute, having a wide network of high-level industry contacts, and being technologically savvy. But foremost, and of greatest urgency, is to be a money guy, says Sill. "The bleeding has got to stop instantaneously, even if the new CEO cuts way too deep. The inexperienced guys are the ones that do multiple cuts because they can't get it right."

But the immediate financial problem is by no means the only one. While stabilizing the patient, the future basis for recovery must be established, something that is often as much a public relations exercise as it is a means of forecasting market demand. Turnaround specialists typically get on the road early into their appointment, spending the best part of the first two or three months calming the nerves of existing customers and asking them where they would like the company to go next.

Such customer interaction begets an initial candor. Tom Wilson, who took on the job of saving Seer Technologies from oblivion, says he could hardly believe some of the activities at the application development company. "At $90 million the company hit a wall. It was a mess. They were spending money wildly. The lights were on but nobody was home, except for the techno-Nazis who controlled the company, even though the customers were saying [some aspects of the] product sucked."

On arrival, he swiftly cut $19 million out of expenses and closed offices, including one of the two offices in London and the half-used 50,000 square feet facility in New York. When the company got back into profit mid-last year—albeit with earnings of a 1 [cent] per share—Wilson presented each employee with a single penny encased in clear glass as a symbol of its turning point.

Maximizing Value

When they get it right, the results of turnaround professionals' effort can be highly impressive. When he took over the running of Tektronix, Yocam found the company with dwindling earnings, stagnant revenues of $1.3 billion and only 22% of sales coming from new products. By the time he left after three years, profits had bounced back to $81 million, revenues had grown to $1.5 billion and an impressive 55% of sales were coming from new products.

Not every company can be saved, though. There has to be a certain base level of revenue and expertise that can be built on. "You have to make sure you keep the products that are paying the bills while starting new product initiatives that implement the new strategic direction you set for the company," says Yocam. But if the company is short on those, there are still other tactics that can be applied.

When Peter Boni came to Bachman Information Systems, the computer aided software engineering (CASE) firm that pre-dated Cayenne, he had to deal with the fact that, in a matter of quarters, the share price had fallen from $37 to $2. The collapse was linked to Bachman tying its future to IBM's life cycle development strategy, AD/Cycle, something that had led Bachman to focus on mainframe tools and IBM's OS/2.

Boni's strategy was to shift the R&D base towards client/server tools for modeling and database design, and also to start embracing object-oriented modeling and construction technology. The first of those new lines came out in 1Q95 and by December of that year, the company's software license revenues were again growing. That helped push the share price from $2 to $6, a swing that allowed the company to acquire object-oriented tools vendor Cadre Technologies in July 1996. Now half of the company's revenues come from those newer product lines, compared to a year ago when two thirds came from OS/2 and mainframe software.

It may seem like a tortuous process, but Boni insists there are no quick fixes. "Company's don't get into problems in weeks and it takes more than a quarter to make them buoyant again." And at Cayenne the turnaround is far from complete—or even certain. The company closed 1997 with a share price just over $2.

In comparison to Boni's two decades of turnaround experience, many get drawn into the role somewhat reluctantly. Yocam, for example, had not planned on another active management role after Tektronix. Having retired for a second time, he had turned down many approaches from the boards and investors of weakened companies before he was persuaded by a veteran Borland board member that there was an intriguing and potentially lucrative opportunity he could not let pass. "After five years of declining revenues and net income, they were going down for the count," he says.

On joining as CEO in December 1996, he set what seemed unrealistic goals: "Stability, profitability and revenue growth within six months." He brought in a completely new management team and speeded up a previously sluggish flow of new products, releasing at least one major new product every quarter. That helped regulate revenues but to put the company on the road to profitability, in February 1997 he axed headcount by a third. At the same time he went out and found fresh funding in the form of a $100 million line of credit.

But the key for Borland—as with many turnaround candidates—has been to move the company out of its tired market niche and to apply its traditional skill base to areas where demand is stronger, margins more attractive, and competition less fierce. The company's strategy has been to shift away from its traditional base of shrink-wrapped programmer's products and to re-position as a vendor of cross-platform, corporate development/middleware software.

At the end of March 1997, Yocam's new business plan was in place for fiscal year 1998. By the end of the first quarter at June 30, Borland was showing revenue growth of 10% and $79,000 of profit versus a loss of $21.9 million in the previous year. The next quarter, revenues rose 8% to $42.5 million and net income jumped to $1.5 million from a $14.3 million loss.

That gave Yocam confidence to go after additional technology for growth. The previous management had bought Open Environment Corp, a middleware application development company that had used DCE (the distributed computing environment) to help corporate customers integrate different vendors' software. The follow-on acquisition—of Visigenic, in November 1997, for $130 million in stock—added products for meshing applications with standard relational database technology, allowing such systems software to better reflect a corporation's individual business model.

The pattern of Borland's product base has already shifted dramatically: A year ago 8% of revenue came from client/server or enterprise products; by late 1997, 47% of revenue was coming from that higher-priced, higher margin area.

What has made those efforts at Borland a success so far, is the latitude given to Yocam by the company's board. Wresting control from the incumbent management team and founders is crucial, says Sill at the GenevaGroup. "Turnarounds are tough to engineer unless you have full control."

That was something Ian Stewart insisted on when appointed at CEO of UK-based applications software company QSP. Stewart was working in Dallas for telecoms switch maker DSC, "sorting out their international sales operation" when QSP's chairman made contact after a desperate period in 1995/96 when profits had evaporated and the share price had collapsed by two-thirds.

Stewart attacked from the top downwards, cutting out most of the nine board members, including CEO and founder Alan Mordain. The new CEO also set about changing the revenue base of the company: The 2 to 1 ratio of product licenses to service was moved to 1 to 1 and will go to 1 to 2, says Stewart. That will help "de-risk" the company, stopping a dependence on individual product orders. The product strategy is to leverage the company's strong base of existing applications by integrating them with the Internet. QSP will finish 1997 with net profits up from a negligible amount in 1996 to £2 million ($3.3 million), on revenue up 18% to £30 million ($50 million), say financial analysts in London.

Money From Nothing

As such turnarounds start to kick in, resumes again begin to flow, with candidates keen to pick up low cost stock options that have lots of potential. That too is the primary motivator for the turnaround artists themselves. "What gets people involved in turnaround situations? Personal wealth," says Yocam unequivocally. When he arrived at Tektronix, his large block of options was priced at $15.50 per share. When he left three years later, he sold out in the $50 to $60 range. At Borland, his options are $5.50, and in the first year the value of those has doubled. His aim is to double that again this year and next.

But for such executives the lure of engineering a turnaround is more than just that financial bonanza. It almost always goes back to the idea of making an impact that Yocam read about in 1992. "It is putting everything on the line for the chance of success," he says. "It is risk-taking coupled with luck, where luck is the point where experience meets opportunity." And there is lots of opportunity.

2.3   HOW TO AVOID STEPPING IN SOMETHING

Failure fighting must begin long before the White Knights and Red Adairs of the world are called in, of course. The people intimately associated with a failure-to-be are the first line of defense, the failure-fighters who have first cut at trying to stem the oncoming disastrous tide.

What can the people most intimately connected with a potential failure do to ward it off? How can they see it coming? The article that follows, "When Bad Things Happen to Good Projects," answers those questions and several more.

For example, it lists

1. the seven deadly sins of project management (the ones most likely to help cause a failure),

2. 10 signs of an onrushing Information Systems project failure,

and then

3. three criteria for canceling a project.

Talk about covering all facets of the dilemma!

In this final section of chapter 2, we are still involved in fighting failure. The author of the article to follow says "It is better to make a decision, be wrong, and then fix the situation than to make no decision at all and let the world pass you by." The hope or expectation is that, with appropriate early action, failure can be averted. Or if it cannot be averted, then there are good ways and bad ways to go about canceling out. In other words, we are still in the rah-rah phase of failure stories.

In the section after this one, though, we will begin swapping true failure stories in earnest. Be patient!

WHEN BAD THINGS HAPPEN TO GOOD PROJECTS

by Tom Field

In 1993, the Oregon Department of Motor Vehicles embarked on what was reported to be a five-year, $50 million project to computerize its paper-based records. By improving the DMV's access to license and vehicle registration data, state officials thought they could downsize the DMV workforce by one-fifth and save $7.5 million annually.

After two years, the five-year project's completion date crept to 2001, and the estimated total budget ballooned to $123 million. Finally, in 1996, a prototype was rolled out, but, according to one consultant brought in to examine the project, the system was fired up on a Monday, and by midweek the DMV test office had longer lines than ever backed up around the block. The new system was a total failure. Soon after, in response to public outcry, state officials killed the project. In the aftermath, the only downsizing that occurred was among the DMV officials who oversaw this disaster, and now there's an active movement among voters to privatize Oregon's DMV.

If only that case were the exception among IT projects. But it's not even the only DMV meltdown—California's $45 million boondoggle in the early '90s earned great notoriety—and it's just one dramatic example of project failures that plague most IS organizations. The Standish Group International Inc., a Dennis, Mass.-based consultancy whose landmark 1995 "Chaos Report" opened people's eyes to the ugly realities of IS project failure, has turned up some new findings in its current research:

♦   Forty percent of IT application development projects are canceled before completion;

♦   Thirty-three percent of the remaining projects are "challenged" by cost/time overruns or changes in scope;

♦   Together, failed and challenged projects cost U.S. companies and government agencies an estimated $145 billion per year.

Some IS projects are doomed by complicated corporate politics or technological evolution—both business needs and IT tools, after all, are subject to change. James H. Johnson, chairman of The Standish

Originally published in CIO, October 15, 1997. Used with permission. Reprinted through the courtesy of CIO. © 1998 Communications, Inc.

Group, has a pet catch phrase built around this theme: Complexity causes confusion and costs. Beyond Johnson's "four C's," project management experts say, IT projects often die simply because IS departments fail to follow the basic project management principles that help ensure project success in the engineering and construction industries. "It's all very basic," says Tom Jones, an Electronic Data Systems Corp. (EDS) account manager who brings to his engagements 25 years of engineering/construction project management experience. "There are a lot of excuses [among IS professionals] about how the new technologies are unstable or the IS organizations are constantly changing, but to me, project management is project management."

Why Projects Fail

IS projects are often doomed from the start because developers fail either to properly assess users' needs or to accurately define the project's scope—or both. The Oregon DMV case is a prime example of the latter. "All the [state's procurement and development] rules were followed," says Peter M. Dolan, president of PhDesigns Group Inc., an independent Ukiah, Calif.-based consultancy, who was called in to assess the project in its latter stages. "The vendor delivered everything it said it would, when it said it would." The problem was no one ever thought to have the vendor actually *integrate* the new system." There

---

Lost Along the Way
10 signs of IS failure

1. Project managers don't understand users' needs
2. Scope is ill-defined
3. Project changes are managed poorly
4. Chosen technology changes
5. Business needs change
6. Deadlines are unrealistic
7. Users are resistant
8. Sponsorship is lost
9. Project lacks people with appropriate skills
10. Best practices and lessons are ignored

was no requirement for there to be a tangible result [of the project]," Dolan says, "just that there be a strict process."

Jones, who currently manages EDS's engagement at engineering giant Bechtel Group Inc. in Houston, tells a similar horror story from his past experience: Two years ago, a large engineering/construction company was hired by six nuclear power plants to design a system that would measure radiation levels in employees who work in the plants' "hot" areas. Soon after signing a lump-sum, multimillion-dollar contract, the developer ran into trouble. No detailed scope of work for the project existed—it was all conceptual—and there was no definition of "complete." The nuclear plants and the developer had far different ideas about when and how this project would end. Eventually, all parties ended up back at the bargaining table to resolve these differences, and in the end, no one was happy, Jones says. "The company lost $7 million to $8 million on the project, and the clients didn't get everything they thought they'd get," Jones says. "It was lose-lose."

The other failure factor that goes hand in hand with scope definition is scope creep: midcourse project changes that often lead to cost and time overruns. In traditional construction projects, proposed revisions are subject to a strict review and approval process—they require formal change orders. Not so in IS projects, where unchecked changes often wreak havoc on deadline and budgets. "There is a reluctance to tell customers—especially internal customers—that they can't change their minds without paying more," Jones says. "But I'm a big believer in internal contracts" that spell out a formal change process.

Other common causes of project failure include loss of executive sponsorship and lack of people with appropriate skills dedicated to the project. Blame also can be shouldered by external consultants, who almost ensure project failures, says The Standish Group's Johnson. "They're not paid on the success of a project," Johnson says. "They're paid on hours billed."

Gopal K. Kapur, president of the San Ramon, Calif.-based Center for Project Management (CPM), points a finger at IS management. "CIOs are one of the major reasons for project failure," Kapur says. "Too many are not fluent in project management practices and principles. They couldn't recognize them if their lives depended on it." As a result, Kapur says, IS projects commonly fall victim to what he calls Management's Seven Deadly Sins:

◆   Mistaking half-baked ideas for viable projects

◆   Dictating unrealistic project deadlines

◆   Assigning underskilled project managers to high-complexity projects

◆   Not ensuring solid business sponsorship

◆   Failing to break projects into manageable "chunks"

◆   Failing to institute a robust project process architecture

◆   Not establishing a comprehensive project portfolio to track progress of ongoing projects

In general, IS departments are big on best practices and lessons learned but not when it comes to project management, Kapur says. Rather than assess what went wrong with failed projects, IS departments are simply inclined to start new ones. "Projects are abandoned like puppies," he says. "Unfortunately, there is no humane society to treat abandoned projects."

Wrong Way

One company that learned from project failure the hard way is Galileo International, a provider of electronic global distribution services for the travel industry. Galileo, which recently went public with a $900 million offering, provides travel agencies at approximately 36,000 offices worldwide with the ability to access schedule and fare information, book reservations and issue tickets for 525 airlines. Galileo also provides subscribers with information and booking capabilities covering 48 car rental companies and over 200 major hotel chains worldwide. In 1995, Galileo's Denver-based operations unit began work on project Agile, which proved to be anything but. Budgeted at $400,000 and scheduled to be completed in just a matter of months, Agile was a software management project designed to help Galileo programmers manage code smoothly between two independent transaction processing systems (TPS), one in Denver and another in London. The goal was to save training time and operating costs by consolidating the systems in a bigger, quicker application based on London's TPS. Senior management's patience wore thin as months ticked by without results.

Meanwhile, the project team continued to report, "We're very, very close."

Finally, Joan Hannan, a senior manager in Galileo's GlobalFares Development organization, was brought in last year to rescue what appeared to be a failing project. "Joan was picked primarily because she was a project manager in one of the larger applications areas, and she had good experience in the company," says Jim Lubinski, Galileo's senior vice president of information services and operations. "She also was considered to be one of our toughest people when it came to managing projects."

Hannan's diagnosis confirmed management's fears: Agile had no definition of scope and no clear deliverables, and the developers demonstrated no customer focus. "The technicians were pure technicians," Hannan says. "They had written some really great code, but the customer focus wasn't there. Every time they gave the [prototype] system to the user groups, it wouldn't work."

In an attempt to salvage the project, Hannan went back to the basics. She handpicked a new development team with business, people, and technical skills. Then the group started at square one, identifying users, setting system requirements and evaluating what had been built versus what was needed. Finally, after seven months, Hannan's team recommended that Galileo scrap Agile and simply retool the Denver system as a company standard. Given the green light, Hannan's group had the expanded Denver system up and running in six weeks.

On paper, Galileo spent hundreds of thousands of dollars and untallied staff hours on a doomed project, but Agile wasn't a total loss.

Warning! Warning!
How to spot impending doom

* Benchmark goals aren't met
* Unresolved issues outnumber deliverables
* Communication breaks down within project team and with customers
* Project costs escalate

Hannan says, Galileo eventually did achieve the efficiencies it projected from system consolidation, and it also gained basic project management skills such as scope definition and continuous deadline/budget review. Those skills were previously applied in different ways by different groups throughout the enterprise and are now recognized as essential and applied uniformly with every project. "We spent a lot of time and money we won't ever get back, but ultimately we did make the right decision," Hannan says. "And we learned a great deal."

Obey All Signs

Often it is possible to turn around a failing project, but one must first recognize the symptoms of impending failure. The most frequently overlooked warning sign is missed deliverables: deadlines, budgets and just plain results. No matter the length of a project, it's imperative to have a series of agreed-upon milestones along the way to track and demonstrate progress. But once your project begins failing to meet those milestones, pay heed. As Hannan says, "I'm not a big believer that if you miss your first five milestones, you're going to meet the next five."

Similarly, says CPM's Kapur, keep an eye on unresolved issues that develop regarding the project. "If the number of issues is equal to or exceeds the number of deliverables, then your project is in trouble," Kapur says.

Miscommunication is another key warning sign. "There is no such thing as too much communication," says Andrew Duncan, Atlanta-based senior manager for Coopers & Lybrand's Solutions Through Technology practice. Key signs of communication trouble are when project team members say one thing about the project to team members and something different to people outside the team and when business users are unable to articulate the project's goals. "Communication gets even worse with international projects, where you have to deal with cultural issues," Duncan cays. "You can be in Italy explaining a project to a group of Italian business partners, and they might be sitting there nodding their heads, but you'd better not interpret that to mean they're agreeing with your outline of the project. They might must be saying, "Yes, we understand what you're saying in English.""

Once the warning signs have appeared, project teams must regroup and perform what project management author and guru Edward Yourdon calls "triage," where one reads the project's vital signs—time line, budget, deliverables—and assesses which areas need priority treatment (see "Are You Part of the Death March?" next page). After this diagnosis, create an action plan that includes a detailed to-do list and an updated time line. "Then if you see the time line slipping again," Duncan says, "the project may not be as successful as you thought."

Proceed With Caution

Frank P. Saladis, project manager with AT&T Corp.'s Information Technology Services group in New York, recently oversaw a successful project turnaround. The project: to divide and share the voice and data network equipment when Lucent Technologies Inc. split from AT&T in 1996. The problem: the sheer size of the project's 30-member core team. "Before we could do anything, we needed 29 people to agree," Saladis says. Consequently, team members spent so much time communicating among themselves that the workers in the field—the ones actually splitting the networks and equipment—felt ignored. "We were telling people what their plans were without ever asking them for their input," Saladis says. "There was a lot of demoralization— 'You're telling me what to do but not giving me what I need to know.'"

To solve the problem, Saladis went directly to the project personnel, painted the big picture for them and opened the lines for constant communication. Then he dissolved the 30-member core team and replaced it with a smaller, more manageable group. "We cut out all the layers [inhibiting communication], and we managed to turn things around," Saladis says. The project was subsequently completed without a significant hitch.

Pulling the Plug

Sometimes it doesn't matter whether you can read that sign up ahead; project failure is unavoidable. To prepare for these circumstances, Kapure advises project managers to consider this question upfront: "Under what conditions would I be willing to shut down this project?" Typically, the answer is "when projected costs far exceed expected business benefits" or "when critical deadlines continue to be missed." But often project leaders don't consider this issue until failure is

Are You Part of the Death March?
"Mission Impossible" projects don't necessarily mean you're doomed

You need 12 months to complete your software development project, but you've only got six. There should be 20 people assigned to a project of this scope; you've got 10. You're hogtied by a fixed-price budget, but realistically you could spend twice that amount—especially since the users keep piling on new requirements.

You've just entered the Death March Zone. But that doesn't mean you're doomed.

Death march is what project management author and guru Edward Yourdon calls "mission impossible" projects, and it's also the title of his new book (Prentice Hall PTR, 1997), which defines the problem project as "one for which an unbiased, objective risk assessment . . . determines that the likelihood of failure is greater than 50 percent."

Typically, death march projects require from project managers a lot of long hours, hard work and a flair for risk-taking. When they fail, they can fail miserably, but when they succeed, they can pay off big for businesses and project teams alike. "The death march is not really a bad thing," says Yourdon, who also publishes *American Programmer Magazine*. "In fact, a lot of folks say this is one of the most glorious things you can get involved in—like climbing Mount Everest or finding the pot of gold at the end of the rainbow. But everybody knows it's risky going in."

Some organizations—Silicon Valley startups and Big Six accounting firms among them—thrive on this approach to project management, Yourdon points out. The style keeps the groups lean, flexible and open to new business needs and technologies. But to survive in this culture, he adds, one must recognize and embrace the lifestyle. "The CIO needs to decide whether death march is the way he wants to run things," Yourdon says. "Is this something that happens accidentally or deliberately? If the latter, then the CIO needs to train project managers to deal with [the approach] proactively."

Specifically, this strategy must be articulated upfront, and its success requires talented people, cohesive teams, decent working conditions and incentive rewards for project completion.

"Ultimately, this is a personal choice, based on personal values," Yourdon writes in his introduction to the book. "Though I believe that I'm much less naive than I was 30 years ago, I'm still attracted by entrepreneurial opportunities. Show me a sufficiently exciting risk/reward formula, and I'll sign up for yet another death march."

—T. Field

already staring them in the face. Then it can be too late to save their project *and* their job.

At AT&T, project managers use a Project Evaluation Review Process (PERP) to monitor ongoing projects and help decide when to pull the plug. "A lot of time a project moves along well, but then there's a breakthrough in technology, and you have to re-evaluate whether this is the best project to do," Saladis says. With PERP, Saladis explains, the operative question is, "How do the projects benefit the business?" It is applied three ways: creating new value for the customers, the business and the employees. Once subjected to PERP, a project is labeled "go," "on hold" or "eliminated."

Joe Thompson, newly appointed CIO of the federal government's General Services Administration, might be the king of project plug-pullers. Last year alone, his previous office reviewed $25 billion worth of IT projects and ultimately called a halt to 10 major projects worth a total of $7.3 billion. The common theme among these failures, which included some high-profile efforts at the FAA and IRS, was "off-schedule and overbudget," Thompson says. And although he reviews these projects at the highest level—after they've been approved and funded by agency heads, the Office of Management and Budget and Congress itself—Thompson asks very basic questions that often uncover fundamental failings. "Do you have a plan?" he asks. Most of the failed projects did not. "Are the projects linked to the business? Do you have a schedule? Are there metrics in place to review the projects?" he asks. Again, most of the failed projects fell short. In many instances, he says, the host agencies' executive leaders weren't even reviewing project status, and if they were, they were

Let's Call
the Whole Thing Off
When to call it quits

*   When costs exceed business benefits
*   When deadlines continue to be missed
*   When technology and/or business needs
    evolve beyond project's scope

looking more at process than results. "The project management skills in the public sector are about the same as in the private sector," Thompson says. "They're not good."

If at First You Don't Succeed . . .

Although "failed project" doesn't look good on anyone's rèsumè, it isn't necessarily a career-killer—especially if one reads the tea leaves and warns senior managers before the failure occurs. "Circumstances occur," says AT&T's Saladis. "If you can't prevent failure, you'd better be telling people about it. Management doesn't want to be blindsided.

In the case of the Oregon DMV, where officials essentially ran from the truth until the project failure was inevitable and messy, jobs were lost—and deservedly so, given that project's end-to-end mismanagement. But at Galileo, where Hannan ultimately failed to salvage project Agile, her boss came away impressed with Hannan's hard work and honest answers when it came time to pull the plug. "I don't have any problem with letting people go down the wrong path," Lubinski says. "Better to make a decision, be wrong and then fix the situation than to make no decision at all and let the world pass you by."

Keep Your Eyes
on the Enterprise:
Stories of Corporate Failure

So much for the rah-rah side of computing failure. The previous chapter might be referred to as the "sweet lemons" view of failure stories. Sweet lemons, some say, are the opposite of "sour grapes"—in sour grapes, we take a dim view of what has happened, perhaps even getting carried away with how terrible it all is. In sweet lemons, by contrast, we take a Pollyanna view of the bad things that have happened—"if life hands you lemons," says the rah-rah crowd, "make lemonade."

Well, no more of that lemonade stuff. In this chapter of the book, we look at the hard-core failure stories with no lemonade embellishment. In this section, a failure is a failure, pure and simple. Whole companies fall by the wayside. Projects and products are ground into the dust. Concepts thought to be promising whither and die on the computing vine. It isn't pretty; but in that perverse way that humans laugh at pies in the face and pratfalls down stairs, it is, in the end, fun. At least, that's our intent in providing you with these stories. Have fun!

We start off with a section called "Big Vision, Small Result." This is the pyromaniac's section of the book. Here, companies go on spending sprees, burning great gobs of (usually, venture capitalist) money. In the end, there remains very little except for a pile of ashes. You can almost imagine the charred visages of pictures of ex-presidents from the greenbacks lying in the heap. "I can't protect the money—close the whole show down" cries one consultant brought in to give advice on what to do. It would have been good advice to give the leaders of any of the companies in this section.

The next two sections have a sort of "smaller is better" flavor to them. In the first, "Together We Fall," companies that have merged in order to increase their strength (have you ever heard of "synergy"— the notion of the whole being more than the sum of its parts?) find instead that they collapse from the sheer weight of what they have done. If the section above was characterized by an ash heap of money being all that remained at the end of the failure, in this section it is the corporate cultures too different to permit the mergers to work that are the ash heap that remains. In the second of these two sections, "smaller is better" takes on a totally different meaning, as we find companies that choose to build so-called "supercomputers" succumbing to the reality that collections of "smaller is better" microcomputers have the potential to do the super job better than their supercomputer competitors ever proposed to do. One by one, supercomputer companies die, another contribution to the ash heap of failure we are accumulating here.

The following section takes a people focus. Here, we tell the stories of "Crooks and Spies and Other Guys," a strange bedfellows collection of stories where people are the cause as well as the victims of failure. The people in this section cheat and steal, lie to and spy on each other, have major, bigtime conflicts, and tear things down faster than they or their colleagues can build them up. One of the stories is a farce, another feels like the retelling of the famous Japanese story Rashomon (we'll explain that a bit later), one is a tale of friends falling out, and many of them fall into what one expert calls the "classic founder vs. new leader problem." The mess these people make of their lives and companies does not a pretty picture make!

In the final section of this chapter, we provide a new twist to the failure tail. Here we find a collection of companies that have succeeded, are among the best-known and strongest in their fields, and then fail! "Grasping Failure From the Jaws of Success" tells the stories of Wang Labs, Commodore (and its renowned "Amiga" computer), and Atari—all leaders of their respective computing niches—that, in the end, ended up just as dead as all their less-successful-along-the-way competitors. Getting to the top, we learn here, is by no means a guarantee of success. There is a strange lesson-within-a-lesson in this particular collection of stories. One of the key factors that turns success into a failure, we see in these stories, is an incoming corporate head who is unable to sustain the success that his predecessors have handed him. I find this collection of stories particularly sad and scary; today's successful company, we see here, may well end up on tomorrow's corporate ash pile.

Corporate failures, here we come!

3.1   BIG VISION, SMALL RESULT

The rapid growth of the computing field has brought about an inter-esting dilemma. Which is the worst entrepreneurial sin—to think too large, or to think too small?

Thinking too small, of course, can lead to a tiny niche company that struggles along hand-to-mouth and, quite possibly, eventually withers on its own vine.

Thinking too large? That's perhaps an even more common problem in the computing field, and the result is even more disastrous—and glaring. One rarely hears about a company that thought too small and failed. Those companies simply die with a whimper. But the ones that fail big time? They get splashed all over the press. This is a collection of big-time, big-bang failure stories.

What generally accompanies a company whose vision is larger than its potential is a huge financial conflagration. Companies like that seem to burn money at an enormous rate. With the help of venture capital—it's always more fun to burn someone else's money than your own!—the financial conflagration flames hot and heavy.

In this section of the book, we're going to play pyromaniac! We're going to see those huge financial fires burning, at rates so rapid as to stagger the imagination. One company is "burning a million dollars a month." Another "burned its way through $70 million in free-flowing funding." At one company, the executives were said to be behaving "like kids in a candy store" and "spending money like drunken sailors." At another, every employee was given a $900 chair, like it or not, and "nobody was happy about it."

Money can turn thinking people into maniacs. One of the stories that follows is said to be "a tale of inflated egos and unrealistic ambi-tions." Another is about a company that "set up shop in a grand style" because of its "outsize ambition," only to find that its "reach exceeded its grasp." Yet another company is said to have "lurched from one cash infusion to another." And, in the final story of this set, the company projected first-year sales of $17 to $20 million," but "no purchase order ever came through."

In the first story, which is about the "Lost Company," we mix in an international element. A well-known American company, eager to get started in the software tools business, buys a Dutch company with a product head start. But the resulting subsidiary never managed to blend its European and U.S. cultures and goals. In the end, a turnaround specialist brought in to figure out how to recover from the mess said "I can't protect the money—close the whole show down." The financial fire was totally and almost literally out of control.

In the second, the essence of the story is "a great idea, but poor execution, and bad timing." The company was trying to start up an internet business at a time when no one saw a clear way to make money on the net, and, the author says, the corporate leaders ended up "shooting in the dark." The money burned as rapidly as it did because the company staffed up, especially in sales, before either electronic commerce or its own products were ready to take off. They "swung for the fences"—and ended up striking out.

The third story in this section is about a promising company whose product looked like the proverbial "next killer app"—a software application that will sell as many copies as the spreadsheet or the word processor, the first software killer apps. In this story, the small entrepreneurial firm was bought by a larger, well-known company. What happened next was a function of who was doing the talking. The small company people said things like "we were robbed at gunpoint," and were subject to "abuse of control." The large company called those accusations "the dying gasps of a Silicon Valley startup that oversold its potential." At the end, as the small company reluctantly closed its doors, a sign appeared there which said "Game Over."

And in the final story of this section, a promising small company dissolved in litigation before it could receive its first purchase order.

Before you read on, don some fire-resistant togs. It's going to get hot in there!

THE LOST COMPANY

by Kenny MacIver

The glass wall in the lobby of the Unisys tower at 1000 Marina Boulevard, Brisbane, California reads 'USoft Worldwide Headquarters'. It suggests the heart of a global software empire, one strategically centered between San Francisco and Silicon Valley. And if all had gone according to plan, inside that HQ several hundred people would be working today for a $100 million application development software powerhouse, the proof that entrepreneurial acumen can be seeded, nurtured and matured by a mainframe-era computer systems giant.

But within the USoft Headquarters, just 11 people remain, and they have been told they will be gone by March 31. Not even the senior management team is present. It is 3,000 miles away in Blue Bell, Pennsylvania, where USoft's owner Unisys is presiding over a final, painful chapter of what must be one of the most catastrophic technology adventures in the history of the software industry.

This is a tale of misjudgment, strategic blundering and excess on an almost unprecedented scale. It is a tale of how, over two and a half years, Unisys allowed USoft to burn its way through $70 million in free-flowing funding, acquisition payments and the cash it generated. It is a tale where the object was to create a $150 million, Wall Street-listed development tools company over three years, but where there is now nothing to show for the efforts and the vast expenditure. It is also a tale of inflated egos and unrealistic ambitions.

Within the twists of the USoft story, however, are lessons for businesses of many types: For large multinationals hoping to successfully diversify into new areas; for European and Asian companies and their venture backers seeking to break into the all-important American market; and for managers who might be tempted to push too hard too fast.

The story does not begin in 1995 with the founding of USoft, but in 1994 when ailing computer systems and services giant Unisys started looking for new avenues of growth. At that point, CEO Jim Unruh and his operational number two, Alan Lutz, called in a seasoned software industry executive to help them formulate a plan for grafting

---

Originally published by Global Technology Business, *March 1998. Used with permission.*

entrepreneurial skin onto the tired computer firm. Mike Seashols had been the driving force behind the Oracle sales team during the 1980s, a visionary always able to see where the greatest potential for the company and its products lay.

As a consultant for Unisys, Seashols got into analyzing the company's former flirtations with application development software. Previously, Unisys had licensed the Ally development environment from Encore Corp, but that had been deemed a failure largely because the Ally development and sales management had been given no latitude. This time things would be different, Seashols and the Unisys executives decided. Whatever product the company acquired as a seedbed for software expansion, the management would be autonomous.

Seashols was given the green light to go shopping. Armed with a commitment from Unisys that it would put $50 million into an initial investment pot over three years, he focused most of his attention on European products which had a strong reputation in their national markets, but which had yet to make it in the US.

After looking at Nat Systems and Four Seasons, among many other companies, Seashols, through a mutual friend, was introduced to Max ten Dam. Over seven years, ten Dam had built TopSystems International into a solid business centered in the Benelux region (Belgium, The Netherlands and Luxemborg), focusing on large corporate customers in need of application development expertise and tools.

For Seashols, TopSystems was the ideal vehicle for USoft. Revenue growth at the Naarden, Netherlands-based company was on a sharp upward curve: After a 30% rise in 1993 to Dfl 11 million ($6.2 million), the company reported revenues of Dfl 17.5 million ($10 million) in 1994—an expansion underpinned by five years of unbroken profitability. It had achieved that through a classic high-end tools strategy. Corporate users of the TopSystems product were required to fully embrace its idiosyncratic, but extremely powerful approach. That meant the software component itself accounted for only a fraction of revenues—around 10%—with the rest coming from related implementation services.

Top Deal

In February 1995, Unisys concluded its deal to buy TopSystems for an initial $9 million, with further results-based payments due that could push the total to $20 million. Having gone this far in his consultancy role, Seashols could not resist the temptation to take the CEO's chair, and he threw himself into ramping up the company at astonishing speed.

Profitability would be put on hold as the company expanded in the US and elsewhere in Europe. Also key to the agenda was ploughing money into R&D in order to productize what was acknowledged as a consultant's tool and make it ready for the US market.

The prize was certainly alluring. USoft estimated that by 1997, when it would be firing on all cylinders, the market for client/server tools would be worth $4.4 billion. With a chunk of that firmly in its sights, the company started writing checks. It quickly built up a sales force in the US of around 60, and exhibited a confidence in its staying power by signing up long leases on large offices in half a dozen US cities and in countries around Europe. "The plans assumed we were going to grow gangbusters," says David Dawson, former US product marketing manager at USoft.

By US standards the spending at home was relatively modest. The excesses were in Europe, where little control was exerted. "The Dutch management had lived off retained earnings. They had never had VC money," says Seashols. "Now they were like kids in a candy store."

Sales staff in the UK, Germany, France and in Benelux were hired on high, fixed-income salaries, with top of the line Jaguars, BMWs and Mercedes dispersed freely among them. There were plenty of other signs that spending was running wild. USoft Germany, for example, with an established 2,000 square feet facility in Frankfurt, suddenly added a second 4,000 square feet office in Dusseldorf, after a newly-appointed country manager decided he preferred to work from his home town. "They were spending money like drunken sailors," says Alf Goebel, a former sales manager at the company.

Former USoft executives recall how in one sales kick-off meeting in February 1996, Seashols promised a Rolex watch to everyone who made target. He also promised that the next '100% club' reward for the best sales people and their partners would be on the Pacific island of Bali.

Marketing money was also being squandered. A laughable example was the extension of a UK ad campaign to London cabs. Emblazing the USoft name on taxis certainly confused London's shoppers, but it was "a stupid medium" that never fostered a single deal, says one ex-

USoft manager. Nevertheless, the company was locked on a target of 100% growth for its products.

But quickly Seashols realized that the infrastructure phase was not being accompanied by sales. "It never even started to take off in the US," says Goebel. The French office was opened then closed over 12 months and the UK and Germany were disappointing. One year in, USoft's head-count had hit 250 (62 in the US) and the company was burning its way through $9 million a quarter without any evidence of success. "There are good reasons why venture capitalists give companies a little money at a time and keep a close eye on how they spend it," says Dawson. "Unisys was not watching the money."

Clearly, someone had to pull the brake on the wild ride.

Burning Cash

In late 1995, Bob Ney was sitting having pizza with Jim Unruh in the staff café in Blue Bell. Ney, a former Oracle sales star and CEO of a document imaging systems start-up, had taken a call at home from Alan Lutz a few weeks earlier. The Unisys number two had offered Ney a 'million dollar plus' deal to take a year off from his business. The job: Fix the USoft problem before it got worse. Ney, who had never heard of USoft, almost fell off his seat when he learned he would be reporting to his former sales colleague from Oracle, Mike Seashols.

On that day in Blue Bell, Ney was in a taunting, provocative mood. After having seen first hand the effects of the huge downsizing that Unisys had been going through he leaned across the table and remarked to Unruh, "It's like a morgue in here. Tell me, what's it like steering the Titanic?"

Ney was there to be brutally honest about other matters too. "I was called in to keep an eye on Unruh's investment," says Ney. But what he saw at Unisys did not inspire much confidence in his new job. Flying into JFK airport in New York for his meeting with Unruh, he was met at the flight gate by a Unisys executive and ushered to the corporate helicopter to make the hour and a half journey to Blue Bell. He recalls saying to himself then, "Now I know why this company is in such deep crap."

When Ney returned to report to Unruh for the last time in September 1996, he again did not hold back. Things had gone too far, he said. He could not find any way to make it work. "USoft was like someone with his arm ripped off. You might be able to squash it back on and stop the bleeding, but by then there's not going to be enough blood left to keep him alive." Ney left the following month, a vote of no confidence that started an outflow of others. His parting advice to Blue Bell: "I can't protect the money—close the whole show down."

Instead, Unisys brought in its own operational people. What they found confounded the notion that they were dealing with 'crazy Californians', says Seashol's executive assistant at the time, Bonnie Radojevich. "They thought of us as underdressed, laid-back Californians who regarded Blue Bell as old, stuffy, and straight. They were right about that last part."

"When Unisys brought in a chief financial officer, she just went crazy," says Radojevich, "especially about the lack of controls in Europe." But those were just the details. How USoft got into such deep trouble in such a short time was more connected to some fundamental problems. Nothing could be more fundamental than getting the business model of the company wrong, as its managers observe.

"TopSystems was a consulting firm that had software, and the challenge was to make it into a software firm that had consulting," says Dawson. "The big issue was that the Europeans wanted to stay with the traditional model and we tried to position it as a software product. It really couldn't do that."

"Mike Seashols tried to turn it into a Silicon Valley shrink-wrapped product start-up," says Goebel. "It definitely could not be sold as a shrink-wrapped product," says Marcel Smit, formerly head of USoft Benelux. "It was and is a great product but you have to teach companies how to work with it."

The buy in is certainly high. "You have got to take a leap of faith and jump over the cliff, to buy into the GUI, the development environment and the whole nine yards," says Dawson. He cites how users like textile manufacturer Burlington Industries in North Carolina have experienced incredible return on investment. The trouble was: The services infrastructure was not there in the US to hold organizations' hands as they took that leap of faith.

Even Seashols agrees that was probably the company's biggest misreading. But at the time he felt the ends would justify the means. USoft had to be a product company in order to have a chance of getting to the Holy Grail of an initial public offering on Wall Street.

The trouble was, the Europeans were not convinced. Says Smit: "The Europeans were saying we have shown you how to make sales—a complex package in which you transfer the knowledge." "They never became a team: It was always two different worlds, the Dutch versus the Americans," says Radojevich.

Those factors began to be manifest themselves in the field as US sales people were rebuffed time and time again. A different breed from the European team, they neither had the sales skills to do the consultancy sell, nor the established back-up services organization or developers to offer a follow through service. "We needed to make this thing an American company as fast as possible," says David Dawson. "And that never happened. Leaving the development team in Holland undermined that. The big dog got the bone—they were supporting the European not the US agenda."

Marketing Gaff!

At the same time as the internal struggles, the company's primary marketing message had completely missed the boat. USoft had been launched in 1995 with the tag "The Server/Client Software Company', implying that its client/server technology put a greater emphasis on server-side processing than the market leader, Powersoft, whose PowerBuilder application code ran only on clients and used the server only to dish up data. That had earned PowerBuilder the 'fat-client' applications tag.

But the reversing of the client and server words was pure hype—as technicians at prospective customers soon discovered. "We had a good story but the product didn't match the story," says Dawson. "The product was fat client city. Implementation was extremely client-centric. That was one of the big killers."

But the errors of judgment did not stop there. Seashols made what turned out to be another crucial mistake: He announced that USoft would not use the vast Unisys' global sales force to sell its software. "In one swoop, he blew away the only friendly sales channel he had," says Ney.

There was a feeling that the Unisys sales force was too undynamic to project the hot Silicon Valley start-up image that USoft was trying to cultivate. As Smith says: "It was a company run by accountants, but we were a start-up. Combining these cultures was pretty hard, so working closely together was not so successful."

But there were good decisions too. Seashols himself was a great choice for leader. "He is a brilliant ideas man, brilliant at reading sales situations and a super-convincing sales guy," says Goebel. Smit echoes that sentiment, with some reservations: "Sometimes he was too much of a visionary, perhaps a few feet too high above the ground."

But Seashols is not good at detail, they concur. During a meeting, he would come up with four big ideas—great ideas—and then say "go implement them". But those four ideas would break down into 4,000 separate 'to-do' tasks.

However, the people around him were not always capable of picking up those ideas and running with them, says Radojevich. And many of them were far from being his first team choices.

Limited Options

Unisys had a reputation as a fallen giant, a profile that cut short many USoft executive recruitment calls. Also, its status as a division (rather than a subsidiary) within Unisys meant it could not offer stock options, the lifeblood of high-tech start-ups. "I never anticipated such problems," says Seashols. "It took an awful lot of persuasion without options."

He was not always successful. "Mike is a big thinker and he had to build up a team that was, in many cases, of average intellect or below average," says Radojevich. People were not up to the challenges he set them. "Mike is not the world's greatest line manager. When he gives someone something to do, he expects that they will be able to carry it out. He never goes back and asks them if they did it."

Adds Smit: "We recruited a lot of the wrong management in Europe. In the UK and Germany they just screwed up and [some] filled their own pockets instead of building a company." The upshot to all this was that while sales continued to rise in the Benelux countries (in 1997 they continued to account for 80% of worldwide revenues and had brought the European operation back into profit), the promised revenue surge from the US simply "never happened" says Smit.

Seashols says the company's total revenues peaked in 1996 at around $25 million, where they remain today.

The fact they were mostly still coming from Benelux was something that Seashols never tried to hide from the Unisys management. But he did use his consummate salesmanship to keep their faith. His quarterly reports to Blue Bell always resulted in the green light—and more funding. "We used to say as he left for Blue Bell each quarter, 'Go do your magic'," says Radojevich. But by 1997, the magic had stopped working. USoft's main supporter within Unisys, Lutz, had departed for Compaq and without him, Seashols was made to carry the can for his mistakes. Over the year Unisys had grafted on more and more of its own people and corrupted the culture of the start-up. And in July 1997, Seashols was finally forced out of USoft and a caretaker manager from Unisys, Dave Drechsel, appointed in his place.

While Drechsel was trying to fathom what had transpired over the previous two years, the European management signaled it had had enough. Behind Unisys' back, they got together with a venture capital company and proposed a management buy out. Offering $15 million to $25 million (depending on what assets went with the buy out), the team would wind down the US operation and take the company back to its Benelux roots. Unexpectedly, and to their complete dismay, Unisys snubbed the approach.

Why should Unisys walk away from a deal that solved one of its irksome problems? Seashols, for one, cannot understand. Others have their own theories: "Unisys was just too embarrassed to sell it back to the TopSystems team," says Bob Ney. "After all, Unisys had had four adventures in software tools—LINC, Mapper, Ally and USoft—and made a mess of all four." Still, something had to be done to clean it up.

The Remains

The developers at USoft in Holland have their own informal museum. It chronicles the evolutions of the company in printouts of early code, original marketing literature, manuals and software packaging, but lately it has been getting a bit neglected. "Maybe you should add a gallery of current and former vice presidents," a visiting US executive recently suggested. "The wall is no way big enough," shot back one USoft developer.

USoft has seen a huge turnover of executives in its short three-year history. That is symptomatic of a company in pain, and Unisys is in the process of trying, once and for all, to end that pain—and its own.

Since Drechsel took over as interim and then permanent CEO last year, USoft has been trying to find a path forward. Drechsel has cut costs, closed unused facilities and dropped headcount even further.

According to Howard Kearns, USoft marketing VP, the workforce now stands at around 40 in the US and 160 in Europe. But others who have recently left the company refute those numbers, saying the US figure is less than 20 and worldwide it is a little over 100. Drechsel's changes, however, have gotten USoft close to break even and prepared it for a sell-off.

Several US and European software vendors report that the company has contacted them with proposals. But also back on the table is a revived management buy out, and even a remodeling of the company around a new business model and an applications focus. What is unlikely is that the USoft story will end here. Everyone who has ever got close to the company swears that its technology is sensational. That alone may be enough to ensure a sequel.

THE HOLE IN NETS INC.

by Art Jahnke

Around Pittsburgh, Donald Jones was known as a local boy who made good. Very good. By 1990, when he was 53, he had started and sold four manufacturing-control companies and he was teaching at the Donald H. Jones Center for Entrepreneurship at Carnegie Mellon University, which he had personally endowed with $1 million. Jones's fifth startup, which sprang from a suggestion by one of his students, was an attempt to bring together regional buyers and sellers of manufacturing equipment. Originally called Automation News Network (ANN), the company printed monthly magazines of industry news and, every six months, produced an industrial directory diskette.

Jones intended his paper and disk products to be a starting point; the endgame would be a kind of electronic clearinghouse for manufacturing news and products. Customers were to be connected via an electronic pager that would download information that was customized by need. As it turned out, Jones's plan was ahead of its time; so, unfortunately, were his estimated costs for pagers, whose actual higher costs kept the electronic clearinghouse stuck in the drawing-board phase.

But when the Internet reared its head, Jones saw immediately that it could do everything he had hoped to do with a proprietary system for a fraction of the cost. By the end of 1995, he had changed the name of his company to Industry.Net and posted much of the information from his print catalogs and diskettes on the Web. If you needed a ball valve, 5,000 miles of coaxial cable or 600 glue guns, you could find them on Industry.Net. And you could find them fast, thanks to Industry.Net's search capability. The Web site also offered links to trade associations, trade show listings and job postings.

Jones knew that the next step—moving from Internet publishing to Internet e-commerce—would require a serious infusion of capital. And even though Industry.Net had more than 4,000 vendors each paying several thousand dollars a year to post catalogs and was reportedly taking in about $2 million a month, it couldn't round up the money needed to make the leap to full-fledged e-commerce.

Originally published in CIO Web Business, October 1, 1997. Used with permission. Reprinted through the courtesy of CIO. © 1998 Communications, Inc.

Late in 1995, however, Jones managed to persuade the high-tech investment house of Hambrecht & Quist LLC to invest about $15 million in Industry.Net. But the price, one source says, was high: H&Q wanted the company to be run by someone whose name was known on Wall Street.

Someone, for example, like Jim Manzi, the 44-year-old software ex-CEO who had helped build Lotus Development Corp. into such an attractive property that IBM Corp. paid $3.5 billion in 1995 to make it part of the Big Blue stable. Manzi himself garnered $78 million from the sale, but in January 1996, after it had become clear that he would not be tapped to run IBM's growing software division, Manzi left. He surfaced in the Pittsburgh offices of Industry.Net.

The promise of Industry.Net had already attracted investments from such savvy high-tech movers and shakers as Bill Gates and Perot Systems Corp. CEO Mort Myerson. Now the appearance of Manzi, whom *The Wall Street Journal* had described as "the enfant terrible of the software world," would attract the attention of the business press, generating high visibility and high expectations for Industry.Net.

In theory, at least, Industry.Net—whose name would change to Nets Inc.—promised to exploit all of the aspects of the Web that Web enthusiasts had been so bullish about: content, community, commerce and customization (the four C's). In the dreams of Don Jones and Jim Manzi, the company would get a jump on the market for online business-to-business e-commerce, generating vast revenues from membership and transaction fees. In fact, the company predicted that its services could help many manufacturers and resellers double their profits.

As for Nets, its profit potential was thought to be nearly inestimable. Every credible online speculator believed that the big money was right where Nets was headed: in business-to-business e-commerce, estimated (at least in the near term) to be 10 times the value of the slow-growing consumer market.

In Internet circles, the rise and fall of Nets Inc., which declared bankruptcy in May, now bears the status of a kind of virtual morality play; along with the requisite twists of fate, there are lessons about good and bad business practices in every scene. There are also some disconcerting questions about the most basic assumptions of the Web's potential.

"There are a million issues that branch off this," says Erica Rugulies, an industry analyst at the Giga Information Group, based in Cam-

What Went Wrong?
Expert opinions on the fall of Nets Inc.

BRUCE GUPTILL
Research director, Electronic Commerce and Internet Strategies,
Gartner Group Inc.
"Nets was a great idea with poor execution and bad timing. The market
wasn't ready. The fundamental problem was that it did not provide utility
to users. If they had just been able to do the transactions, that would have
kept them afloat."

ERICA RUGULLIES
Giga Information Group Industry analyst
"If you look at it as a mall, it's not a good idea. If you look at it as a business-
to-business buying-and-selling community, it is a good idea. But they lacked
focus. There is no way that they would succeed by being all things to all
people. In this industry, where technology is immature, things change fast
and business models have to be tightly defined and close enough in focus to
be architectible. They were shooting in the dark."

TOM DAVENPORT
Author, professor and director of the Information Management Program
at the University of Texas at Austin, and CIO columnist
"My view of Nets is that they were overly ambitious in several ways. They
staffed up in advance of the work in a world where e-commerce is still a
slow sell. They assumed that a common set of product categories could be
developed across industries, when that took decades in an EDI context. They
assumed that a small player [themselves] could create substantial changes in
how multiple industries do business, which in the past has only been done
by powerful customers [e.g., Wal-Mart Stores Inc. and General Motors]. It's
possible that all this might have worked eventually, but it was impossible for
it to work within the time frame of Nets Inc.'s funding."

bridge, Mass. "One is the mall concept and whether that will work.
Another is the timeliness of e-commerce." The Nets Inc. experience
seemed a portent to Gartner Group Inc. as well, where Bruce Guptill,
research director for Internet and Electronic Commerce Strategies at
the Stamford, Conn., researcher, wrote a special report on the
bankruptcy and its implications.

LESSON 1
Never mistake means for ends

Nets' race to develop transaction software became all-consuming, monopolizing resources and attention that should have gone elsewhere—to customer relations, publishing and sales. Nets became, in effect, a software company.

Some of this post-mortem scrutiny, of course, arises from Manzi's high profile. But a great deal is driven by belief in the high potential of the model Jones was pursuing. "An honest broker like Nets has some great advantages," says Gregory Wester, research director for Internet markets at the Yankee Group, a research company based in Boston. "They can pull together all of the participants in a market segment and provide side-by-side price comparisons."

The first jolt to this foray into Web community building occurred in March, two months after Manzi came on board. When Don Jones suffered his third heart attack, he relinquished leadership of his company forever. Manzi, who reportedly invested $2 million in the company, took an even firmer grasp of the wheel and headed in the direction of additional capital investment, overruling the idea of a public offering and seeking private money instead. He approached Cahners Publishing Co., the country's largest publisher of industrial trade magazines, hoping to swap one-third of Nets for an amount reported to be $175 million. Cahners declined the offer.

Still, recalls Jim Sabol, former director of information technology at Nets Inc., "There was a lot of energy at that time. Everyone was talking about big deals with Cahners and various venture firms and how people would be millionaires based on the value of their stock."

In July, Manzi succeeded in trading equity for cash when he gave AT&T 18 percent of the new company that would be called Nets Inc. In addition to an undisclosed amount of money, the deal gave Nets control of AT&T's New Media Services, an online publisher of business news, regional industry newsletters and parts catalogs on diskettes. On the surface, the deal made everyone happy: Nets got the benefit of the AT&T brand, and AT&T got rid of a white elephant that, a year-and-a-half earlier, it had spent $50 million to acquire from Ziff-Davis Inc. But problems would follow.

"Buying [New Media Services] was a complete debacle," says Sabol. "Everyone was excited about the AT&T name, but the dark side was that the expenses were unbelievable. They were burning through $3 million or $4 million a month, and their revenue was insignificant. But Manzi had a vision: He wanted to get bigger faster."

In fact, one of the few things that the customarily tight-lipped Manzi would say in the wake of the AT&T merger was that he planned to expand the Nets Inc. model beyond the bounds of manufacturing.

Predictably, Manzi's deal making attracted attention and second guessing from industry analysts some of whom were quick to suggest that expanding the client base was the last thing that Nets Inc. should have done.

"[The company] cast its net far too wide," says Yankee Group's Wester. "They tried to serve all sorts of industry segments. If you want to build a community, you have to capture the gestalt of that community; you have to know its language and its customs. I think they bit off more than they could chew."

Just how far beyond manufacturing Manzi wanted to expand remained a company secret. But those who heard Manzi's dreams of creating divisions to be called Travel.Net and Pharmacy.Net began to wonder exactly where they should begin the expansion. "Had the analysts known we were thinking about going into the travel business, they would have fallen on the floor," says one former employee who was close to Manzi.

LESSON 2
Perform many hours of community service

An online community is a powerful marketing tool, but Nets' zeal to expand into other niches before securing authoritative mastery of the one it had pioneered diffused energy internally and squandered a sense of community among its customers.

Wester and other observers believed all along that Nets Inc.'s success would depend on its ability to harness transactional capabilities and command a piece of the action of the deals consummated in its online space. Manzi seemed to agree. Almost immediately, he began paring down AT&T New Media Services, getting rid of its online newsletters. Trouble was, insiders say, the newsletters were the company's primary revenue producers, and Nets needed all the revenues it could get.

At the same time—in a move that would prove to be critically divisive—Manzi moved Nets' executive offices to his old neighborhood in Cambridge, hired a half-dozen former Lotus executives and generally set up shop in the grand style to which he had been accustomed in Lotus's heyday. That rankled employees of the Pittsburgh office, who were used to a somewhat more Spartan existence.

To pull together the data that would catalog, order, inventory and sell just about anything that could be sold, Manzi hired Mark Taflian, a highly regarded software technologist whose reputation rested on his tenure as vice president of strategic systems and advanced technology at United Airlines. Taflian, whom Manzi named chief technology officer and vice president of engineering at Nets, had most recently been president of Covia Technologies, a promising developer of message-oriented middle-ware that shut its doors around the time of Manzi's move to Industry.Net.

At Nets, Teflian got busy fast, hiring programmers to build what he calls CANS—Commerce Architecture for Nets. And hire he did. Within months, Nets Inc. would have more than 50 programmers on staff.

Throughout fall 1996, Nets' editors struggled to migrate print catalogs to HTML, management tried to come up with new products, and programmers worked to develop software that would put the business end of the business online. Time was passing, and many at Nets knew they weren't the only company trying to build a business-to-business online marketplace.

"Our belief was that if we could aggregate enough merchants in our electronic mall, we would be the first place somebody would shop," says Sabol, Nets' former IT director. "But there was always the wolf at the door."

In October, Cahners put up Manufacturers Marketplace, a beta site that posted information from 30,000 manufacturers and linked to 13 of the company's manufacturing-related magazines. It was easy to see that Cahners was heading in the same direction as Nets. Manzi, who had tried to deal with Cahners just a few months earlier, took note.

A second, and arguably more serious, threat to Nets sprang from the global procurement group at GE Lighting, which had been using an Internet-based Trading Process Network (TPN) to send customized bid packages to regular business partners. The company found that TPN reduced procurement times by 50 percent and costs by 30 percent and was predicting that by the end of that year it would be spending about $1 billion on purchases made over the internet.

GE Information Services (GEIS), which runs GE's Internet commerce operation, realized that what was good for GE Lighting was good for most manufacturing companies, and in fall 1996, it made its procurement service available to buyers and sellers of manufacturing materials and factory supplies. (Textron Automotive Co. in Troy, Mich., one of the handful of businesses that have signed on, will use the service to shop for $500 million in materials.)

Like Cahners, GE had money, clout and a database of 40,000 suppliers. More important, they also had in place the kind of e-commerce transaction software that Nets was still aggressively hiring programmers to create.

At the same time Nets was so actively recruiting programmers, it was jettisoning salespeople, cutting its direct sales force from 60 to 30, and eventually to 15. "Our customers were not happy," says Sabol. "The salespeople weren't there to service the accounts."

But some former employees say that revamping the sales force was necessary, both to cut the relatively high costs of sales and to scale up to a business as large as that envisioned by Manzi. "Cutting the salespeople was Jim's idea of the best way to scale this thing," says Hank Howie, Nets' director of business development and now general manager of Internet projects at Restrac, a maker of personnel-recruiting software. "If you have a direct sales force, you can't get the mass-market distribution that you need with something that large."

It was certainly true that Nets' new products—such as a business card that would be posted on the site for one year for about $500 and a business card with a link to a customer's site that would be posted for about $1,500—could be sold more cost-effectively by telemarketers than by a direct sales force. But those sorts of products—intended to provide a graceful segue from catalog to shoppers' paradise—also presented a problem.

In a medium that was supposed to thrive on customization, says Sabol, Nets found itself pushing products that appeared less custom than the postings of Industry.Net. "We talked about customization," says Sabol, "but we looked like McDonald's, with various products that all looked the same. We shot ourselves in the foot."

More fundamental, sources say, was that the selling of just about anything never seemed to be a priority of Nets' management.

For some of those within Nets, the salvation was not in what it had, but what it would have—when technology permitted. The company was, after all, being run by the former CEO of a software powerhouse. Quickly, Nets was beginning to look a lot more like a software company than like the publishing company turned online communitarian venture that had spawned it.

"Nets is very typical of technology companies," says David Maland, Nets Inc.'s former director of inside sales. "It was being moved by technologists rather than marketing people. And they wanted to have the ultimate solution before they did anything. The many-to-many idea that Nets was working on was a good idea, but we were not able to market products or services quickly enough."

Speed was a problem elsewhere. According to one source, Taflian had promised Manzi that he would have CANS up and running by the end of 1996, but when the end of 1996 came around, Teflian revised his forecast. Perhaps, he told Manzi, he could have CANS up by the end of 1997. Manzi knew he was in trouble. According to a confidential report by the investment-banking firm of Lazard Freres & Co., Nets' 1996 revenues were only $12 million, and the absence of salespeople continued to take its toll. In January, Nets reportedly tapped Goldman, Sachs & Co. in an effort to get an infusion of $50 million, but Goldman passed. No one was buying.

LESSON 3
It's always the customer, stupid

Same as it ever was, if customers aren't happy, they're gone. In one year, Nets' revenues from sales dropped from $2 million a month to $85,000 a month as customers stopped coming back.

LESSON 4
Choose would-be suitors carefully

When you seek to ally with a potential competitor that might not really need you, you risk giving up more than you get. A year-and-a-half after Jim Manzi tried to cut a deal with Cahners Publishing, Nets is dead and Cahners' Manufacturing Marketplace Web site is going strong. So is General Electric's TPN, which partnered wisely and well with Thomas' Register.

"I guess if they'd had a really good transactional-software platform, they might have had more enthusiasm from investors," says Wester. "But they still would have needed customers."

At the same time, Nets found a way to reduce costs. It killed what was left of the AT&T merger and laid off 54 people. Still, money was flowing out of the company much faster than it was coming in. Nets spent $5 million on a Pittsburgh data center that was completed in February 1997, and Manzi moved his Pittsburgh contingent out of 17,000 square feet in an office park to 40,000 square feet in a fashionable office building. In most companies, a gleaming new office with Steelcase furnishings is a way to boost morale, but in the case of Nets, the move served mainly to fuel a class war that pitted the economy-minded Pittsburgh contingent against the lifestyles-of-the-rich-and-famous crowd from Cambridge. Everybody, says one former employee, got a $900 chair, and nobody was happy about it.

They were even less happy later that month, when the already powerful GEIS Trading Process Network announced a new partnership with Thomas' ConnectsUs, the Web-based version of Thomas' Register—the well-respected publisher of manufacturers' catalogs—which included 55,000 product headings. GE predicted that within 18 months, the value of transactions on the new joint venture would exceed $4 billion (it reports it is on track to hit those numbers).

Competitors proliferated. On March 3, Teflian, whose influence at Nets continued to grow, circulated a list of nine of them, including TPN Register, IBM's CommercePoint and Cahners Manufacturers Marketplace.

Two weeks later, at the National Manufacturing Week trade shows in Chicago, Cahners officially unveiled its imposing entry in the field. While it wasn't yet transactional, Manufacturing Marketplace was an impressive sourcing guide that was being promoted in Cahners magazines, with a total circulation of 1.2 million.

Nets, too, had taken a booth at the show. But instead of heralding the launch of the site, Manzi announced a partnership with Cambridge, Mass.-based PSDI, a vendor of software that tracks the history and costs of maintaining equipment. It was a promising alliance, says one former employee, but because visitors to the Nets booth at the show kept asking when the site would become transactional, the PSDI deal indirectly emphasized the company's inability to get a working product up and running. Within Nets, people began to anticipate the end.

On April 14, new Nets President Catherine Hapka did something that all but verified the company's imminent demise: She sent a memo to all employees that denied the rumors. "Let me address the most serious rumor by borrowing a phrase from Mark Twain," Hapka wrote. "Rumors of our demise are premature."

Hapka's memo was off the mark. Revenues, says one former employee, had sunk to $85,000 a month, down from $2 million a month the year before. Expenses were still off the charts. Ten days after Hapka's misguided attempt to boost morale, Manzi started to underwrite the payroll himself, kicking in about $500,000 a week.

"On May 9," says Sabol, everybody knew something was coming. The big rumor was that we were going to be acquired by Cahners and everybody would be laid off."

Manzi, who had made a fortune at Lotus popularizing such distributed technologies at Notes, put another distributed technology to good personal use that day. While the 200 employees of Nets huddled around speaker phones in conference rooms in Cambridge and Pittsburgh, he spoke to them from his home in the tony Boston suburb of Chestnut Hill. Nets Inc., he said, was dead.

WERE JIM MANZI'S BIG IDEAS TOO BIG?

by Paul C. Judge and Stephen Baker

When employees of Nets Inc. in Cambridge, Mass., and Pittsburgh were summoned to a meeting on May 9, they knew the news couldn't be good. Nets had been on the edge for months and layoffs were likely. But there also had been rumors that a financial savior, possibly from Malaysia, was near. Just days earlier, managers had assured workers that Chief Executive Jim P. Manzi "wouldn't let the company go bankrupt with his name on it," as one recalled.

Yet Manzi, talking from his home in Chestnut Hill, Mass., told employees gathered around speakerphones that it was "the worst day of my life." Nets, he announced, had filed for Chapter 11 bankruptcy protection. Despite his best efforts, including lending at least $1 million of his own money to keep Nets going in the previous few weeks, Manzi hadn't been able to land new investors.

It was a devastating crash landing. In January, 1996, when he took over at what was then called Industry.Net, Manzi boasted of building an entirely new electronic marketplace where buyers and sellers of industrial parts—from fasteners to turbines—could hook up through computer networks. Last June, when he merged his little company with AT&T's New Media Services, an online information provider, Manzi spoke of networks that would lower the cost of commerce for professions such as law and medicine. Nets was out to blanket the globe, collecting a commission on every transaction on its network.

But from the start, Manzi's reach exceeded his grasp. In bidding to lead the new market for electronic commerce, say insiders, customers, competitors, and analysts, he erected a much more expensive enterprise than Nets could support. He moved Nets' headquarters from Pittsburgh into tony Cambridge offices and hired high-priced executives from Lotus Development Corp., the software company he ran for nine years before selling out to IBM in 1995. He also spent heavily to develop the complex software required to realize his technological vision. "Jim wasn't going to do this as a small-time play," says one Nets executive. "He was swinging for the fence."

Originally published in Business Week, *May 26, 1997. Reprinted by special permission, copyright 1997 by The McGraw-Hill Companies, Inc.*

By the end, 5,000 subscribers a week were joining the online exchange, according to Nets. But most registered for free, and the big suppliers, which Nets had hoped would pay up to $200,000 per year to sell their wares online, never logged on. Investors were scared off by the lack of big customers as well as by the E-commerce efforts of giants such as General Electric Co. and IBM. Nets' monthly revenue fell from around $1 million when Manzi took over to $100,000 recently, according to insiders. (The company won't disclose financial results.)

Financing Flop

Manzi declined to be interviewed. But employees say that at the core of the company's many problems lay a cultural tug-of-war between the free-spending, outspoken Manzi and Nets' flinty founder, Donald Jones. Homespun and well-connected to old-line industrial companies, Jones ran a tight-knit company, and was commonly found smoking on the loading dock with his workers. He also owned 32% of Nets' stock.

Jones hired Manzi to take over, hoping his connections would bring in long-needed financing. But on Mar. 29, three days after Manzi opened the Cambridge offices, Jones suffered a severe heart attack. During his months of recovery at the Cleveland Clinic, Manzi shifted the core operations from Pittsburgh to Cambridge, hiring 60 new engineers. Jones declined to talk to *Business Week*.

Manzi had his own ideas about funding. He nixed plans for a public offering and retained Goldman Sachs to arrange a private placement—which never happened. Insiders say that later in the spring, Manzi approached Cahners Publishing with an offer to sell a third of Nets for $175 million. Cahners didn't bite. Then, in July, he completed the AT&T New Media Services deal. From the outside, it looked like a coup: The new company was allowed to use AT&T's brand name along with its business network, which Manzi figured he could use to draw business to Nets. In return, he gave AT&T about 18% of Nets' stock.

Sources familiar with the deal say New Media Services was barely breaking even. But with the AT&T unit under his wing, Manzi began shutting down what he viewed as the low-tech side of the business: regional newsletters and parts catalogs on diskettes. Insiders claim the discontinued businesses were generating cash while electronic commerce was not. "Most of our leads were coming from the printed publications," says one. "Most of the industrial users were low-tech."

Startling Retreat

Nets' cash flow began to dwindle. By January, it was clear to some insiders that Manzi's strategy was faltering. AT&T Business Network, essentially a Web site that collected business news, wasn't attracting many customers. But it was eating up at least $5 million a year in costs. In late January, Manzi pulled the plug on that business. He also announced a startling retreat: Instead of trading billions of dollars worth of industrial goods, he said Nets would focus on connecting customers and suppliers in such prosaic business services as maintenance.

At the time, the company was burning cash at a rate of $1 million a month, and Manzi and his team still were struggling to sign up customers. Nets retained Lazard Fréres to sell a third of the company for $55 million—30% of what Manzi had sought a year before. By April, the asking price was $52 million for 40%. Jones and two associates resigned from the board on Apr. 9.

By May, Nets' money had run out. Supporters say Manzi by then was working around the clock to find new capital, in addition to fronting the company $500,000 a week for two weeks in late April. "He's an unbelievable fighter," says one Nets executive. On May 9, though, Manzi sent an electronic concession of defeat to employees. But, he assured them, "I believe in our vision and that this is one of the major business opportunities for the next decade."

Manzi's supporters say he simply underestimated the task of building an electronic commerce system on the scale he envisioned for Nets. "This is the kind of thing that happens when a company tries to break new ground," says Michael Porter, a Harvard business school professor who sits on the Nets board. "The odds here were always on the thin side." Manzi's outsize ambition, though, did little to improve those odds.

SCRAMBLED SIGNAL: Innovative Start-Up Flops, and a Lawsuit Against TCI Follows

by Mark Robichaux

John Malone always called it a "killer application"—interactive software that allows home viewers to play along with TV sports or game shows for prizes.

Three years ago, the powerful chief executive of cable giant Tele-Communications Inc. chanced upon the one such system he thought would take the TV world by storm: a sleek black, software-driven gadget developed by upstart Interactive Network Inc. Mr. Malone seemed convinced that its real-time capabilities would revolutionize the way people use their television sets, and be the first real hit in the hot, lucrative new niche known as interactive TV.

These days, however, it is Interactive that is using the word killer— as an accusation against TCI. Virtually bankrupt, with seemingly little way to raise new capital, Interactive is accusing TCI of using hardball tactics and questionable business practices to wreck Interactive and snatch its business patents.

"I feel liked I've been robbed at gunpoint," says David Lockton, the intense, 58-year-old chairman and founder of Interactive. His case is laid out in a lawsuit filed in California state court charging TCI with, among other things, a breach of fiduciary duty, conflict of interest and "abuse of control."

So intensely personal has the dispute become that Mr. Lockton posed his 200 employees for a photo—all of them with raised fists, their middle fingers extended. "I told them this one was for John Malone," he says.

TCI dismisses Interactive's complaint as the dying gasp of a Silicon Valley start-up that oversold its potential and ran into a lot of bad luck. Whatever the case, the clash makes one thing clear: In the race to roll out new technology in an evolving, multibillion-dollar industry, the ground is often shifting and slippery, and the pain often exceeds the gain.

Originally published in the Wall Street Journal, *February 26, 1996. Reprinted by permission,* © *1996 Dow Jones & Co., Inc. All rights reserved worldwide.*

Today, numerous cable giants around the country are halting interactive tests over delays, high costs and concerns about whether consumers really want it. Instead, many are focusing on using their wires to offer access to the Internet.

Others are still actively in the hunt in an industry that some say could be worth $14 billion in the next five years. One example: In a pilot project that should provide some indication of interactive TV's direction, Time Warner Inc., the nation's second-largest cable operator, wired the last of 4,000 interactive homes in Orlando, Fla., two months ago. Among the earliest practical applications will be video-on-demand, which allows viewers to choose from scores of movies at the flick of a remote-control unit.

"There will be interactive TV of some sort," insists Gary Arlen, a Bethesda, Md., research consultant. "But it's going to have a long, long gestation period."

For Mr. Lockton, a Yale-educated entrepreneur who helped start 12 companies before Interactive, the outset of 1992 seemed auspicious. He initially called his idea for Interactive "TBO"—for "The Big One"—and boldly predicted as many as one million subscribers in the first year after launch. "It was frightening," he says of the company's market potential.

Indeed, the company's gizmo started a huge buzz among media companies, and some jumped in to give seed money or loans, including General Electric Co.'s NBC, Gannett Co., Motorola Inc., Sprint Corp., Cablevision Systems Corp. and A.C. Nielsen Co.

The main attraction: Using a black control unit with a keypad and display screen, viewers could play along with 50 different TV programs, including "Jeopardy" and "Wheel of Fortune," and Major League Baseball and National Football League games. They could even predict story lines in shows such as "Murder She Wrote."

Says Massachusetts Institute of Technology's Media Lab director Nicholas Negroponte, an early adviser to the company, "The fundamental idea was terrific."

Paul Kagan, owner of a leading cable-industry research firm in Carmel, Calif., became an investor after his first brush with Interactive's system. "It was very successful in my house," says Mr. Kagan, who adds: "Analysts who said the game doesn't work are wrong. It works."

It was Mr. Kagan who, in early 1993, got Mr. Malone interested in Interactive. In April of that year, Mr. Malone got his first peek at the system at TCI headquarters in Denver. There, with Mr. Kagan in attendance, Mr. Lockton and Robert Brown, a senior vice president, got the TCI chief to play a game of Interactive "Jeopardy." A smiling Mr. Malone was hooked.

At the time, hype over interactivity had reached a frenzy, and cable, telephone and computer industries all were tripping over themselves to stake their claims. So, in June, TCI began investing roughly $13 million for a 22% stake in the company, and Mr. Malone declared that the Interactive Network system would be "the industry standard for interactive television." TCI installed Gary Howard, a TCI vice president, on Interactive's board.

Eventually, TCI would sink $30 million in equity and loans into Interactive. Not only did Interactive seem to offer a prize system that made watching TV compelling, it had a bonus application: With antigambling laws being repealed in various states, Interactive's technology seemed a perfect way to break into the lucrative gaming and lottery business by allowing users to pick lottery numbers or bet on televised horse races.

Never mind that, like many start-ups, Interactive Network had lurched from one cash infusion to another, posting a loss of $24.8 million on revenue of $1.1 million in 1993. It had drawn enough viewers in test markets in San Francisco and Chicago to keep investments coming; in the Bay Area, Interactive claimed 3,000 customers paying an average $25 a month for its service.

Fading Enthusiasm

It wouldn't be long, however, before the honeymoon turned sour. For one thing, TCI insisted that it could more-efficiently market Interactive's system by installing Interactive's software on new high-capacity digital-cable boxes. Equipment makers promised to deliver these boxes by 1994, but the delivery date came and went—and the boxes never (and still haven't) arrived. Interactive, expecting a quick national launch, found itself cooling its heels and considering other options—all the while burning up precious capital.

Meanwhile, TCI, still convinced that Interactive had a critical lead over rivals, continued to increase its stake in the company. But to hedge its bets, TCI had also taken a stake in a rival interactive start-up known as Zing Systems. Interactive considered this a perplexing annoyance at first; later though, Zing itself would flame out, filing for bankruptcy in December. Interactive would judge it a disaster for its own fortunes when a divided TCI management seemed, at a critical juncture, to be throwing its weight and energy toward Zing.

All the more galling to Mr. Lockton was an episode in 1994. When TCI learned that Mr. Lockton was planning a $22 million public offering at a discount to offshore purchasers, Brendan Clouston, president of TCI's cable operations, called Mr. Lockton to Denver, where he persuaded him to halt the offering.

Mr. Lockton recalls that Mr. Clouston said, "If anyone is going to buy this company at a discount, it's going to be the guys who brought you to the dance." TCI told investment banker Lazard Freres to "stand by" at a meeting in April 1994 while TCI prepared a financing plan to roll out the service, according to the Interactive Network lawsuit. Both Mr. Clouston and Lazard Freres declined to comment on these events.

A new investor—Sony Corp.—also emerged when Mr. Lockton presented the company's financing needs and national rollout plans to lead investors TCI and NBC. Sony, which distributes popular game shows, had started Game Show Channel on cable and saw potential for Interactive's system. Under the plan, TCI proposed a $65 million public-rights offering, to be guaranteed by TCI and Sony; an additional $30 million in equity would be sold to TCI and Sony, with NBC as a junior partner, according to Mr. Lockton.

As it worked on a joint marketing plan with TCI, Interactive Network started adding employees, buying computers and equipping a new 80,000-square-foot production facility. Earlier, it had ordered 50,000 control units—backed by a letter of credit from TCI.

But at the last moment Sony, without explanation, pulled out. The move, Interactive's suit says, "left Interactive with no financing, and with $20 million in obligations incurred at the direction of TCI for the national launch." Sony declined to comment. But people close to Sony said the talks fell apart in August 1994 over terms that Sony thought favored TCI.

With Sony out, TCI began to play hardball, proposing a plan that would give it even greater control over Interactive. Atop its $20 million equity stake, TCI agreed to give Interactive an additional $10 million as a convertible secured loan. But, as a condition, Interactive would first have to obtain $15 million more from other TCI-approved investors, as well as $25 million in new equity—a total of $40 million, all within a scant two weeks.

TCI, the suit goes on, also demanded that the title to the patents, software and technology be deeded immediately to the secured creditors. Then, as the largest creditor, TCI designated an agent for the secured creditors—itself. Interactive could only regain full title to the patents and software by raising an additional $45 million, according to its lawsuit.

TCI says the terms, though tough, gave Interactive another shot at going big time while salvaging TCI's interactive investment. But most on Interactive's board saw it differently. "We had no choice," says Interactive board member Jerome S. Rubin, founder of Lexis and Nexis electronic-information systems. "It was take it or go under."

People at some of Interactive's other minority partners say they were privately aghast at TCI's moves, but were unable to stop them because TCI had other significant relationships with them. NBC badly needed TCI to carry its CNBC and America's Talking cable channels. Motorola was making new TV set-top boxes for the cable giant. Sprint was getting roughly $1.3 billion from TCI as part of a financing for a new wireless-telephone venture.

Most of Interactive's investors declined to comment. NBC, in a statement, said: "It is NBC's view that Interactive Network had a high degree of potential to be a leading interactive system. We were very disappointed that the company's plans did not come to fruition."

Rise Before the Fall

In August 1994, Interactive says it agreed to TCI's terms—and, surprisingly, raised $15 million from NBC, Motorola and Sprint, and more than $20 million in an offering of shares in Europe. Immediately, the company paid debts outstanding, and used the remainder as operating capital.

But Mr. Lockton says that TCI, as secured creditor, began quashing proposals to raise new revenue, such as a unit to license its technology for gambling. TCI says it had serious concerns about the viability of such proposals.

If this weren't trouble enough, Interactive also found itself in an internal TCI power struggle between high-ranking TCI executives, some of whom were sold on Interactive's technology and some of whom were touting TCI's other Interactive bet, Zing. At one point in 1994, Mr. Lockton, at a meeting in Denver, informed Mr. Clouston that he had sued Zing for patent infringement in federal court in San Diego. Mr. Clouston, who had been an Interactive ally, replied: "Good."

The management conflicts boiled to the surface on a trip in January 1995, when Interactive executives flew to Denver to present what they considered to be better than expected results of a TCI-approved marketing test of their system in Indianapolis. Mr. Clouston, Interactive's champion, wasn't at the meeting. Instead, Interactive executives say they found themselves facing hostile questions from Zing supporters who clearly were intent on disparaging the Interactive system.

"There was a lot of hostility," recalls Gordon Wade, an Interactive board member and president of a consulting concern. "It was apparent to me there were warring factions within TCI."

Says TCI's Gary Howard: "The management team at TCI is like any corporation—you can have healthy tension. Everybody is looking at the bottom line."

Though Zing would also fall by the wayside, Mr. Lockton says that meeting convinced him that he was being abandoned by TCI. In the following months, he tried unsuccessfully to lure other giants such as ITT Corp., News Corp. and Bell Atlantic Corp. as investors.

But by mid-1995, Interactive was broke again. Its once-promising San Francisco and Chicago pilots never attracted more than 5,500 subscribers and are now defunct. The company, since 1987, had raised and raced through $130 million without ever getting its national roll out.

Two Options

Its stock, which had traded at an all-time high of $15 a share on the Nasdaq Stock Market, dropped to 25 cents, and the company was delisted last spring. One by one, for a variety of reasons, Motorola, Sprint and Gannett had resigned from Interactive's board.

For now, Interactive seems to have two options: file for protection under Chapter 11 bankruptcy laws, or be forced to do so by creditors. TCI, as its chief lender, stands to gain all its remaining assets—including the technology, software and patents.

Interactive now charges in its lawsuit that TCI's goal was simply to snatch Interactive's patents. It also asserts that Mr. Howard, TCI's designee to Interactive's board, had a clear conflict, divided between the interests of Interactive's shareholders and safeguarding TCI's Interactive investment.

TCI dismisses Mr. Lockton's assertions. "When the whole digital world got delayed, (Mr. Lockton's) ability to get his cost down was delayed, too," says TCI's Mr. Howard. "We're not used to writing off $30 million."

He adds: "No one around here wants to be part of a failed effort." In suing TCI, Mr. Lockton is "stretching to find a reason why his business failed," Mr. Howard says.

Mr. Lockton has moved his handful of remaining employees to a hangar-sized warehouse in Silicon Valley, where thousands of the Interactive black boxes are collecting dust. He makes calls from a car telephone—the office phone was cut off. Back at the entrance of the white, mirrored offices of Interactive Network, a sign says: "Game over."

AMBITIONS OF STARTUP FALL SHORT: Lofty Goals of Terry Software Thwarted by Mistakes, Conflict

by Richard Burnett

Leaving a trail of dashed hopes, broken friendships, and empty pockets, Terry Software Development Corp. has melted like soft-serve ice cream in a Central Florida summer day.

What began as a team effort has dissolved into a pool of conflict, pitting friend against friend, partner against partner.

At the beginning, Terry Software's owners envisioned their company growing with success and themselves basking in millions of dollars.

But when the big sales failed to materialize, employees and rent went unpaid, investors lost money and the vision was shattered.

"The company had a lot of potential," said Byrd Marshall Jr., an Orlando lawyer who represented Terry Software in some deals. "But any technology company like this in the development stages has capitalization problems. Theirs just lasted longer than they anticipated."

Terry Software was born in the summer of 1988, the brainchild of three former engineers from Martin Marietta Corp.'s defense operations in Orlando.

Its demise two years later came after a torturous series of mistakes and false promises, said Bob F. Terry, the company's founder.

Terry, who became the target of several lawsuits and legal judgments, considers himself the victim more than the victimizer in the downfall of Terry Software.

"This has been a major learning experience for me," he said. "I was a very trusting individual, but I learned that you have to be very careful what you do in business."

"Ninety percent of the people I got involved with came to me saying they had all these abilities to do wonderful things. But what it all boiled down to was they allowed me to do all the work."

In the beginning, the partners of Terry Software—Terry, Mike A. Bialota and H. Ron Fisher—wanted to parlay their high-tech experience into private enterprise. In less than a year, however, the threesome had split, and litigation was imminent.

Originally published in the Orlando Sentinel, *Feb. 25, 1991. Used with permission.*

As a software engineer for Martin, Terry helped write computer programs for the Air Force's Lantirn night-vision system. Bialota also worked on the Lantirn, as a logistics engineer. Fisher was a software engineer on other programs.

In late August 1988, Terry left Martin and started Terry Software. Several months later, Bialota and Fisher joined him and they began to develop a business plan.

Terry had already laid the groundwork for the company's first product, a data security software system for personal-computer networks. Terry and Fisher were the software programmers, Bialota was the marketing chief.

In spring 1989, the three hired their first full-time salesman, Mike Seaman, who had been a data processing equipment salesman in Tampa.

Success seemed within reach, and the Terry Software team was loose and confident, former employees say. Terry and Bialota, former military officers, talked like old war buddies. Terry, then 29, and Seaman, then 25, were fellow musicians and pals who socialized together and lived in Terry's house.

Business relationships were informal. Money exchanged hands routinely with few records kept. They trusted each other.

Terry promised to make them all millionaires, former employees said.

The company appeared close to signing a number of multimillion-dollar deals for its product, PC Security System Plus. It was, the company proclaimed, virtually fool-proof against unauthorized access to computer files.

"We've had Fortune 500 companies that take a look at our system come back to us and ask us how in the world we did this," Terry, the company's president, said in June 1989.

Officials of the Naval Training Center in Orlando and McDonnell Douglas Corp. in St. Louis said then they intended to buy the software.

Encouraged, Terry Software optimistically projected first-year sales of $2 million to $20 million.

Reality was far different.

"No sale ever went through," said Bialota, the former vice president of marketing who invested more than $20,000 in the company. "Nothing ever materialized of substance, and no purchase order ever came in from the companies."

The bond began to break during the summer 1989. In June, Fisher resigned as vice president of engineering.

In a court deposition six months later, Terry claimed that Fisher allowed the software-security system to infringe on the copyright of software by other companies. Former Terry Software officials said it was unclear who caused the alleged infringement. Fisher could not be reached for comment.

Suddenly, many of the potential customers were finding fault with PC Security System Plus, Seaman said.

"It was complicated to use, cumbersome and not as user-friendly as a lot of other software products on the market," he said.

In an attempt to regroup, Terry Software bought the right to Genesis, a disaster-recovery program for data-processing systems.

By then, however, the company needed money badly, former officials say. In August, the company hired Lance Woodworth, an Orlando business consultant, to obtain new financial backing.

Woodworth, who would later become chief executive officer, said he was hired "to rescue the company from insolvency, raise the necessary money to continue operations and complete the development of its software products.

Woodworth said he obtained capital from a friend and business associate, Bruce Simpson of Gainesville, who invested at least $300,000 from 1989 through 1990.

In the meantime, Woodworth and Terry began a housecleaning at the company. The two developed a plan to oust Bialota and renegotiate Seaman's employment contract, which promised him an annual salary of $50,000, according to court records.

By September, Bialota agreed to resign and gave up his company stock. In turn, Terry pledged to pay back more than $28,000 that Bialota and friend Kathleen Dabney had invested in Terry Software, according to court records.

Two months later, after Seaman agreed to renegotiate his contract, Terry fired him. Court records later stated that the company had never formally paid Seaman, although he received some money on a personal basis from Terry.

By January 1990, everyone was in court. Bialota, Dabney and Seaman filed suit against Terry Software Jan. 26, seeking to recover lost investments and unpaid salaries.

In the litigation that followed, the former Terry Software officials alleged that Terry had breached contracts and refused to pay them, according to court records.

Although initially resisting payments to Bialota and Dabney, Terry and Woodworth agreed in an August 1990 out-of-court settlement to pay the two a total of $20,000 plus interest over a two-year period.

Seaman continued his suit to trial Aug. 17. Seaman said Terry misled him from the start about so-called multimillion-dollar deals that were "imminent." For almost six months, Seaman worked without pay, he said.

Terry said Seaman's employment contract was invalid, because Seaman had misrepresented his work experience prior to employment and has misled Terry about his work on company accounts. Seaman also had breached his work agreement by misusing the company telephone for personal calls, Terry said in court records.

The one-day trial ended with Orange County Circuit Judge William C. Gridley ruling in favor of Seaman. Evidence and testimony indicated that Terry knew Seaman's qualifications when he hired him; that he did not misrepresent work; and that any alleged misuse of the telephone was not relevant to the suit, the judge ruled.

In September, the judge entered a final judgment of $43,982 for Seaman. Later that month, Seaman's attorneys garnished a company account to obtain $13,881 of that judgment.

The remainder is unpaid, Seaman said.

"Bob (Terry) was real good at selling a dream," he said. "But I don't believe he ever put any of his own money into the company."

Terry said he befriended Seaman, allowed him to stay in his home and paid his household expenses and utilities because the company was short on capital.

"Mike knew we didn't have any money," he said. "He knew we were a startup company in the basic entrepreneurial environment."

Terry said he went out and obtained more financial backing with the help of Woodworth and Simpson, who became the major investor. But Simpson wanted Seaman and Bialota out of the company, Terry said.

"It became obvious that we had to make some major organizational changes," he said.

About a year after Bialota and Seaman left Terry Software, the company came in for more changes. Terry said Simpson decided to break his partnership with Woodworth, and in late October 1990, Simpson and Terry voted to fire Woodworth.

Subsequently, Simpson, who owned all the assets of Terry Software, sold his stake to the Quantum group, a real estate company in Orlando, Terry said. A new company was formed, called Quantum Software, with Terry as chief engineer, he said.

Terry said several companies are evaluating the products he developed, but there still have been no sales.

In the meantime, Woodworth said he has been stung by his ouster. He said Terry and Simpson "secretly" negotiated the Quantum deal.

Simpson would not comment on the deal.

More legal action is in store.

Terry's settlement with Bialota and Dabney has collapsed, according to court records. Earlier this month, they reactivated their claims after Terry failed to make a Dec. 1 payment. Terry now owes them more than $37,000, according to records.

3.2   TOGETHER WE FALL

"United we stand; divided we fall." That is a basic truism that every American school child understands. It tells an important story from the Revolutionary War, that we must act together if we are to win. The lesson of that truism, for the most part, is valid both internationally and throughout time.

This section of the book is about counterexamples to that truism! Here, we look at companies that decided to band together, and failed because they did so! While "bigger is better" has worked for a lot of computing companies—some would say that, during this era of computing company shakeout, only those that become strong through growth and merger will survive—it has not been a universal solution. (We will see, in the next section of this book (on supercomputing), another example of where "bigger is better" turns out to be simply untrue).

Here, we present two stories. The first is about the merging of Novell and WordPerfect, a marriage that many thought at the outset was made in heaven. As the world's most successful software company, Microsoft, continued its dramatic growth, other software companies began to fear that its growth would result in their own inability to compete, and their eventual demise. Some resorted to attacking Microsoft on legal grounds, a path that is still unfolding through U.S. Department of Justice antitrust action as this book is being written. Others chose the path of Novell and WordPerfect, merger.

That marriage made in heaven ended badly. Basically, the two companies had very different cultures. Success-focused Novell collided head on with lifestyle-focused WordPerfect. WP execs saw their Novell counterparts as "rude invaders of the corporate . . . Camelot." Novell executives began to suspect that WordPerfect had overvalued itself in merger negotiations. Phrases like "repeatedly fought" and "significant clashes" and "debacle" are scattered throughout the story to follow, like litter after a tornado has moved on. "Personality issues," one pundit is quoted as saying, "cannot be ignored in the computer industry's rush to consolidate."

Eventually and perhaps inevitably, there was a divorce, with WordPerfect being sold by Novell to another struggling software house. The losses were colossal. The sale price was 1/7 of the original $1.4 billion purchase price! Someone in the midst of the wreckage is quoted as saying "It was four years of wasted time." "It might have worked if it was executed perfectly," another guru said. "Instead, the strategy was disastrous, one of the costliest in software history."

It is not just in software where we see the phenomenon "together, we fall," and the littered wreckage of a merger that failed. Probably the most important computing mergers that failed stories are connected with AT&T.

That leading telecommunications company is just completing a fairly bad half-century. They suffered an anti-trust breakup at the hands of the U.S. Justice Department a few decades ago. They found serious and hostile competitors on their doorstep almost immediately, and began a vicious level of competition to which all the competitors have contributed and which many Americans are fairly sickened and disgusted by. They attempted to recoup from their losses in several ways. One, trying to get back into the local telephone business (from which they had been barred in the anti-trust resolution), is still dangling out there just out of AT&T's reach. The other, trying to get into the computing business, is what our story that follows is about.

Each time AT&T has tried to muscle or buy or otherwise get into the computing business, the failure has been manifest. Some promising avenue for entering the field is chosen, and the execution driving down that avenue turns out to be so atrocious that the whole thing falls apart. That, in fact, is what happens in our story of the attempt to combine AT&T and the long-time computing company NCR (once known as National Cash Register).

The story of the AT&T/NCR merger is surprisingly similar to the previous Novell/WordPerfect story. There was an immediate culture clash (an NCR spokesman said "they destroyed our culture"). There were disagreements about the financial viability of NCR prior to the merger (the merger was, to a large extent, an unfriendly one). In this case, key NCR people were dismissed in multiple waves of cost-cutting and culture-snuffing.

And, eventually, AT&T had to admit failure. They turned NCR loose. It is still trying to regroup and return to its former level of success. Meanwhile, the general view of the industry is that the failed merger was "financially disastrous" to AT&T, and the whole ugly result represents a "stinging rebuke to AT&T."

"United we stand"? Not in these stories!

NOVELL NOUVEAU: Software Firm Fights to Remake Business After Ill-Fated Merger

by Don Clark

Robert Frankenberg wants to take his company back to the future. But first he has to escape its past.

Mr. Frankenberg became chief executive of Novell Inc., the second-largest personal-computer software company, 20 months ago. The job has turned into one of the toughest in the industry.

Novell was once a money machine as profitable as industry leader Microsoft Corp., which tried to buy it in a secret $10 billion bid in 1992. Mr. Frankenberg's predecessor, Raymond Noorda, rebuffed the overture and instead embarked on an expensive acquisition binge to fight Microsoft on all fronts, culminating in a March 1994 deal to buy WordPerfect Corp. for stock then worth $1.4 billion.

Mr. Noorda's concept was to meld WordPerfect's popular word processor and other programs with Novell's operating systems, a business model similar to Microsoft's. It might have worked—if executed perfectly. Instead, the strategy was disastrous, one of the costliest in software history. WordPerfect lost most of its market share, virtually imploding last fall.

One reason is obvious: fierce competition from Microsoft. But the other key factor, known to few outside this foothill community, is an extraordinary clash between the staffs of Novell and WordPerfect that crippled the merger and compounded lethal management errors.

WordPerfect executives came to view Novell executives as rude invaders of the corporate equivalent of Camelot. They repeatedly fought with top members of Novell's staff in San Jose, Calif., over issues ranging from expenses and management assignments to Christmas bonuses. Mr. Frankenberg sided with the San Jose contingent in a strategic mistake: dismantling a WordPerfect sales team that would be needed to push a long-awaited set of office software products.

Mr. Frankenberg now is trying to sell WordPerfect—minus nearly all of its top executives and about 3,600 employees—in the next three weeks. WordPerfect is expected to fetch one-seventh or less of its $1.4

billion purchase price. "The cultures were very, very different," Mr. Frankenberg says. "Melding those two was interesting and difficult, and there were significant clashes."

Dangers of Dithering

The debacle provides the latest evidence that personality issues can't be ignored in the computer industry's rush to consolidate. It also points up the dangers of dithering in a fast-paced Microsoft-dominated world. While Mr. Frankenberg was doing damage control, Novell was distracted from more aggressively expanding its core business—providing software that ties PCs into networks, a market into which Microsoft is making sharp inroads. Novell's stock sank 56% while the issues of other network companies soared, and its market value now is roughly half of what Microsoft offered nearly four years ago.

"I count four years of wasted time," says Craig Burton, a former Novell executive who heads a market-research firm in Salt Lake City. Of technology's all-time missed opportunities, "Novell ranks right up there," contends Rich Edwards, an analyst at Robertson Stephens & Co., the San Francisco brokerage house.

But it's too early to count Novell out. It still has a net profit margin—about 15%—many companies would envy, and about two-thirds of the market for PC network software. Mr. Frankenberg is refocusing the company on network-related products, pushing Novell into hooking together entire corporations, letting companies electronically merge selected operations with customers and suppliers, and even linking people with their appliances and cars.

Noorda's Nemesis

Other companies are banking on Novell to succeed in keeping Microsoft from dominating network computing. "From a user's standpoint, it's very important that there be alternatives to Microsoft," says Richard Shaffer, principal of Technologic Partners, a New York research firm. "The strongest alternative at the moment is Novell."

Some former Novell insiders claim the WordPerfect misadventure began because of Mr. Noorda's obsession with William Gates, Microsoft's chairman. They say Mr. Noorda believed Mr. Gates had strung him along during two rounds of merger discussions that failed.

Mr. Noorda denies such passions. He says he saw a time coming when corporate customers would prefer to deal with just one supplier for both networking software and applications. And Novell's NetWare operating system, working in the background, was a piece of technology that PC users never noticed, while Microsoft not only had an operating system but many programs that created user loyalty.

"We needed to get NetWare in your face," says Mr. Noorda, who is 71. "It wasn't obsession with Microsoft."

At any rate, Mr. Noorda jumped at the chance to acquire WordPerfect for $1.4 billion in stock and buy Borland International Inc.'s spreadsheet business for $145 million. Closely held WordPerfect had been battered by its failure to develop products for Microsoft's Windows operating system and to match Microsoft's move into low-priced combinations called suites. "We saw it as a merger of two great companies to make a greater third company," says John C. Lewis, a former WordPerfect executive vice president.

Investors disagreed. They dumped Novell's stock and drove the value of the stock transaction down to $855 million by the time the deal was closed in June 1994.

Mr. Frankenberg, a Hewlett-Packard executive who was consulted about the deal before joining Novell in April 1994, saw a credible chance to create links between desktop PC programs and networks that would rebuild WordPerfect's sagging market share. But former WordPerfect executives, including co-founder Bruce Bastian, say the attitude of other Novell executives toward WordPerfect appeared to be poisoned to begin with; this was particularly so, they add, among San Jose-based members of an inner circle called "the executive suite."

"The California people never liked the WordPerfect deal, me included, because it didn't make financial sense at all," says Kanwall Rekhi, a former Novell executive vice president who resigned from the board in September.

The Novell executives' fears were confirmed when WordPerfect sales dropped 14% in 1994 to $600 million.

In retrospect, there were reasons for skepticism. WordPerfect was close-knit and insular. Employees typically left at 5 p.m. to attend to family and Mormon Church responsibilities: highly paid programmers blew off steam by piloting remote control boats in a nearby canal. Customer support was generous, and the sales force never had quotas.

"It's hard to explain how magical it was," says Dale Taylor, a former WordPerfect product manager who left Novell in November.

Novell, by contrast, was fractious and tightly focused on profits. Its revenue per employee was about $225,000 at the time of the merger, compared with less than $140,000 for the 5,000-employee WordPerfect. Executives from both companies agreed that WordPerfect's expenses had to be cut sharply, particularly in sales.

But WordPerfect people became demoralized as Novell people received most sales-management jobs and WordPerfect's manufacturing and telephone sales were contracted out.

Christmas 1994 became a symbol for the tensions. WordPerfect had a tradition of paying holiday bonuses. WordPerfect employees complained bitterly, Mr. Frankenberg says, when he decided after the merger to give bonuses only to networking businesses that hit financial targets. WordPerfect people griped that in merged departments, only longtime Novell people got bonuses. "That was one of the turning points in people losing hope in the possibility of us being an integrated company," says Claire Averett, WordPerfect's former vice president of human resources.

Dismantled Sales Force

WordPerfect's managers committed a crucial mistake, failing to deliver a new suite in time to take advantage of Microsoft's launch of a new operating system, Windows 95, last August. But Mr. Frankenberg may well have committed one of his own, by agreeing with his staff to disband WordPerfect's sales force to cut costs. Novell's sales organization, adept at selling networking products to a network of independent resellers, had little experience in selling low-priced application programs to retailers or corporations. Dismantling WordPerfect's sales team penalized sales of a new suite of application programs, called PerfectOffice, which began shipping in early 1995.

"They were sitting there with product and no one to sell it," says Adrian Rietveld, WordPerfect's chief executive at the time of the merger.

But Mr. Frankenberg balked at the cost of rebuilding a new applications sales force. "Right or wrong, it was my decision," Mr. Frankenberg says. "I simply could not afford to have two separate sales structures around the world."

Because of the errors on both sides, Novell's application sales were only $49 million in the fiscal fourth quarter ended Oct. 28—far below the $144 million of the second quarter—causing Novell to badly miss earnings estimates for the fourth period. The company also learned in October that the Windows 95 suite wouldn't be ready by January 1996.

Mr. Frankenberg concluded that time had run out. He received approval from Novell's board to sell the division on Friday, Oct. 27. Working throughout the weekend, he announced the decision in a videotaped message and electronic mail to the group and its 1,800 employees.

"The synergies that were hoped for at the time of the merger had gone away," Mr. Frankenberg says. "I knew it was the right decision, but it was still very difficult."

'Easy Scapegoat'

Jeffrey Tarter, an industry watcher who publishes Softletter in Watertown, Mass., blames the Windows 95 delay and many other problems on WordPerfect's earlier failure to keep up with Microsoft. W. E. "Pete" Peterson, WordPerfect's president from 1980 to 1992, adds, "Novell makes a real easy scapegoat."

Some analysts think Novell may get up to $300 million for the former WordPerfect operations, though Mr. Peterson predicts the price may be as low as $50 million. Several well-financed software companies, such as Oracle Corp., have said they aren't interested. Bidders are believed to include financial groups hoping to team up with former WordPerfect managers. "You have an established franchise," says Will Fastie, an industry consultant who failed to find financing for a bid. "It's too bad Novell didn't do what was necessary."

Mr. Bastian, the WordPerfect co-founder, faults Mr. Frankenberg for letting his Novell troops run roughshod over WordPerfect's. "I want him to run it for what's best for the company, not for his executive staff," he says. Mr. Bastian resigned as a Novell director after the decision to sell WordPerfect. His Novell stock has declined by nearly $90 million in value since the merger. "I don't like Novell," he says. "I don't like the way they treat their people."

Mr. Frankenberg bristles at the suggestion he played favorites or didn't take decisive action. He has recruited new managers, installed budgeting and reporting procedures and repaired problems with Novell's latest NetWare line.

His main challenge now is to try to compete with a juggernaut. Microsoft's Windows NT operating system lets people share files and printers, like Novell's NetWare, but also is good for running business applications. Although 1995 NetWare sales rose a healthy 21% to 825,000 units from 680,000 a year earlier, researcher International Data Corp. estimates that Windows NT Server sales will nearly triple to 353,000 units from 115,000.

While complaining about some Microsoft tactics, Mr. Frankenberg has met with Mr. Gates to help NetWare work better with Windows NT and Windows 95. The goal: to make NetWare a neutral tool providing network connections.

Over the longer haul, Mr. Frankenberg wants Novell to play a major role in the evolution of world-wide communications, working with AT&T Corp. and other big players to marry the Internet with private NetWare networks.

One Novell weapon, not yet matched by Microsoft, is a directory technology that helps identify computer users and determines which corporate databases and other computing resources they can tap into without the need for multiple passwords. Mr. Frankenberg also has high hopes for a simpler variant of NetWare that can connect machines, appliances and even cars to computer networks.

Rick Sherlund, a Goldman Sachs analyst, says Mr. Frankenberg "has done a terrific job of rationalizing the business." But questions about growth remain. In the fiscal fourth period, sales of the latest version of NetWare were flat with the third period, while sales of its older version fell 23%. Novell predicted that total first-quarter revenue will be about flat with the fourth quarter's $481 million.

Selling WordPerfect presents its own risks. Microsoft can bundle Windows NT at discounted prices with its popular desktop application programs and create attractive technical links between them, as Novell had originally planned to do with its products. Though Novell hopes to retain close ties with WordPerfect's buyer, companies that use its two product lines may be easy targets for Microsoft. "I think the analysis that this is smart for Novell is wrong," argues Gordon Eubanks, chief executive officer of Symantec Corp. and a veteran of software-industry mergers.

Mr. Frankenberg says it makes no sense to remain in businesses half-heartedly, force-fitting two sales structures that don't mesh. Above all, the episode taught him the importance of retaining focus. "This is a much harder job than I thought it would be," he says.

DISCONNECTED LINE: Why AT&T Takeover of NCR Hasn't Been A Real Bell Ringer

by John J. Keller

Forced marriages rarely result in happy unions. The one between AT&T Corp. and NCR Corp. has proved financially disastrous.

A perennial loser in computers, AT&T in 1990 feverishly pursued NCR, finally paying $7.48 billion in stock to acquire the stubbornly independent company. With NCR, AT&T would "link people, organizations and their information in a seamless, global computer network," AT&T Chairman Robert E. Allen vowed.

This week, it will become clear how wrong his forecast was. AT&T is expected to take a $1.2 billion charge, lay off up to 10,000 people and substantially narrow the computer unit's business. Losses are said to have hit almost half a billion dollars since January. Some insiders say an outright sale of the unit, now known as Global Information Solutions, may loom.

It is a stinging rebuke for AT&T, a company unaccustomed to failure in its mainline telecommunications business. How could this happen? The NCR deal has failed so far because of myriad miscues. AT&T ignored warning signs and continued pursuing a company that was far weaker than anyone first realized. It let many top NCR executives exit, then rankled an embittered and balky work force by imposing its own culture on the new property.

Taking Over

AT&T declined to make Mr. Allen and other executives available for interviews about problems at the computer unit.

AT&T waited through a voluntary two-year hands-off period to take full management control of NCR. Then it appointed its own executives to run the unit—even though AT&T managers had flopped in steering the parent company into computers. The AT&T team tried to put in a financial-reporting system that made it tougher to gauge profitability as products moved from production to market. They reorga-

---

Originally published in the Wall Street Journal, *Sept. 19, 1995. Reprinted by permission,* © *1995 Dow Jones & Co., Inc. All rights reserved worldwide.*

nized sales, confusing customers. And they ultimately dumped the NCR name—successor to the century-old National Cash Register Co.—in favor of the sterile GIS.

"AT&T destroyed our culture and the esprit de corps we had here," says one veteran NCR manager who now fears losing his job in the new cutbacks.

AT&T's fatal attraction for NCR was a bold attempt to buy its way out of a record of failure in the computer business. After the breakup of the old AT&T empire in 1984, the company hoped a foray into computers would jazz up its image and let it shed the mantle—and the lower stock multiple—of a boring, slow-growth utility.

"We're not Ma Bell anymore," Chairman Allen would remind employees.

Strategic Struggles

Everyone had hyped the coming "convergence" of computers and communications, but AT&T lost as much as $3 billion over five years in the late 1980s as it struggled to make its own strategy work. NCR's fortunes in computers, by comparison, looked like a prize.

So, AT&T made an unsolicited offer of $6.03 billion in December 1990. The companies looked like a terrific fit. NCR was trolling for new markets and had won praise for selling "open" computer systems based on the Unix software invented by Bell Labs. NCR's ties to retail and banking markets might stir more revenue if NCR customers used AT&T's communications network to transmit data.

But NCR would have none of it. NCR Chairman Charles Exley had taken a company that made its name in boring cash registers and put together a well-managed expansion into electronic systems and software that, by the late 1980s, had made NCR one of the industry's most profitable companies and a hot stock.

Digging In

NCR had a proud heritage. The company helped build Dayton, Ohio, over the past 80 years, and it gave a young salesman, Thomas Watson, his start selling business machines. When Mr. Watson departed, he started his own company—International Business Machines Corp.—and borrowed much of NCR's buttoned-down, white-shirt approach.

Mr. Exley had no intention of letting NCR become a mere AT&T unit. He wrote to Mr. Allen saying, "We simply will not place in jeopardy the important values we are creating at NCR in order to bail out AT&T's failed strategy."

Over four months, he and AT&T waged war. NCR's chairman said that AT&T was targeting the wrong company, and that NCR was just beginning to execute its open-systems plan and couldn't afford the distraction of a long takeover battle.

In reality, NCR already was beginning to slide. But as it reluctantly started negotiations with AT&T, NCR offered up some rosy predictions about its future. Mr. Exley's team said NCR's 1991 revenue would hit $6.62 billion, a 5% rise over the year earlier, and net income would be $386 million. Going out several years, NCR told AT&T that its profit in 1995 would hit $897 million on revenue of $10.3 billion. AT&T sweetened its offer by $1.4 billion.

NCR later acknowledged that its forecasting was flawed. In September 1991, right before the merger was consummated, NCR filed papers with the Securities and Exchange Commission saying 1991 revenue and profit would be "materially below" projections it made to AT&T during the talks—in fact, even below 1990's showing.

"They have never hit their internal forecasts since AT&T got them," says Jack B. Grubman, an analyst at Salomon Brothers Inc. "Not once."

Mr. Exley declined a vice chairman's post at AT&T after the merger and quietly left the company. His generous exit package includes close to $700,000 a year as part of the merger settlement, plus the roughly $35 million he made in the stock swap with AT&T. Mr. Exley, 65 years old, is sailing in the South Pacific and not able to take calls, according to his secretary.

The New Boss

Mr. Exley's successor, NCR President Gilbert Williamson, vowed to make the marriage work. But some of his actions repelled AT&T officials. Mr. Allen, sticking to his hands-off pledge, put what was left of AT&T's computer business in Mr. Williamson's hands, urging him to work with managers of AT&T units.

A crack salesman at NCR in the 1970s, Mr. Williamson had risen through the ranks on his ability to put up big numbers. Under AT&T, he favored the NCR line and gave scant support to one of AT&T's few real successes in the computer market: a new kind of laptop.

AT&T wanted to cash in on the mobile computing trend with its own unique machine. Snappily named Safari, it had communications features that dazzled the experts and trade writers.

At one of his regular product reviews a short time after the merger, somebody asked Mr. Williamson what to do about AT&T's Safari, a machine superior to NCR's own laptop. An executive who was at the meeting says Mr. Williamson snapped: "Give it a number," as other NCR machines have. When the person noted that this might hurt sales, "Gil said 'Discussion over,'" the executive recalls. Never aggressively marketed, the Model 3170 bit the dust. Today, AT&T resells laptops from NEC Corp. of Japan. Mr. Williamson recalls the Safari meeting but says, "The nomenclature was used to show where it fell in our 3000 family of computers. Maybe what you've heard is a reverse attitude problem on the part of some former AT&T computer people."

Still embittered over the takeover, NCR management never warmed up to AT&T. When AT&T sent a copy of its planned annual report, Mr. Williamson and his team passed it around and "just dumped on it," says one person. "Word got back to AT&T." Says Mr. Williamson: "I don't believe that ever happened."

Regarding talk of strained relations between himself and 60-year-old AT&T Chairman Allen, Mr. Williamson says, "Look, the NCR management team was doing its best to execute the strategy that was in place. That's what AT&T and Bob Allen wanted us to do." He adds: "We were executing that transition well and making a profit."

Juice and Enthusiasm

When Mr. Williamson, 58, left NCR in early 1993, AT&T scurried to make the unit more AT&T-like. NCR workers in Dayton were asked to attend pep-talk breakfasts with their new chief executive officer, Jerre Stead, an AT&T executive. Mr. Stead, who had helped to turn around AT&T's struggling office-phone-systems business, used a chipper delivery and sloganeering to motivate workers. "Delight your customers," he would say.

Moving quickly to make NCR more "open," Mr. Stead had the conference room at NCR's Dayton headquarters rewalled in glass so people could see senior managers in action. He called managers "coaches" and lower employees "associates." In a satellite conference call to employees, Mr. Stead gave out his home phone number and pressed other NCR executives to do the same.

Mr. Stead's was an open-door policy—literally. He had the doors on senior executives' offices taken off so that workers could wander in and chat. NCR President R. Elton White returned from a trip to find his door gone. Infuriated, he told a custodian to replace it, but Mr. Stead countermanded the order. A 27-year veteran, Mr. White quit a short time later. He confirms the incident but declines to comment further.

AT&T began to insinuate itself into NCR culture in other ways, making workers adhere to an AT&T code of values called the "Common Bond." Some NCR employees felt hounded by recruiters from AT&T's "employee resource groups" representing specific segments within AT&T—women, blacks, homosexuals, Asians and others. "If you tried to say anything about [the employee groups] like 'What are they doing here?' or 'They have no business doing this here,' AT&T sent you to sensitivity classes," one manager says. An AT&T spokeswoman says, "Nobody was forced to do anything."

But the change that truly disturbed NCR came in early 1994 when Mr. Stead changed the unit's name to AT&T Global Information Solutions. Down came the NCR logo from the building on South Patterson Boulevard, named for NCR founder John H. Patterson; up went the AT&T logo of a blue-striped globe.

The following July, Mr. Stead got snagged in a local political spat, perhaps innocently. A Dayton-area school board decided to spend $1.2 million on IBM personal computers rather than the $1 million NCR had bid on the project. AT&T sent letters to employees who lived in the Centerville district relating how the school board had just declined to grant Mr. Stead a reversal. The letters mentioned a recent bond issue that was voted on to pay for it. Some folks in Centerville, who thought AT&T was trying to meddle in its affairs, saw Mr. Stead's hand behind the letter. But, says an AT&T spokesman, "Jerre didn't send the letter. It was purely informational."

When Dayton Mayor Michael R. Turner met with Mr. Stead, the executive "acted sort of new age, talking about his glass conference room walls instead of about his products," Mr. Turner says. "I wouldn't expect glass walls and casual dressing for employees to be one of the top three things on the mind of a CEO."

But Mr. Stead labored hard to bring substantive change. Attempts to change GIS's profit-tracking proved too cumbersome to implement. The unit fell further into the red. Most of senior operations officials—

NCR veterans—either were forced out or quit. Only about five of the original 30 remain today at GIS. Mr. Stead chose as replacements AT&T executives, some of whom were involved in the company's earlier failure in computers.

Seeking what he called "profitable growth," Mr. Stead aimed to serve big corporations with huge database needs and expand GIS's franchise beyond retail store systems, automated teller machines and mom-and-pop businesses. He pushed the company into numerous new markets divided among such industries as transportation and consumer-goods manufacturing where the unit had little presence. He set up "customer focus teams," each with its own sales people, product specialists and customer-service technicians.

Costs skyrocketed. NCR was developing special systems and software for individual accounts and set up 500 teams in more than 100 countries to cater to them. "They tried to be all things to all people and lost a lot of money doing it," says computer analyst Jon Oltsik of Forrester Research in Cambridge, Mass.

Recovery was further hampered by three sales-force reorganizations in two years. Customers accustomed to dealing with the same rep for years were hit with a new face very few months. "In the old NCR, when a customer called they knew who they were going to get and who to complain to," says a GIS salesperson in Denver and a 22-year veteran of NCR.

GIS was partly done in by a shift in the market to smaller, more reliable systems. Older machines required a lot of profitable maintenance work. PCs, by contrast, rarely break down, offering little margin on the service.

Higher-end, mid-range systems were existing, but weren't selling enough to cover losses. Analysts say IBM and Hewlett-Packard Co. lately have been scooping up the kinds of orders GIS needs to remain a viable player in mid-range computing. The falloff in orders has been dramatic: GIS sold only $9 million of high-end computers in August instead of the $61 million it had expected to sell, according to a person who has seen its books.

Mr. Stead was able finally to eke out a profit of $45 million in last year's fourth quarter by selling NCR real estate in Hong Kong as well as the unit's Microelectronics division, according to the person familiar with the books. Several insiders say Mr. Stead projected an operating profit at GIS this year of $400 million. But GIS has already lost

$475 million through August, according to one insider. An AT&T spokesman says, "We're not going to discuss presentations Jerre made to the board or our profit goals."

Mr. Stead, 52, was lured in January to Legent Computer Corp. with the promise of a generous salary and a huge stock package. A few months after joining, he announced an agreement to sell Legent to Computer Associates International. Mr. Stead left Legent this summer after the acquisition, which netted him $15 million in severance pay and a hefty profit from stock options. Mr. Stead didn't return phone calls to his home requesting comment.

The Ax Man Cometh

Now the job of fixing AT&T's computer mess has fallen to Lars Nyberg, 43, a former executive of Philips Electronics NV. Known for wielding a sharp ax, AT&T's 10th computer chief in 11 years has begun a retrenchment that will cut GIS's annual costs by at least $1 billion. People close to GIS say Mr. Nyberg has decided to stop the unprofitable business of manufacturing PCs and instead is negotiating resale pacts with suppliers such as NEC, Intel Corp., Compaq Computer and South Korea's Hyundai. "We're not going to comment on that," an AT&T spokesman says.

Mr. Nyberg is basically dismantling most of what Mr. Stead erected. Up to a fourth of GIS's work force of 43,000 will be cut. Separation packages are being offered. Extended benefits would be given in return for a commitment from workers not to sue AT&T. "I'll take it," says one executive, sounding glad to get out.

To refocus GIS on its core business, Mr. Nyberg has put an end to most of the unit's expensive customization work in software and hardware. He has also carved GIS's core business of retail and banking systems into smaller self-contained units, each with its own headquarters.

Analysts say such a restructuring presages future asset sales. Mr. Nyberg and AT&T aren't commenting. Clearly, though, AT&T's decade-long quest to make it in computers is nearing an end. Despite $8 billion of computer losses since the 1984 breakup, a defiantly proud AT&T vowed to stay the course. Now, when a spokeswoman is asked whether the company will remain in the business, she pauses for several seconds. "We're not going to comment on that," she says finally.

3.3 NOT-SO-SUPERCOMPUTING

This is probably the strangest section of a generally strange book! The remainder of the stories you see in this book tend to be about a company, a project, or a product that failed somewhere along the way (and those are pretty strange phenomena, given that most of the computing field was thriving during the time of these failures). But this section is about the failure of a whole industry!

"Bigger is better" seems to have been a continual cry for most of the early history of the computing field. With the advent of the microcomputer, however, "smaller is better" became a competing cry. It took a while for those two viewpoints to collide, but when they did, massive damage came to those still operating under the "bigger is better" theory. These are the stories of that massive damage.

The "supercomputer" was the generic name the field applied to computers bigger than the norm. Those supercomputers took various forms, ranging from massive uniprocessors to massive multiprocessors to heterogeneous collections of smaller processors. But what characterized all of these supercomputers was that they were intended to be useful in solving equally massive problems.

And for a while they were. They became the darlings of two very different worlds—the federal government, especially the Departments of Energy and Defense, which did indeed have massive problems to solve; and academic researchers, at several major universities, who saw the coordination of such massive machinery as a challenge in itself, independent of the applications to which they were put. The feds put up the money, and the researchers constructed the sandboxes and played with the toys. It seemed like a win–win game that could last forever.

But then two things happened. The Cold War ended, resulting in the feds having fewer massive problems requiring immediate solutions. And the "smaller is better" phenomenon began to win the battle, resulting in a David beating Goliath kind of phenomenon. Both the need, and the mechanism for satisfying the need, came into question at the same time. What followed was probably inevitable.

The handwriting went up on the wall fairly early. In the third and fourth articles, below, we see the 1989 story of Control Data Corp.'s (CDC) supercomputer spinoff ETA, with the head of that branch of

CDC saying at its death announcement "We ran out of money . . . I can't make it any simpler than that." One computing pundit, at that time, was quoted as saying ETA may have produced "the last of the traditional supercomputers."

Hardly anyone paid any attention. Bigger still seemed to be better, and besides, federal money and research interest seemed to the true believers likely to continue on forever. In fact, we begin our collection of supercomputer stories not with the 1989 CDC–ETA demise, but with the much more recent 1995 story of a much more spectacular failure, that of the highly-touted Kendall Square supercomputer maker.

One of the chronic problems with supercomputers, especially those that use a parallelism approach (running several pieces of a program simultaneously in different parts of one or more computers), was software. To be blunt, no one has ever figured out how to build software that can be easily divided into the multiple pieces that the supercomputers needed to do their thing. The problem was not new—it had been understood since the late 1950s—but hardware optimists ignored the problem, apparently figuring that "if we build it, they" [the software people] "will come."

Returning to our introduction to the story of Kendall Square, that problem was acknowledged by the company, and, if you believed their public pronouncements, solved. "They had a real good idea [for] how to solve the programming nightmare of massively parallel computers," we will hear one pundit claim. (In retrospect, it is not clear how successful that idea was, since it does not seem to have been used by other supercomputer experts as far as I am aware). Meanwhile, others were attributing much fainter praise to the company's product. We hear another pundit saying that their products "crashed less than similar supercomputers."

Whatever the truth of the technology was, what finally did in Kendall Square (aside from the ongoing malaise of the supercomputer industry that we have already discussed) was what some called "accounting irregularities." Basically, on one or more occasions, they cooked the books. The intent may have been relatively harmless—for example, they sold a computer to a university, bought back enough time on that computer to balance the cost, and yet claimed the sales figure as income on their books—but the result was an accounting disaster. Chapter 11 was the refuse bin into which the high hopes of Kendall Square were poured!

Threaded all through the history of the supercomputing field is the name "Seymour Cray." Cray started CDC (which was the first company to succeed with something called a supercomputer), saw the spinoff of CDC's ETA (discussed above), and then broke with CDC to form two companies with his own name on them. Cray Research, the first of them, struggles on to this day, now swallowed up by Silicon Graphics. The story of Cray Research's sequel, Cray Computers, appears in this section. It, along with Kendall Square and another supercomputer company whose story I have not been able to capture for this book, all succumbed financially and went Chapter 11 in a nine-month period in 1995. Cray seemed particularly saddened by the death of that company. He is quoted in the story as saying, "Somehow we have to go home and think about how to get on with the rest of our lives." He was to die a couple of years later.

It was becoming obvious to most of those in the computing field that supercomputing was no longer super. In the final portion of this section, we see three computing field observers noting (in 1994) that it is time for computing research to acknowledge what the supercomputing industry was already (and reluctantly) being forced to understand, that the era of supercomputers was at best in some kind of suspended animation, and at worst was dead.

For a graphic picture of the death throes of the supercomputing field, read on.

MISSING THE BOAT: Yachtsman Bill Koch Lost His Golden Touch With Kendall Square

by William M. Bulkeley

In a life graced by wealth and good luck, William Koch has been many things—oil man, yachtsman, philanthropist and collector of rarities, from precious coins to fine wines.

At nearly everything he has tried he has succeeded, parlaying family wealth into a personal fortune of more than $600 million. Perhaps his most audacious feat came in 1992, when, as an upstart sailor rated by Las Vegas as a 100-to-1 shot, he won the America's Cup.

But at Kendall Square Research Corp., Mr. Koch's winning ways have ended. As the Waltham, Mass., company's main bankroller, he dreamed of building a high-tech colossus based on innovative supercomputers. This year, taking over as Kendall Square's chief executive, Mr. Koch tried to extricate the company from an accounting mess that had inflated reported revenue. But it was too late, and last month he laid off all but a skeleton crew and shut down computer-making operations.

Kendall Square has been dogged by an accounting scandal, which resulted in a Securities and Exchange Commission investigation and at least a dozen shareholder suits accusing management of making misleading statements. Mr. Koch has already been involved in one expensive settlement, in which he had to invest another $25 million in the company, atop the $40 million he had previously put in. Kendall Square, valued at $360 million by the stock market only 14 months ago when its shares sold for over $25 apiece, now trades at less than five cents a share.

Seduced or Overreached?

How could a man who had once succeeded so conspicuously stumble so badly? Mr. Koch contends he was, in essence, seduced by Henry Burkhardt III, a computer whiz who founded Kendall Square and who was ousted as chief executive last December after auditors uncovered a pattern of booking questionable revenue. "We got sucked in because

Originally published in the Wall Street Journal, *October 27, 1994. Reprinted by permission,* © *1994 Dow Jones & Co., Inc. All rights reserved worldwide.*

of Henry's brilliance, Henry's vision and the desire to make a lot of money in a short amount of time," Mr. Koch says.

But Mr. Burkhardt says Mr. Koch knew what he was doing as an investor. "Bill saw the big changes in the industry and saw an opportunity to create an interesting business," Mr. Burkhardt asserts. He and some other current and former Kendall Square employees contend Mr. Koch overreached—that he assumed his business skills could apply to high technology.

They also say Mr. Koch spread himself too thin: Even while trying to fix Kendall Square this year, Mr. Koch has been managing his Oxbow Group, a $500 million energy and trading firm in West Palm Beach, Fla. He also has been fighting over foreign claims to his coin collection; starting an all-woman team to vie in the next America's Cup qualifying races; battling Massachusetts over taxes; and heading the Koch Crime Commission, a Kansas crime-fighting initiative.

Mr. Burkhardt says; "Bill made a big mistake by thinking he could run the business by bringing in a few of the slogans he'd used to win a sailboat race. It's a very complex business."

Koch Industries

Mr. Koch (pronounced "coke"), who is 54 years old, followed his brothers to Massachusetts Institute of Technology, where he studied chemistry. He later joined them at Koch Industries in Wichita, Kan., a privately held energy company started by his father. After launching and losing a proxy fight for control in 1980, he was fired. A bitter court fight still continues over how much Mr. Koch is entitled to for the 21% stake he held, even though his brothers in 1983 bought out his interest for $470 million.

Mr. Koch used that money to start Oxbow, and then began to dabble in venture capital. He had met Mr. Burkhardt, now 49, a co-founder of Data General Corp. in Westboro, Mass. "I was restructuring my life," recalls Mr. Koch, who says he was charmed by Mr. Burkhardt's brilliance. "We became very good buddies."

In 1986, he backed Mr. Burkhardt's effort to start a company to create a new kind of supercomputer that would use many small processors working together. A few others were already making these "massively parallel processing" computers, but they were hard to program. Mr. Burkhardt had a design called "shared memory" that he said could make them as easy to program as a mainframe.

Mr. Koch claims Mr. Burkhardt predicted a product in two years and "had a goal of a $1 billion company in five or six years." Mr. Burkhardt replies that while he thought it was possible to build a $1 billion company, "there wasn't any timetable."

Two years later, the company sought funds from experienced venture capitalists. One who came aboard was Arthur J. Marks of New Enterprise Associates in Baltimore. "It was a wonderful idea," says Mr. Marks, who became a director. They had a real good idea of how to solve the programming nightmare of massively parallel computers. They were the first."

In 1991, Kendall Square finally shipped its first computer. The buzz in the super-computer business was that the brash newcomer had something special. In March 1992, still with no earnings, Kendall Square raised $40 million in an initial public offering.

Business surged. Users said Kendall's KSR1 was simpler to use and crashed less than similar supercomputers. But Mr. Koch says the board was frustrated as early as 1992 by Mr. Burkhardt's refusal to provide cash-flow analyses or detailed marketing plans. Mr. Burkhardt intimidated them, Mr. Koch and some other directors claim.

Riding the Fat Pig

Louis Cabot, former chairman of the Brookings Institution, who recently resigned as a Kendall director, says, "Burkhardt didn't really want anyone looking closely over his shoulder. When Bill got people like me on the board, we also were asking tough questions. Burkhardt didn't always answer as fully as it turns out he should have."

As business improved and the stock rose, directors swallowed their misgivings. "We were riding the fat pig," says Mr. Koch. Kendall sold $43 million more in stock in April 1993, at $16 a share. But short sellers started betting against the stock because of its widening receivables—often a sign that customers aren't paying.

Mr. Koch says that Mr. Burkhardt insisted that the company's auditors, Price Waterhouse & Co., stay out of the building until just before the end of each quarter—ostensibly because they might interfere with crucial deal closings—and then would push them to work round the clock to bless the financials. Mr. Burkhardt replies that auditors worked on a schedule and never complained of their access to information.

But last year, Mr. Koch says that a new Price Waterhouse auditor discovered a side-letter about a sale to a Greek company that indicated the customer could return the computer at any time. That proviso led the auditors to reject the sale and start looking for "more snakes in the woodpile," Mr. Koch says. When they gave directors details of some other deals, the board was astounded. One insider says people referred to them as "Gong-show deals."

Generous Terms

Mr. Koch says that unknown to him, Kendall Square, starting in late 1992, made astonishingly generous arrangements with customers, some of whom never paid. When William Goddard, a chemist at California Institute of Technology, was pleased with his first supercomputer, Kendall asked him if he would buy another; Dr. Goddard says he replied that he would have to apply for a grant to afford it. But, he says, Kendall Square shipped it immediately in March 1993. The grant still hasn't come through, Dr. Goddard says. But Kendall booked a $1.4 million sale.

In 1992, according to company documents, Kendall Square received $1 million for a computer sold to the University of Houston and booked it all as revenue without subtracting the $420,000 in "grants" it promised to pay the school.

In another case, internal documents show, Kendall converted the loan of a computer to the University of Manchester in the U.K. to a sale at the end of 1992. Letters between Kendall salespeople and the university show that the university agreed to acquire the computer at the end of 1992 for about $450,000 payable the next year, with the proviso that it would rent back to Kendall Square half the time on the machine for a price "that will exactly cancel out our obligation to pay them." In effect, Kendall Square gave the university the computer and called it a sale.

Mr. Burkhardt "was paying customers to give us sales and not disclosing it," Mr. Koch asserts. "My personal opinion is that some of this activity was basically fraudulent."

Mr. Marks of New Enterprise says, "There were definitely problems with management revealing the information the board wanted." William H. Congleton, another venture capitalist and director, tells of Mr. Burkhardt's avoiding direct questions from directors: Henry dances around; he's very persuasive."

Mr. Burkhardt says he produced the reports directors wanted and says the notion that he wouldn't answer their questions is "ridiculous."

He denies knowing about questionable accounting practices. He says that he made many decisions "that in retrospect were wrong" because he believed the sales were valid. "As soon as I found out what was wrong, I immediately made the directors aware," he says, adding that he lost $1.5 million himself in Kendall. He says he is sorry Mr. Koch "feels I intentionally misled him. I'm not surprised he's bitter."

Mr. Burkhardt says that if the company hadn't fired him last December, he could have rebuilt its reputation. "If I'd been there, the outcome would have been different. There's no way to argue that point," he says.

A Dual Role

As the auditors' questions piled up, the board turned to Chief Financial Officer Karl Wassmann III with questions of its own. Mr. Wassmann served a dual role, which directors now say was a conflict of interest: He had to approve the terms of Kendall's sales, and he also was the designated "closer," taking over from the salesperson to clinch sales. "Karl was a very effective deal maker. He enjoyed doing that," says James B. Rothnie, executive vice president, development. "It's very clear in retrospect that the guy who has responsibility to keep score shouldn't be a deal maker." Mr. Wassmann didn't return calls seeking comment.

At the end of October 1993, Kendall said it was delaying its third-quarter financial report because of revenue-recognition questions. The shares lost a third of their value, falling to just over $16. A few days later, a shareholder suit was filed citing SEC insider-seller filings by Mr. Burkhardt covering the sale of more than $1 million of stock in August, mostly at around $20 a share.

Later suits also mentioned stock sales by Mr. Wassmann and Peter Appleton Jones, Kendall's top sales executive. When Price Waterhouse removed its certification from the 1992 results, which had been cited in the second stock offering, more shareholders suits were filed. The stock sales by insiders also set the SEC investigation in motion.

The directors eventually forced Messrs. Wassmann and Jones to resign, before dismissing Mr. Burkhardt. Mr. Koch says he made the shareholder suits the first priority after he took over as CEO. The company needed funds, but Mr. Koch says he and other investors wouldn't pour in money only to watch it go for legal expenses. The company's increasingly public problems fed the reluctance of customers, who already were questioning Kendall's long-term viability. Mr. Koch, with his deep pockets, was a highly visible target for lawsuits.

Mr. Koch says he could have settled the shareholders suits for $10 million and liquidated the company in January. But he says he felt a responsibility to customers and shareholders, including his family and crew members on his winning America's Cup team, to whom he had given stock. Moreover, some customers raved about the KSR1's capabilities.

Mr. Koch reassured existing customers and sought payments for shipped computers. He personally collected $3 million from Canon Inc., Kendall's Japanese distributor, after a quick trip to Tokyo. But other customers drifted away, and when auditors were finished, they halved the 1992 revenue and said 1993 revenue was only $18.1 million—far from the $60 million once forecast by Mr. Burkhardt.

In March, Mr. Koch reached a tentative agreement with shareholders under which they would take about $5 million in cash and considerable stock and warrants on the condition that he would inject $25 million into the company. He provided a loan, but the litigation talks dragged on. Mr. Marks says the raft of troubles made it nearly impossible to recruit an experienced high-tech CEO.

Still, by late summer, things were looking up. Lawrence Reeder, a venture capitalist and board member, agreed to become CEO. Kendall announced two computer sales. Philip Morris Cos., whose executives Mr. Koch treated to a yacht race off Newport, R.I., decided to buy a machine to run the company's vast database of smokers, he says.

But experts hired by the directors concluded the company's newly announced second computer, the KSR2, was too slow and inherently unreliable. Steve Frank, Kendall's vice president for architecture, says that after Mr. Koch decided to try to revive the company in January, "no one felt a sense of responsibility or urgency. There was a lot of Brownian [random] motion. Nobody wanted to tell the boss the bad news."

Mr. Koch discovered that developing a third computer would take at least two years and $30 million, and by then rivals would be ahead. Kendall tried to find a partner that would inject cash to license the technology. Individuals close to Kendall say Compaq Computer Corp. was interested, but it hasn't acted so far. Compaq won't comment.

On Sept. 16, Mr. Koch provided the $25 million he had promised under the suits, settling them. A week later, he ended computer man-

ufacturing and sales and laid off all but 50 of the company's 170 workers. The stock collapsed from over $2 a share to less than 10 cents on
the Nasdaq Stock Market. Glenn DeValerio, an attorney for the suing
shareholders, says he was surprised by the decision to end computer
sales, but he believes Mr. Koch acted in good faith.

Mr. Koch says he still hopes Kendall can create a business licensing
technology, although he concedes there aren't any immediate prospects.

Once supremely confident, Mr. Koch now says he is chastened. Last
year, when Kendall Square was still booming, Mr. Koch startled Hollywood by declaring an interest in buying troubled Metro-Goldwyn-
Mayer Inc. from Credit Lyonnais SA. Today he says, "I'll put that under
wishful thinking. It's an industry I don't know about."

CRAY COMPUTER FILES UNDER CHAPTER 11, ENDING QUEST TO BUILD SUPERCOMPUTER

by William M. Bulkeley

Cray Computer Corp. filed for bankruptcy-court protection, ending a quest by 68-year-old computer legend Seymour Cray to build the world's fastest supercomputer again.

Six-year-old Cray, of Colorado Springs, Colo., never sold a computer and ate up at least $200 million in capital. It filed for Chapter 11 protection against creditor lawsuits in Denver after failing to find investors who would put up another $20 million to complete building and testing its Cray 4 model. "To not complete such a long effort is very disheartening," Mr. Cray, chairman and founder, said in a letter to the company's 360 employees.

Cray's fate is another sign of the troubled state of the supercomputer industry, where two other firms have filed for protection in the past nine months. Shrinking defense and security budgets since the end of the Cold War have reduced demand for the powerful computers—used in weather forecasting weapons design and crytography—that cost $5 million to $40 million apiece.

The action leaves Cray Research Inc., Eagan, Minn., virtually alone at the high end of the U.S. supercomputer market, although three Japanese firms continue to make supercomputers. Intel Corp. also makes high-performance supercomputers, but with a different design and a smaller market.

Cray Research, now selling its new T90 supercomputer, may benefit from not having to fight a price war with Cray Computer. But Robert Ewald, president of Cray Research, said "I don't anticipate any near-term financial benefit since Cray Computer didn't have any customers." He added he is "really saddened" by the filing because "Seymour is the father of supercomputing, the icon of the industry."

Mr. Cray built the first supercomputers for Control Data Corp. in the early 1970's and later founded Cray Research Inc. which became a high-performance leader. But in 1989, Cray Research balked at the escalating cost of funding Mr. Cray's new design using gallium arsenide semiconductor chips. Cray Research spun out Cray Computer with $100 million in capital and considerable technology. In July 1991, Cray Computer raised $65 million in a public offering, and later raised another $40 million in private placements.

Its first-generation computer, the Cray 3, was two years late to market and never sold. Mr. Cray had expected the market would embrace the Cray 4, a higher-performance machine that was scheduled to be ready in a few months.

In Nasdaq trading, Cray Computer fell 73%, or 68.75 cents, to 25 cents. In New York Stock Exchange trading, Cray Research was unchanged at $17.75.

Charles Breckenridge, Cray Computer's executive vice president of marketing, said "we're exploring options as to how we might continue completing the Cray 4." He said many prospects in federal government agencies and laboratories were interested in the computer, but "clearly many of them were very concerned about our financial viability." He said that because of tight government budgets, the company couldn't have made any sales until October.

Observers were dubious that much can be salvaged from Cray Computer. "My guess is you're talking about tenths of pennies on the dollar invested," said Gary Smaby, a Minneapolis-based market researcher. "When you build a technology as exotic as Seymour's, it's all intertwined. In isolation none of the parts or processes has the same value."

Mr. Cray wasn't available for comment. But his letter to employees sounded like a coda on his career. Government buyers, he said, are cutting costs and "do not want to take any risks at the moment." He added, "Somehow we have to go home and think about how we get on with the rest of our lives."

CDC BIDS ETA FAREWELL

by Jerome D. Colonna with Ken Juran

Goodbye ETA Systems. Control Data Corp.'s decision last week to pull the plug on its six-year-old ETA Systems supercomputer subsidiary left ETA users dismayed. Says Walter McRae, director of the University of Georgia's Advanced Computational Methods Center, "It's like an unexpected death."

CDC's solution to its current financial troubles left ETA customers scrambling to comprehend the long-term impact of the loss of ETA.

"We had major development efforts under way with ETA," explains McRae. "A staff of four ETA scientists were working here full time. Those people have been terminated." The future of that development work will be one of the topics McRae discusses with CDC representatives as the two organizations work out an arrangement for future maintenance support.

Speaking in New York, CDC chairman Robert Price said that such arrangements for future service and maintenance will be made on a "customer-by-customer" basis in face-to-face meetings over the next few weeks. Price made it clear, however, that no more ETA products or enhancements will be manufactured.

One of the customers hardest hit by the company's decision to cut its losses on ETA was Florida State University. FSU has long been a supporter of CDC and its supercomputing efforts. A CDC customer for 25 years, FSU was the first to take delivery on the ETA's first machine, the ETA10. Indeed, the university's commitment to the architecture and the company led to its decision last year to purchase the first ETA10G; the machine, which began to be installed just a few months ago, is scheduled to begin full-scale operations this week.

Dr. Robert M. Johnson, FSU's vice president of research, graduate studies, got a call from ETA last week telling him that FSU's ETA10G would be the only 10G produced. He says, "We are on the cutting edge of computing with our class-seven; machine and when you remove that class of machines, you hurt us."

Johnson believes that while the loss of ETA won't hurt FSU's long-term abilities to do advanced computational research, it might adversely

Originally published in Information WEEK, *April 24, 1989. Copyright 1989 by CMP Publications, Inc., 600 Community Dr., Manhasset, NY 11036. Reprinted with permission.*

affect FSU's ability to fulfill its large contract with the Energy Department. "Hopefully that won't be affected, but I have no idea if that's in jeopardy," he says.

The decision also surprised staff members. Rumors of a sale of ETA had been circulating for weeks, but no one expected CDC to simply close shop. "I guess from their standpoint, it was a banker's decision," Johnson concludes.

The Money Ran Out

Johnson may be right. A visibly exhausted Price faced a host of reporters at conferences in New York and Minneapolis. In New York, the day after the news broke, Price said the decision to abandon the supercomputer was difficult but necessary. Turning to a reporter and throwing his arms in the air, Price said, "We ran out of money. I can't make it any simpler than that."

CDC's money troubles have been substantial since 1985, when it sustained a loss of more than $500 million. Since that time, Price explained, the company has embarked on an evolution that has included the sale of many subsidiaries, such as Commercial Credit for $800 million. A restructuring at the beginning of the year saw the departure of Tom Roberts, then vice president of the company's computer systems division, and the ascension of Lawrence Perlman to president and COO.

Price positioned the shuttering of ETA as part of that evolution. In its six years of existence, it lost more than $100 million a year; CDC, as a result of the closing, will write down $490 million.

While Price did point to unforeseen changes in the supercomputer market, he took full responsibility for the failure of ETA. Leaning into his microphone, his voice unshakeable, Price declared, "I am the CEO. I have total responsibility. No qualms. No excuses. No apologies."

The chairman's willingness to take the heat did little to stem the rising demand for hardware-independent system software such as Unix. Such software, said Price, contradicts the basic fundamentals of the way CDC conducted business. He pointed out that during the company's long history in supercomputing (CDC built the first machine to which that name was applied—the 6600—in the mid-60s), successful vendors sold proprietary hardware systems and left the application development to the users. ETA's inability to win back market share for

CDC was because of those changes, not technological failings, according to Price.

But the failure of ETA is more complex than that and hints at more fundamentally troubling problems. While the technology team at ETA is considered by many to be among the best in the country, ETA has lost key sales simply by being outperformed by Cray Research Inc. Wilbur Wynn, manager of corporate computer services at Advanced Nuclear Fuels Corp. in Washington state, for example, just canceled his remote supercomputing service contract with Control Data and is bringing in a Cray. "One of the reasons we went with Cray was that we weren't at all convinced ETA was viable—technically or financially," Wynn says. Just last week, Wynn cut the cord to the remote Control Data sites.

Beginning this week, Wynn will slowly migrate all of his operations, including processing now done on Cybers and Prime minicomputers, to the Cray. He expects eventually to link the Cray engineering data with finance and administration data now on IBM mainframes.

In Search of Profits

Wall Street analysts welcomed the "streamlining" of the company's operations, adding that CDC's decision to concentrate efforts on core businesses should help return it to profitability by the third quarter, although the company will still face a losing year.

E. Magnus Oppenheim, president of E. Magnus Oppenheim & Co., an investment bank, says that "by cutting back, surviving entities will be strong and profitable." Oppenheim also believes that the streamlining is far from over: "They've got this big drain [ETA] out of the way, and they'll shave off other operations." But overall, CDC has "very good management. [Perlman and Price are] doing a bang-up strategic job."

A return to profitability is uppermost in the minds of Price and Perlman. Perlman helped bring about the turnaround of the company's storage peripherals business (which last year was spun off into a separate subsidiary named Imprimis) and is highly regarded on the Street. Imprimis, according to Price, contributed just over $1 billion to the company's $3.6 billion in revenue last year.

The decision to focus on the company's core businesses, such as aerospace and engineering, was also welcomed by Cyber users. Even

FSU's Johnson believes that cutting ETA's losses is good news for the users of CDC's Cyber mainframes. "CDC is strong enough, and big enough, to survive," he says, adding, "Ford developed the Edsel; did they go out of business?"

At Rockwell International's Information Services Center, Greg Pritchard, adviser for scientific and engineering computer applications, says Rockwell has two Cyber 990s and 960s and had run the ETA machine through some benchmarks, but decided to buy a Cray. In the end, ETA's drain on CDC's ability to put resources into the Cyber line was too much. Adds Pritchard, "Getting rid of ETA is a positive thing."

FEDERAL EXPERTS LAMENT LOSS OF CDC'S ETA

by Gary H. Anthes

For supercomputer maker ETA Systems Inc., the operation was successful, but the patient died.

In a move that will entail a one-time charge of $350 million and the loss of 800 jobs, Control Data Corp. last week said it will dissolve its ETA subsidiary and abandon its 6-year-old super-computer business.

Federal experts in high-performance computing praised ETA's hardware technology while deploring the loss of a key player in the small but strategically important supercomputer arena.

The termination of CDC's ETA Systems unit follows weeks of rumors that the supercomputer subsidiary was for sale. Analysts had speculated that Unisys Corp. or a foreign firm might pick up ETA, but CDC apparently could not find a buyer for the costly and trouble-prone operation.

The ETA-10 supercomputer, a descendent of CDC's successful Cyber 205, was introduced in 1986 amid much fanfare. The top-of-the-line model, the liquid-nitrogen-cooled ETA-10G, had up to eight processors, a 7-nanosecond clock speed and an advertised peak performance of 5.1 billion floating-point operations per second (Gflops).

That seemed to ensure formidable competition for Cray Research Inc., whose fastest machine at the time had four CPUs, a clock speed of 8.5 nanoseconds and a peak performance of about 1 Gflop.

But ETA sold only seven of the large, $22 million systems and 27 of the $1 million air-cooled models. CDC lost $100 million on its ETA operations last year alone, and it said ETA was not soon expected to turn a profit. CDC also cited as a factor stepped-up competition from Japanese supercomputers and U.S. mini-supercomputers.

Gary Smaby, managing director and supercomputer analyst at Needham & Co., said, "The fundamental problem was that their marketing strategy was poorly executed. They thought that if they created a fast box, all else would follow."

It was a fast box, and it is still the top-rated uniprocessor in the Linpack benchmark figures published by Argonne National Laboratory. The problem was that there was little applications software to accompany it, and its operating systems proved slow to debug.

Originally published in Federal Computer Week, *April 24, 1989. Reprinted with permission of Federal Computer Week, copyright 1989, FCW Technology Group. All rights reserved.*

The John von Neumann National Supercomputer Center in Princeton, N.J., one of five centers supported by the National Science Foundation, cast its lot with ETA early, building naturally on its Cyber 205 base by adding two large ETA-10 systems.

Control Data said it will continue to support existing ETA installations, and Doyle Knight, the director of the von Neumann center, said he isn't worried. Control Data will support the hardware, and ETA will keep enough people to maintain the center's existing software, he said. But Knight said it is not clear whether planned new releases of the operating systems will be forthcoming.

Despite his apparent confidence that his systems will continue to get needed support, Knight called ETA's demise a major blow to the U.S. supercomputer industry. "Their technology was very good. This is a critical loss for the country," he said.

William A. Wulf, who heads the computer science and supercomputing programs at NSF, acknowledged that on-going support for installed ETA systems may be a troublesome issue. He called the systems at the von Neumann center "reasonably productive," especially for single large jobs, but he said software bugs remain. "There's a tremendous amount of work to be done to the operating systems," he said.

The United States lost one-third of its supercomputing options at a stroke, with Cray and IBM Corp. the survivors, Wulf said.

The Japanese are gearing up for an assault on the U.S. supercomputer market. Also, IBM is working with designer Steve Chen to develop a supercomputer, and it already has a super-class machine in its 3090 vector computer.

Finally, several mini-supercomputer firms are nipping at Cray's heels.

"IBM will quickly fill the void as the second choice in government contracts," Smaby said. "Cray would probably prefer to compete with ETA."

A spokesman for Cray declined to comment, but other sources at the Minneapolis-based company left little doubt that Cray would move quickly and aggressively to fill the computing needs of ETA's customers and prospects.

While most federal supercomputer experts believe strongly that the loss of ETA deals a blow to U.S. industry, others downplay the loss. One source suggested that vector machines based on very aggressive clock speeds—the approach taken by ETA, Cray and the Japanese—

eventually will give way to architectures with more CPUs built around more conservative components.

One official, who asked not to be named, pointed out that each successive generation of Cray computers costs more and takes longer to bring out. He suggested that the Cray-3, to be introduced next year, may be the last of the traditional supercomputers.

Dieter Fuss, deputy associate director for computations at Lawrence Livermore National Laboratory, which has several Cray supercomputers, rejected that notion. "I talked to Seymour Cray last week, and he's beginning to think about the Cray-4 now," he said.

Fuss said supercomputer centers of the future will need different types of computers adapted to different types of applications. They might have ETA- or Cray-like vector machines, massively parallel computers such as the Connection Machine from Thinking Machines Corp. and lower-cost scalar processors for codes that can't be vectorized.

"We're a long way from getting useful systems using [non-standard] paradigms," NSF's Wulf said. "What we need is an industry with very deep pockets to make a commitment to another paradigm."

PARALLEL COMPUTING: Glory and Collapse

by Borko Furht, Florida Atlantic University

A decade ago, university researchers were in love with parallel computers, and the US government amorously responded. Those were the days of glory. Times have changed. The market for massively parallel computers has collapsed, and many companies have gone out of business. But the researchers are still in love.

Glory

Ten years ago, researchers basked in parallel-computing glory. They developed an amazing variety of parallel algorithms for every applicable sequential operation. They proposed every possible structure to interconnect thousands of processors. Federal agencies generously sponsored this research, hoping parallel computers would help gain a strategic advantage in the cold war against the Soviets. Many parallel computer companies emerged, and for a while business was good. They sold machines to the US government for several millions of dollars, and just a few sales generated profit.

Collapse

Today, the few parallel computing companies still in business are struggling to survive and probably won't. According to the Smaby Group study,[1] the scientific and engineering market for massively parallel processing machines has decreased significantly over the last several years to only $300 million in 1993. As a result, there are fewer than 10 parallel computer companies. Two companies, Intel and Thinking Machines, control over 60 percent of the market. Yet Thinking Machines lost $20 million last year and has recently announced Chapter 11 bankruptcy. The parallel computing industry has collapsed. But why? What happened?

Reasons for Collapse

Many researchers[2,3] blame this collapse on the lack of good parallel-processing software. We complained about this ten years ago and we

---

Originally published in IEEE COMPUTER, *Nov., 1994. Used with permission.*

will complain in the future, so we might as well complain today. But this is only one reason. The other reasons are more significant.

First, the cold war is over, and the federal government is no longer willing to spend millions of dollars for these very specialized, expensive machines. The government has dramatically reduced funding in this area and transferred it to new, promising technologies, such as multimedia applications, information superhighways, digital libraries, interactive television, and virtual reality.

Second, there is new competition from personal computers and workstations, which increasingly employ more powerful, inexpensive processors. In distributed configurations, these systems offer solutions to many problems once solved only by parallel computers.

Finally, when W. Daniel Hillis, Thinking Machines Corporation founder, decided to develop a machine with millions of parallel processors to resemble the human brain, was he on the right track? In building computers, should our ultimate goal be to create another human being? Experience indicates otherwise: we need fast and inexpensive sequential machines, which will solve about 99 percent of today's problems. For the remaining 1 percent, small parallel processors (multiprocessors) or sequential machines connected and distributed on networks should achieve satisfactory solutions.

The Research Continues

Despite the parallel computing market collapse, many university researchers not only study, but actually *promote* parallel computing. From 1993 to the present, there have been at least a dozen international conferences on parallel processing, and attendance is increasing. In the last few years, many journals, magazines, books, and papers on parallel processing have been published. Who is sponsoring these activities?

The most appalling trend is that education related to parallel processing has peaked. For his recent article, "The Status of Parallel Processing Education,"[4] Russ Miller investigated over 70 institutions. He indicates that several universities offer both undergraduate and graduate courses on topics like parallel algorithms, parallel programming, and parallel architecture. Some, like Michigan State, Auburn, and University of Central Florida, offer seven to nine courses, but the champion is Purdue University, which offers 10.

Will our graduates ever use parallel computers in real life? Probably not. According to a recent survey of 400 chief information officers by consulting firm Deloitte & Touche,[5] the hot technologies of the future are

♦ multimedia systems,

♦ expert systems,

♦ handheld computers,

♦ voice recognition,

♦ neural networks,

♦ fuzzy logic, and

♦ virtual reality.

This is bad news for the parallel computing community. How many undergraduate or graduate courses do universities offer on these hot subjects? Probably fewer combined than the number of parallel processing courses offered. (And we complain that our graduates cannot find jobs.)

Potential Solutions

Parallel computer companies have three choices: change their focus, file bankruptcy, or allow a larger corporation to acquire them. Some companies (Encore, Hewlett-Packard, IBM, Pyramid, Tandem, Stratus, and AT&T) have already changed their focus to transaction processing and fault-tolerant computing, which are more profitable.

Other companies are trying to find a new niche for their parallel machines. For example, nCube has formed an alliance with Oracle, whereby applications such as on-demand multimedia services and interactive television use nCube's massively parallel computer as a large multimedia server.[6] Similarly, Dow Jones employs two of Thinking Machines' CM-2 massively parallel systems in the interactive media market.[1] These parallel machines are not performing traditional parallel operations such as parallel matrix multiplication or parallel fast Fourier transforms, but are storing and delivering thousands of movies to customers. In other words, instead of operating as massively parallel processors for number crunching, they are operating as large input/output switching systems.

In his excellent article, "Where is Computing Headed,"[3] Ted Lewis tries to predict the future of computing. I agree with his statement that "we can expect multiprocessing to become widely accepted in the practical world of everyday computing," where "multiprocessor systems consisting of four, eight, and 16 processors will be integrated into desktop Pcs. . . ." However, I disagree with his claims that a lack of software will keep massively parallel computers "outside the mainstream of computing" and that "the lack of good parallel processing software languages, tools, and environments makes for fertile areas of research that will continue to attract the research community throughout this decade."

We should stop developing parallel algorithms and languages. We should stop inventing interconnection networks for massively parallel computers. And we should stop teaching courses on advanced parallel programming. Let's turn to the real world. Let's listen to those 400 chief information officers. Let's refocus our research to match industry needs. Let's teach our students something they can use today, something their future employers might want them to know.

Those *still* in love with parallel computing should woo practical applications such as video-on-demand, interactive television, expert systems, or digital libraries.

REFERENCES

1. R. Moran, "Supercomputers: What Happened?" *Information Week,* August 15, 1994, pp. 12–13.

2. Arvind, "Prospects of Ubiquitous Parallel Computing," *Proc. Parallel Processing Symposium, 8th Int'l (ICPP '94),* IEEE CS Press, Los Alamitos, Calif., Order No. 5602-02U, April 1994, p. 2.

3. T. G. Lewis, "Where is Computing Headed," *Computer,* Vol. 27, No. 8, August 1994, pp. 59–63.

4. R. Miller, "The Status of Parallel Processing Education," *Computer,* Vol. 27, No. 8, August 1994, pp. 40–43.

5. "Hot and Happening," *Information Week,* August 15, 1994, p. 52.

6. R. Buck, "The Oracle Media Server for nCube Massively Parallel Systems," *Proc. Parallel Processing Symposium, 8th Int'l (ICPP '94),* IEEE CS Press, Los Alamitos, Calif., Order No. 5602-02U, May 1994, pp. 670–674.

SUPERCOMPUTERS AIN'T SO SUPER

by Ted Lewis

This month celebrates Supercomputing 94, when speed junkies gather in D.C. to schmooze and sell their latest iron. But is this the happy-camper crowd of five years ago when parallel processing, supercomputing, and Grand Challenges were in the hype? I'm afraid not. These days, Kendall Square Inc. wonders where the money went; Thinking Machines is gone; Cray Computer is living on Seymour's mortgaged wealth; and Intel has been wounded by reports that its machine doesn't really work. So what is wrong with America's lead in high-performance computing?

For one thing, the vendors soaked up government money to build fantastic iron, but forgot the software. With a wink of an eye, super-salespeople claimed peak gigaflop performance without mentioning how to program the things. But Gartner Group (Stamford, Connecticut) rated the top vendors according to "software availability" (applications code, not compilers and operating systems), rather than gigaflops, revealing the embarrassing truth about life in the fast lane. Thinking Machines, Kendall Square, Intel, and Cray Research received failing scores ranging from a dismal 1.0 to 3.5 (out of 31 "killer apps"), while top-ranked Silicon Graphics, Digital Equipment, and IBM received scores of 19.75, 14.50, and 7.25, respectively. Does this correlate with failure and success in the market? You bet.

Another factor is price/performance. I could never understand why a 30-processor multicomputer costs as much as 130 workstations when both contain the same commodity chips. Yet many early big-iron vendors—again with a wink of an eye—cashed in on the speed craze at premium prices. The truth is, you can use a network of workstations to simulate a large-grain parallel computer without ripping out operating systems software, breaking and resetting programmers' coding arms, or hocking that prized collection of Peggy Lee recordings. Recently, more than one enterprising computer scientist has referred to this kind of parallel computation as "heterogeneous computing." It's not new, but it is news. Expect to hear a lot about heterogeneous computing at Supercomputing 94's watering hole.

Originally published in IEEE Computer, *Nov., 1994. Used with permission.*

Smaller Footprints

Yet another reality is that computing happens on the desktop these days, and not in some fluorescent, air-conditioned, raised-floor computer center. Almost every National Supercomputing Center has free time to give away, if only someone will take it. But, hey, I can let my workstation run all night long, pick up the answer the next morning, and still beat the queue on a Cray C90 or Intel Paragon at the local Center for Really Fast Iron.

What we are talking about here is gigaflops on a budget. After the hype fades, the bottom line is whether or not your system can be programmed, is on your desktop, has a future when you want to scale up to lots of processors, and, by the way, runs your application fast. Sounds like a Silicon Graphics Challenge, doesn't it? I don't normally take sides in these matters, but frankly, SGI has the most sensible strategy to make supercomputing work (DEC and IBM come close, but no cigar). Before you send all that crank e-mail, let me explain.

First, big memory is more important when running "challenge problems" than lots of processors. Academics like me have had a decade to figure out how to partition a big problem into little pieces that can fit into distributed memories, only to discover that message-passing is very slow. This means (virtual) shared memory and—to keep the processors busy—large-bus cache memory to boot.

Next, you need to run each processor as a workstation (to do real work, like your budgets and e-mail) and then be able to turn around and spread your application across a farm of boxes.

Finally, you need a software strategy so that the installed base of Cray Computer devotees can port their Cray Fortran code onto a new machine with 90 percent lower maintenance fees. (Are you still with me? If not, call SGI, DEC, IBM, or Convex and ask for this stuff.) You need all of this to work today, as well as in three to five years when vendors upgrade to newer hardware and operating system platforms.

The numbers support the strategy. SGI's Koontz (director of marketing) claims 2,500 Challenge systems are in the field. Compare this with about a dozen Cray T3Ds and a handful of just about everything else that strays off the "formula" adopted by SGI. So beware the fast-iron sales engineer. Maybe that wink is actually a nervous twitch.

SUPERCOMPUTING: Same Name, Different Game

by Monica Snell

On the eve of Supercomputing 94, November 14–18 in Washington, D.C., the supercomputing business is doing anything but super. Veteran players, who have carried the supercomputing ball since the beginning, are being forced into retirement as the rules of the game change and a new team of lower priced machines emerges.

Vendors used to competing in a primarily government-sponsored environment are—due to DoD budget cuts—being pushed toward the commercial marketplace in search of customers. And it's going to be a "tough transition" according to David Mills, systems research manager with Dataquest in San Jose, California.

"In five years there will be very few players left in the supercomputing business," Mike said. "Many in the business now will not make it." The reason is that commercial users focus on different features and benefits. Only the companies that can adapt will survive.

Troubled Firms

Thinking Machines, the Cambridge, Massachusetts, firm that initiated massively parallel processing, filed Chapter 11 in August. While the company plans to continue to support and service its installed base and offer upgrades through 1995 to selected customers, it will no longer sell supercomputers. Instead, it plans to provide software tools and applications to the parallel systems market.

Kendall Square Research, Waltham, Massachusetts, announced in September that it will discontinue the manufacture and sale of its KSR supercomputer series. Its troubles began in 1993 when an accounting scandal and 12 class-action lawsuits brought on by shareholders hit the company. However, the company has not filed for bankruptcy. It will continue to support installed computers and plans to license its proprietary Allcache distributed-processing technology to third-party computer and networking manufacturers.

Originally published by IEEE COMPUTER, *Nov., 1994. Used with permission.*

Pricing Strategy

Analysts say price is the main factor that could make or break the companies. As the market begins to cater to business-oriented patrons, vendors will encounter budget-conscious customers, said Terry Bennett, director of technical systems research for Info-Corp in Beaverton, Oregon. "The emphasis is going to shift from the highest possible performance," he said.

Vendors agree that price/performance will be an important factor in determining who stays in the game. Steve Conway, spokesperson for Cray Research in Eagan, Minnesota, said the company is very aware that "everybody is extremely price sensitive." In response, Cray will introduce a "baby" supercomputer next year, the J90. The machine will offer 3.2 gigaflops and sell for about $800,000. This offering, Conway said, is a far cry from the supercomputer Cray offered in 1991. It sold at $10 million and maxed out at 2.67 gigaflops.

Ed Reidenbach, product manager for Silicon Graphic's Power Challenge series in Mountain View, California, agreed that strategy will become a "price/performance story." The Power Challenge machines keep costs down by using CMOS technology, which reduces the need for expensive upkeep such as cooling, flooring, plumbing, maintenance, and support. "With other supercomputers, users can spend hundreds of thousands of dollars on utilities," Reidenbach said.

But Thomas Nolle, president of CIMI Corporation, a strategy-planning consultancy in Voorhees, New Jersey, warned that price cutting can go only so far before it becomes detrimental. When a company sells X number of computers at Y amount below cost to build a base, there is no guarantee that it will continue to sell enough computers to make up the loss, and the profit it would have made is eradicated.

Software

A second factor that will impede the extension of supercomputers into the commercial market is the lack of software. Few developers are doing software for supercomputers, and according to Nancy Stewart, Dataquest analyst, they may not for a while. "It's the chicken and egg quandary," Stewart explained. Supercomputer vendors need applications to get a good installed base, but they need the good installed base to entice software developers to write applications.

AT&T is one company that has the applications area covered. AT&T acquired its supercomputing technology when it acquired NCR, which had acquired Teradata. The 3700 (MPP, or massively parallel processor) and 3600 (SMP, or symmetric multiprocessor) are focused on the standard SQL (Structured query language) database.

Intel has done well in the supercomputing marketplace, according to both Mills and Bennett, but it does have some work to do in the software development market. According to International Data Corporation of Framingham, Massachusetts, last year Intel garnered 27 percent of the MPP market, with $93 million out of a $346.7 million total. Also, Intel's XP/S140 was listed as the most powerful supercomputer in the world by the Linpack Report speed benchmarks.

To compete in the commercial market, Intel's director of operations for the Supercomputer Systems Division, Wendy Vittori, said the company plans to focus on cost and "RAS—reliability, availability, and serviceability. The commercial requirements for success go way beyond the technical," Vittori explained, and Intel will incorporate "commercial, off-the-shelf, desktop aids to help build this product."

The competition the supercomputer faces in the commercial sector comes from both ends of the spectrum—the mainframe and the desktop. According to Nolle, with the enormous increases in desktop performance, it's more practical to solve problems meant for a supercomputer on the desktop. Also, "supercomputer vendors will encounter a tough sell when they go against the mainframe vendors. The mainframe has some big backers and is entrenched in the marketplace," Mills said.

To combat these opponents, supercomputers formed by MPPs, SMPs, and clusters, workstations strung together, are becoming more commonplace. According to Bennett, using "merchant" technology such as standard I/O buses and off-the-shelf microprocessors will reduce costs and help raise supercomputer sales. Bennett foresees more vendors entering the supercomputing market at the low end.

Although the supercomputing industry is not doing as well as vendors would hope, analysts say it will not die out. According to Bennett, the industry is currently in a "lag" where traditional vector supercomputers are fading out and other approaches are maturing. By 1996, Bennett said there should be a reasonable upswing in the high-performance computing business, and the market will continue to grow to over $4.5 billion in 1998.

3.4 CROOKS AND SPIES AND OTHER GUYS

People are what make the corporate world go round. Good, capable people can make the difference between corporate failure and corporate success. Read any corporate annual report—somewhere in those glossy, best-smelling pages, there is usually a tribute to the people of the company, who "made us what we are today" and are "the key to our ongoing success."

But, then, there are the problems that people bring with them. Most computing consultants tell us that when they're called in to solve a corporate problem, it is rarely about technology, it's about people. People problems are the flip side of "people are what make the corporate world go round." And they're all too common.

This section of the book is about people problems. In this section, people cheat and steal, lie to and spy on each other, have major conflicts, and manage to tear down all the good that their capable sides had managed to erect. It would be easy to get discouraged about people and their nature when you're reading this section. (That's one reason why I've buried it in the middle of the book!)

In our first people-focused story, we see two versions of the same story. The first is written in 1989, when a corporate "Dr. Fix-It" has apparently run aground, presiding over a company called MiniScribe that has become a "Greek tragedy." The apparently-successful company is adrift, Dr. Fix-It is only coming to work once a quarter (!), there is "outrageous fraud" being perpetrated, and corporate free-fall is about to begin, fueled by a management team that "believed its own press clippings" about a company sometimes called the "darlings of the industry."

Time passes. In the second version of the MiniScribe story, published in 1993 (four years later), the scene is a courtroom. Dr. Fix-It is accused of "falsely inflating the value of inventory . . . and income," of doing "insider trading" by dumping his own shares in the company before breaking corporate bad news to the public. The descriptions of some of the crimes are graphic—Dr. Fix-It is accused of "ordering boxes to be stuffed with bricks and labeled as inventory."

What went wrong here? How could a man who "only came to work once a quarter" have been responsible for so many detail-level corporate infractions? Our two snapshots in time don't answer all the questions the story raises, but they certainly illustrate the worst of what happens when people things go wrong.

The second people-focused story, by contrast, is something of a farce. A corporate spy, so the story goes, steals the trade secrets of the U.S. company for which he works and passes them on to the French company for which he is spying. A few years pass, the incident is largely forgotten, and the French company sues the American company for stealing the design of one of its products. This litigation wouldn't be worthy of our including in this book, except for one thing—that stolen design is apparently none other than the design originally taken from the American company in the spying episode! In other words, the French company is suing the American company for using a design that the American company originated! People foibles do not always lead to Greek tragedies; comedy is sometimes an equally plausible outcome!

But that's it for humor in this section. The next three stories are grim reminders of how bad people problems can get. In each case, we see a promising startup led by a technically-knowledgeable entrepreneur torn asunder as the company matures and control is wrested away by less technical people. In the first, "Partnership Peril," there is an international flavor, as the American entrepreneur loses control to a powerful and well-known Japanese conglomerate. The story is said to be like "Rashomon," the classic Japanese tale in which the descriptions of an episode differ markedly among the observers of the episode. In the end, the American is not only ousted from his company, but loses his Japanese wife to the strife along the way.

In the second, one of the better-known software methodologists, Ken Orr, is paired in his new startup company with a "hired-gun chief executive" with whom he is totally incompatible. The story's author calls it the classic "founder vs. new leader problem" (which, of course, all three of these stories are). Orr and the new CEO suffer a massive "values collision." In retrospect, Orr says, his success in obtaining venture capital also became a problem—"Venture capital is a lot like steroids—you get pumped up artificially; then you get overly aggressive; then you get paranoid." This story is rather old—it is about a software CASE tool company back when the world thought CASE tools were a breakthrough technology—but it nicely fits with the other two adjacent stories.

The third story is a classic of its own kind. "Four men embittered by life at one company," the author begins, "leave to form a new one. This time, they thought, things would be different."

They certainly were. Things got much worse, and rapidly! The four nouveau entrepreneurs, struggling to start their company, found themselves with disastrously different views of how that company should be run, about how to tell who is contributing the most to the company, and about who should be paid how much. Choosing up sides, the foursome fell into a 2–2 split, then into a 3–1. With that, the one is fired. End of conflict?

Not at all. The fired executive continues to harass his former colleagues, and takes steps to build a new company (his own!) out of the framework of the old. Eventually, there is a massive "coup"—both people and files are cleaned out of the old company in one fell swoop—and the fired executive has both started his new, competing company and found revenge. The author calls the whole scene "Guerrilla Theater."

Perhaps surprisingly, this last story is not really about corporate failure. The old company, as it turns out, rebuilds and thrives. But there is a failure of another kind. One of the former foursome says it best at the end of the story. The failure that matters here is relationship failure—the partner describes a sad kind of "loneliness," and says "I feel I have to be guarded about what I say and whom I say it to."

People failure may be more profound, in the long run, than corporate failure. And now, on to our people-focused failure stories.

WHY 'DR. FIX-IT' OF HIGH-TECH FIRMS FAILED
TO SAVE MINISCRIBE

by Patrice Apodaca

Quentin Thomas Wiles used to be known as "Dr. Fix-It" because of his successful rescues of sick high-technology companies. The Sherman Oaks resident was roving trouble-shooter for the San Francisco investment firm Hambrecht & Quist, which made a reputation for investing in near-bankrupt or start-up high-tech firms.

In 1985 he was sent in to turn things around at MiniScribe, a Longmont, Colo., maker of disk drives that store and retrieve data for computers. Wiles, now 70, went to MiniScribe determined "to show them one last time that he was the best there is," said William Hambrecht, president of Hambrecht & Quist and a MiniScribe director.

For a while, Wiles' magic seemed to work. MiniScribe reported that its sales soared to $603 million in 1988 from $115 million in 1985. Meanwhile, it went from a loss of $16.8 million to a profit of $25.8 million.

But today, Hambrecht calls MiniScribe "a Greek tragedy." Steven Sidener, a San Francisco attorney who represents a shareholders group suing MiniScribe, Wiles and Hambrecht & Quist for securities violations, describes what happened at MiniScribe as "an outrageous fraud."

According to a report issued by MiniScribe's new management, previous senior management was under so much pressure from Wiles to maintain the company's turnaround that it took part in "a massive fraud" to inflate the company's reported sales and earnings for the last three years. Things were so out of control, the report says, that at one point bricks were packaged as finished disk drives and sent off to customers to temporarily boost sales and inventory numbers.

Critics add that Wiles also was seldom present at the company and his product diversification strategies backfired.

The report, which has been given to the Securities and Exchange Commission's enforcement division, doesn't specifically accuse Wiles of fraud. But it offers a stinging indictment of his management. Not surprisingly, MiniScribe's stock has collapsed, from a high of $13.75

Originally published in the Los Angeles Times, *Sept. 26, 1989. Copyright 1989, Los Angeles Times. Reprinted by permission.*

per share in 1988 to $1.625 at Monday's close on over-the-counter trading.

Wiles, who has denied any knowledge of the fraud, quit as Mini-Scribe chairman and Hambrecht & Quist vice chairman in February.

Since then, he has dropped out of sight. "This has been quite a trauma for him," said Wiles' attorney, Cary Lerman. The phone at Wiles' office on Ventura Boulevard has been disconnected, and his name has been removed from the office door.

Born In Nebraska

But for all of the problems at MiniScribe, the puzzling part is that Wiles employed many of the same techniques of management reorganization and cost-cutting there that he did at a dozen or more companies he successfully nursed back to health.

Wiles, who didn't respond to requests for an interview, has been involved in turnarounds since the early 1960s. He was born in Weeping Water, Neb. After graduating from the University of Nebraska with degrees in mathematics and chemistry, he worked for electronic products maker Goodall-Electric Manufacturing in Ogallala, Neb., and eventually took control of the company.

When it was sold in 1960 to the Cleveland-based industrial conglomerate TRW, he went along and began his career as a troubleshooter, turning around several ailing TRW companies. In 1970, he left and joined Hambrecht & Quist. Early on, William Hambrecht decided that Wiles "had a very special talent" for turning around disorganized companies.

His methods were often considered harsh but they usually worked. Wiles worked his magic at such companies as ADAC, a Milpitas, Calif.-based maker of medical equipment; Silicon General, a San Jose semiconductor maker; Rexon, a Manhattan Beach data storage business, and Granger Associates, a Santa Clara, Calif., telecommunications firm. All were either losing money or were marginally profitable when Wiles arrived.

"I've never met anyone who's better at forcing organizational problems to the surface," Hambrecht said. Wiles "had an intuitive sense of what the soft spots were."

Under Wiles' stewardship, for instance, ADAC went from a loss of $33 million in 1984 to $4.3 million in net income in 1987, and was recently named "turnaround of the year" by the Turnaround Management Assn. in Cary, N.C.

So what went wrong with Wiles at MiniScribe?

"I think MiniScribe got too big for his system," said William (Dan) Rasdal, a former Granger executive. Rasdal, now president of Silicon General, noted that MiniScribe is five times bigger than other firms Wiles managed. "When you move into a company like Granger, it's not too hard to break it down into pieces and make sure you're on track," Rasdal said.

MiniScribe's internal report also indicates that Wiles lost control of the firm simply because he wasn't there enough. Wiles wanted to spend more time at home and with his wife, who suffered a heart attack a few years ago, said Edmund H. Shea Jr., a Rexon director and executive vice president of J. F. Shea, a Walnut construction firm. Wiles visited the firm only once a quarter or less, Miniscribe officials say.

In contrast, during Wiles' turnaround of Grange, he owned a home nearby and would visit the company about four days a week, Rasdal said.

Cut Divisions

Hambrecht says it's now apparent that Wiles kept up the pressure of his crisis management techniques long after MiniScribe was in a turnaround phase. "This experience has reinforced for me that it's important to separate the turnaround effort from the later ongoing management effort," he said. "I think the intensity of effort that goes into a turnaround is either wasted or it distorts things later on."

Hambrecht also said MiniScribe's managers were guilty of hubris. "They were the darlings of the industry and Wall Street and they started believing their own press clippings," he said. "They believed they were almost immune to cycles in the disk drive business. So when things did cycle down for them, they kept driving forward, assuming they'd be able to pull it out and continue to grow."

In the past, Wiles whipped companies into shape using Q. T.'s Disciplines," a 12-point guide to management fundamentals, and "Q. T.'s Method of Operation," an eight-point list for identifying problems and solutions.

He eliminated divisions such as production and finance and reorganized firms into small units.

Compounding the problem at MiniScribe, Hambrecht suggested, was that Wiles' former lieutenants—such as Rasdal and Michael Preletz, who now runs Rexon—had left his turnaround team. That left Wiles with younger, less experienced managers not accustomed to his demanding style.

"Q. T. can be very intimidating to a young person," Hambrecht said. "I think [MiniScribe executives] were more inclined to tell him what he wanted to hear than what they really thought."

It also turned out that Wiles' market strategy at MiniScribe didn't work. To capture a bigger slice of the competitive market for disk drives, MiniScribe started making more expensive drives. In doing so, said John T. Rossi, an analyst at Alex, Brown & Sons, "They took their eye off the ball and neglected their bread and butter business" of mid-range drives.

When the expected demand for the high-end drives didn't materialize, business took a sharp downward turn. MiniScribe reported its first loss in more than three years in the fourth quarter of 1988, a $14.6-million deficit.

Critics also charge Wiles with sending the wrong signals to managers. Wiles "understood how investors respond to an appealing story," analyst Rossi said. "People were doing what was necessary to perpetuate the story" of a successful turnaround, he said.

Wiles also became carried away with his success, Hambrecht admitted. "We all tried to talk Q. T. into slowing it down," Hambrecht said. "The tragedy was it could have had 25% less [growth] and it still would have been the best ever."

Hambrecht said his own anger toward Wiles over the MiniScribe fiasco has begun to dissipate. He talked to Wiles recently and said Wiles remains very despondent.

COMPUTER CHIEF WILL FACE TRIAL

By Peter G. Chronis

Q. T. Wiles, former chairman of the defunct MiniScribe Corp., was indicted yesterday on three federal counts accusing him of a wide-ranging conspiracy to defraud the disk-drive manufacturing company's shareholders.

Wiles, now living in Sherman Oaks, Calif., once was considered the financial wizard of America's high-tech industry. But now he is accused of falsely inflating the value of Longmont-based MiniScribe's inventory and pumping up its income figures in reports to shareholders.

The indictment handed up yesterday in federal court in Denver says Wiles enriched himself by dumping more than $1.7 million worth of his own MiniScribe shares while knowing about the company's worsening financial condition.

In one incident noted by the indictment, Wiles ordered boxes stuffed with bricks labeled as inventory.

The counts against Wiles include conspiracy and making false statements, improperly using non-public information and wire fraud.

Thousands of workers lost their jobs and investors lost millions of dollars in the MiniScribe scandal. The company filed for Chapter 11 bankruptcy in January 1990, and most of its assets are now owned by Maxtor Corp. of California.

Named in a separate two-count indictment was Patrick J. Schleibaum, the company's former chief financial officer. Schleibaum, now of San Diego, was charged with one count of conspiracy and making false statements and one count of making false statements in MiniScribe's 1987 annual report. Schleibaum dumped more than $1 million in MiniScribe stock, according to the indictment.

Each count against Wiles and Schleibaum carries a possible five-year prison term and $250,000 fines. Summonses were issued for the defendants.

The indictments capped a federal investigation that began about 3 1/2 years ago.

Originally published in the Denver Post, *March 12, 1993. Used with permission.*

Among other things, the indictments allege:

◆ Schleibaum ordered two company officers to break into locked trunks containing the work papers of MiniScribe's auditors so that inventory records could be altered.

◆ After learning of an inventory shortfall of "millions of dollars" in 1987, Wiles ordered the memorandum reporting the problem destroyed and the shortfall concealed.

◆ Wiles, Schleibaum and others created millions of dollars in fictitious inventory that was supposed to be "in transit."

Bricks, obsolete parts and scrap were packaged to look like finished goods and counted as inventory.

MiniScribe also has been involved in a maelstrom of civil litigation that embroiled its former officers and Coopers & Lybrand, the company's former accountants.

FBI spokesman Tom Cannistra said yesterday that further indictments aren't expected.

Wiles, known as the Mr. Fix It of troubled high-tech companies, came to MiniScribe after Hambrecht & Quist Inc., one of California's leading technology investment companies, pumped $20 million into the company and took control in 1985. Wiles also was associate chairman of Hambrecht & Quist.

According to narratives in the indictments, Wiles, Schleibaum and several unindicted individuals "engaged in an unlawful scheme to defraud" that employed "materially false and misleading financial statements" about MiniScribe's inventory and income.

Falsified financial statements were disseminated to the SEC, MiniScribe shareholders, and "unwitting purchasers and sellers of MiniScribe stock," the federal documents say.

The data also allegedly went to Standard Chartered Bank, an English financial institution with offices in Chicago, Singapore and Hong Kong that lent Wiles $70 million for the company.

A CHIP COMES IN FROM THE COLD:
Tales of High-Tech Spying

by William M. Carley

A trans-Atlantic computer-chip war has ended. And as an American company and a French conglomerate shake off the dust of battle, they leave behind a tale of espionage and bureaucratic bumbling worthy of John Le Carre.

To begin at the end, the story unraveled when the French government-owned Cie.des Machines Bull sued Texas Instruments Inc. in a U.S. court in 1993. the French computer company complained that TI was illegally making a computer chip that Bull had invented and patented.

Had it not been for the prospect of a daunting court battle, TI officials might have found the lawsuit amusing: They replied that *they* had invented the chip—and Bull had it only because a spy inside TI had given it to French intelligence agents, who passed it on to Bull.

Moles at Work

This much is undisputed: In the 1970s and 1980s, French intelligence agents recruited moles in the French subsidiaries of U.S. companies, including International Business Machines Corp. and Texas Instruments. The moles passed secrets about new computer chips and other technology to the French agents.

U.S. government officials say French agents passed the stolen technology on to Machines Bull, although the French company denies getting any stolen data.

The French spy system came to light in 1989, when the moles inside the U.S. companies were fired. After a brief flurry of publicity and with few details disclosed, the matter seemed to fade away.

Fast forward to the 1993 lawsuit in Dallas. TI argued that the judge should reject Bull's lawsuit because of the French company's "unclean hands" and invalid patent. Bull denied any wrongdoing, including getting any stolen TI technology. This week the case was settled out of court on terms that haven't been disclosed.

Originally published in the Wall Street Journal, *Jan. 19, 1995. Reprinted by permission.*
© *1995 Dow Jones & Co., Inc. All rights reserved worldwide.*

But details of the alleged French espionage scheme have emerged in court files. In the documents, Texas Instruments unmasks the alleged spy and charges that he was passing TI secrets to French agents for nearly 13 years.

A Mysterious Package

In 1969, according to documents in the TI case, Jean Pierre Dolait completed his engineering degree in Paris and went to Pasadena to study at the California Institute of Technology. Mr. Dolait got his Ph.D. in aeronautical engineering at Cal Tech, and then his M.B.A. at the University of California in Los Angeles.

Texas Instruments hired Mr. Dolait in 1976, according to a TI personnel record filed in court. Mr. Dolait, starting as a product manager, worked his way up. By 1989, he was based in the Texas Instruments plant near Nice and was European marketing director for semiconductors.

Around that time someone mailed a package from an IBM plant in France, according to an IBM official. But the address label came off or was obliterated, so the French post office returned the package to the company. IBM officials were shocked to discover the package contained highly confidential IBM technical documents.

IBM called in the Federal Bureau of Investigation, which launched a broad inquiry. The FBI found that several U.S. companies had moles feeding technical data to French intelligence agents. Texas Instruments was one of the victims. According to TI's court documents, the mole inside the company was Mr. Dolait.

TI asked Mr. Dolait to fly from Nice to Texas, supposedly to attend a business meeting. Instead, he was questioned by the FBI. According to a TI official, the FBI provided the company with enough information to fire Mr. Dolait on the spot for spying. Mr. Dolait couldn't be located for comment.

TI lawyers said in a court document that "the French espionage agent discovered working as a TI employee in 1989 had been feeding information useful to Bull from TI . . . for 13 years."

The Bull Bill

In 1991 a Bull licensing manager—who apparently was oblivious to all this—wrote to Jerry Junkins, chairman of Texas Instruments. A TI chip family, the TMS 370, seems to infringe on a Bull patent, wrote

Yves Coutenceau. Perhaps TI should obtain a license and pay licensing fees to Bull, Mr. Coutenceau suggested.

A Texas Instruments license lawyer in Dallas—also apparently unaware of the alleged spy game—wrote a routine reply to Mr. Coutenceau saying that he would look into it. Negotiations between TI and Bull ensued, with the TI lawyer even offering to pay a royalty to Bull of up to 6% of the chip's sales. But on Oct. 6, 1993, Bull sued TI for alleged patent infringement.

That set off alarm bells at Texas Instruments. TI's 370 chips are widely used in autos in fuel-injection systems, air conditioners and radios, and bring in tens of millions of dollars in revenue. Texas Instruments lawyers took a closer look at Bull's chip design.

In court documents, TI lawyers say they found the design had been invented at TI by Michael Cochran in 1974, although the company didn't patent the chip, a strategy that avoids disclosing trade secrets. Two years later, TI hired Mr. Dolait—and two years after that, Bull filed a patent application for the same chip design, TI lawyers say. "Because of his placement within Mr. Cochran's division, the French agent had access to the technical information in [the] division during the period between Mr. Cochran's conception of the invention and Bull's filing of its patent application," the TI lawyers state in a TI court document. The Bull design derives from Mr. Cochran's invention, which was stolen from TI, the TI lawyers add.

A Miscalculation?

Bull vehemently denies this, saying its chip was invented by Michel Ugon, a Bull employee in France. As far as Bull is concerned, "the Texas Instruments spy story is a fantasy," says Hadrian Katz, a U.S. attorney for the French company. He adds, "The notion that Bull somehow got this technology from Texas Instruments is silly. For one thing, the Cochran chip concerns a calculator, which has nothing to do with Bull's chip."

Some TI officials, however, suspected Bull would use the lawsuit to get even more Texas Instruments secrets through the civil discovery process, in which both sides exchange documents relevant to the case. TI lawyers, in a hearing in federal court last May, raised that concern.

Robert Kahri, a TI lawyer, asked that the TI documents be kept in the U.S., and restricted to Bull's U.S. lawyers and assistants, a request granted by the court.

Suddenly, the suit was settled this week. What triggered the settlement isn't clear. Lawyers on both sides decline to comment. But there may be another shoe to drop.

Bull, in its court filings, says that several companies have been paying royalties to Bull under the chip patent, including Motorola, Inc. If TI's allegations are true, then these companies are paying royalties to Bull for technology stolen from Texas Instruments. A spokeswoman for Motorola confirms the company is paying royalties to Bull but has no further comment.

PARTNERSHIP PERIL: Chip-Making Pioneer in U.S. Found Grief in Seiko Joint Venture

by Eduardo Lachica

As John Hall drives his well-traveled Buick coupe past his former office at Micro Power Systems Inc., he can only stare wistfully at its handsome Spanish-colonial front. The semiconductor pioneer founded Micro Power and invested 15 of his more productive years in it. In the process, he gave his Japanese partners, the Seiko group, a huge head start in advanced chip technology.

Then, his world crashed around him.

Seiko, the big watch and personal-computer maker, fired him. He lost control of the company and the technology he had spent so long developing. He poured almost all his savings into suing his former associates at Seiko. His old company countersued him, warned customers of his fledgling new company against doing business with him and charged him with stealing trade secrets. His Japanese wife, a former Tokyo nightclub hostess, left him.

Now, financially and emotionally exhausted, he has agreed to settle his complaint for just a fraction of the $110 million in damages he originally sought.

The 57-year-old engineer is a bear of a man, but his voice quavers a bit as he relates his story. As he tells it, he was preparing to take Micro Power public in mid-1986 when Seiko, fearful of losing unfettered access to his technology, ousted him and shooed off prospective underwriters.

He flew to Tokyo for a face-to-face meeting with Ichiro Hattori, then Seiko's president, to negotiate his termination settlement. As Mr. Hattori spoke in his mahogany-paneled suite, his words chilled Mr. Hall to the bone. "He said he controlled enough wealth in this world to win any lawsuit he should be forced into," Mr. Hall recalls. Undeterred, Mr. Hall returned to Santa Clara and sued Seiko in state court here.

Mr. Hall's discharge and more than three years of litigation provide a startling counterpoint to American entrepreneurs' current enthusiasm for high-tech partnerships fueled by low-cost Japanese capital. Of course, Silicon Valley offers many examples of smoothly operating U.S.–Japanese joint ventures. But, noting that they are almost all younger than his operation, Mr. Hall says the Americans in those ventures may eventually wind up not so enchanted with their partners.

"The Japanese don't always honor their obligations," he charges. "They'd strip American companies of their technology, send it back to Japan and use it to increase their own sales in the U.S."

That accusation hasn't been proved. But Mr. Hall's tale certainly challenges the image of Japanese executives as eager to avoid litigation at all costs. Seiko has spent millions of dollars fighting the case.

"Mr. Hall made an unreasonable demand, and we did nothing wrong," contends Tsuneto Enami, the managing director of Seiko Instruments Inc., one of Seiko's four major units. "What we want is an end [to the court suit] with an understanding that we did nothing wrong."

Cross-Cultural Hazards

Finally, Mr. Hall's tale illustrates the difficulties of cross-cultural partnerships. Seiko tried to turn a brilliant engineer from West Virginia into a Japanese corporate loyalist. Mr. Hall tried to go along. But when tough problems arose, Mr. Hall reacted like many an American and sued. Seiko, feeling betrayed, lashed back.

There was little in Mr. Hall's background to prepare him emotionally for his immersion in a Japanese corporate family. In the early 1960s, the shy young engineer focused on semiconductor devices and quickly became a hot ticket for his work at General Electric Co., Honeywell Inc. and Union Carbide Corp.

In 1967, working at Intersil Inc. with another industry wizard, Jean Hoerni, he won his first job for Seiko. The Japanese watchmakers asked him if he could design a tiny chip for their new quartz models. The engineers at one unit, Seiko Epson Corp., doubted it could be done. In nine months, he says, he delivered the devices.

Seiko asked Mr. Hall to come work in Japan. But he didn't want to give up his dream of founding his own semiconductor company. Eventually, they struck a compromise and started a joint venture in Santa Clara, calling it Micro Power.

Seiko still wanted to make Mr. Hall one of its own. So, before starting the venture, it took him to Tokyo in the fall of 1970. For half a year, he tutored Seiko engineers by day and drank with them by night.

He soon became a trusted sword-bearer for the Hattori family, taken along to the geisha houses where crucial business deals are struck. Masukatsu Hamamoto, a Seiko executive whose career included interpreting for Hideki Tojo, Japan's wartime prime minister, became his mentor.

Mr. Hall quickly learned that Seiko, one of Japan's largest privately held corporate empires, was divided into bitterly competing fiefs. Two of its companies, Seiko Instruments and Seiko Epson, make watches for world-wide distribution by Hattori Seiko Co., the group's only publicly traded company. Yet the two units compete at selling other products, such as printers and robotic equipment, in the U.S. "That was mostly Shoji's doing," says Mr. Hall, referring to Ichiro Hattori's father, who made Seiko a global force in watchmaking. "He thought that competition brought out the best in his companies."

Because Mr. Hall was brought into the group by Seiko Instruments, his relations with Seiko Epson were chilly from the start. In addition, he says, Seiko Epson engineers had "lost face" because he had bested them with his fast delivery of innovative watch chips.

Epson denigrated Mr. Hall's work as trivial. But Pentagon analysts trace Seiko's upsurge in the powerful computer chips called complementary metal oxide semiconductors, to his time in Japan in the early 1970s. "Before that, they had nothing. But after Hall, they had a lot," one Defense Department chip expert says.

Two powerful personal forces entered Mr. Hall's life in Japan. One was Fumiyo Endo, an entertainer at the Mikado, a glamorous theater-restaurant and favorite watering hole of Tokyo businessmen. Mr. Hall left his wife, set up Ms. Endo in an apartment and eventually married her.

The Japanese Executive

The other new force was Ichiro Hattori, the president of both Seiko Epson and Seiko Instruments. Though about the same age, the two men differed greatly. Mr. Hall is a soft-spoken introvert at ease only in his workshop; Mr. Hattori, who died three years ago, was a handsome, charming aristocrat; at school, he had been a tennis partner of the Japanese emperor. He also was a Yale-educated internationalist who was proud of the 1,800 jobs the Seiko had created in the U.S. and who urged other Japanese businessmen to be "good neighbors" with the Americans. Yet, in private, Mr. Hattori was "autocratic and impulsive," Mr. Hall recalls.

After opening the business in 1971, almost alone amid Santa Clara's orange groves and tomato farms, Micro Power grew along with the business of making analog integrated circuits, which measure light, heat, sound and other physical properties (unlike digital devices, which simply count). Micro Power's sales soared from about $250,000 in 1972 to more than $25 million in 1985; analog devices now account for 20% of the semiconductor market.

Mr. Hall made chips for Sharp Corp.'s first hand-held calculators and a low-power chip for Medtronic Inc. that could run a pacemaker for 10 years in a patient's chest without maintenance. But best-known were his designs for the use of molybdenum or tungsten gates to interconnect the multitude of transistors in semiconductor devices. His patents for molybdenum gates are assigned to Micro Power and thus effectively under the control of Seiko, the majority owner of Micro Power. Mr. Hall contends that the partners eventually could be worth as much as $10 billion; Seiko values them in the low millions.

Mr. Hall also supplied high-performance chips to two "Stars Wars" contractors, Aerojet-General Corp. and Hughes Aircraft Co. One of Micro Power's biggest sales was $7 million of modules for the B-1 bomber's phased-array radar, he says.

The China Question

His very success with technology, Mr. Hall believes, sparked his dispute with Seiko. In 1980, Seiko was seeking to extend its right to sell watches in China. In return, he says, the Chinese demanded some of his high-speed flash converters, semiconductors that can switch rapidly between analog and digital operations. Mr. Hall, who made six trips to China between 1980 and 1984, says he dropped the project after the Central Intelligence Agency warned him that the converters could greatly improve the accuracy of China's missiles.

Seiko, in a written statement to this newspaper, says Mr. Hall's account of the China matter is "totally wrong" and "slander." It adds that when asked under oath about this as part of the litigation, "Mr. Hall couldn't show any fact as proof."

Courtney Hart, a former Micro Power engineer, says he hasn't any direct knowledge that the China project was scrapped because the

CIA intervened but confirms that the agency tracked the company's dealings with China closely. A CIA spokesman declines to comment.

After Mr. Hall dropped the project, he says, his relations with Mr. Hattori began to cool. That cast a pall over another Hall objective: to sell Micro Power stock to the public to raise the value of the shares and make the company more independent. Mr. Hall contended in his lawsuit that the late Seiko president induced him to produce more technology for the Seiko group with false promises of support for a public offering. Seiko denies the charge, saying it never tried to block the offering.

But in 1985, Mr. Hall, assuming that Seiko would go along, contacted investment bankers about taking Micro Power public. In addition, Arthur Trueger, who heads the San Francisco branch of Berkeley Govett Ltd., a British investment firm, injected $7 million into Micro Power by buying preferred stock.

A Demanding Partner

Mr. Trueger turned out to be a demanding partner, constantly sending deputies to monitor accounts and pushing for a management shakeup. So, Micro Power's board hired Michele Giammarino, a retired Texas Instruments Inc. executive, to help Mr. Hall manage the company.

Whether a public offering would have succeeded isn't clear. Yasuo Sakaniwa, the former president of Seiko Instruments' U.S. subsidiary, who is acting as a spokesman for the Hattori family on the Hall matter, says he invited 10 investment banks to manage a stock offering. "They all told me that Micro Power wasn't ready for it," he says.

Yet a financial adviser retained by Micro Power who asked not to be identified says three major Wall Street firms—Bear, Stearns & Co., Donaldson Lufkin & Jenrette Securities Corp., and Smith Barney, Harris, Upham & Co.—expressed interest. Then, he says, "Giammarino came in, and suddenly there was no deal."

Clifford Gookin, who was then at Bear Stearns in San Francisco, says his initial impression was that Micro Power was in shape to go public. "Then I was told the owners had changed their minds," he recalls. Wendy Lane, who worked on Micro Power for Donaldson Lufkin, says she can't recall whether the company was ready to go public. A Smith Barney spokesman says the officials involved have left the firm and can't be reached.

To the board's dismay, Mr. Giammarino and Mr. Hall squabbled from the start. The board first kicked Mr. Hall upstairs to be chairman. Then, in June 1986, it charged that Mr. Hall had "misappropriated" money and suspended him as chairman. A month later, it fired him, although he retained his stock. Despite losing both his job and his wife, he received little consolation from industry colleagues.

"We do a lot of business in Japan," admits the chairman of a major semiconductor manufacturer. "It wouldn't be helpful for us to get involved in this matter."

Judicial Rulings

Over two years, two judges and a court-sanctioned master denied Seiko's request to dismiss most of Mr. Hall's complaints. Another judge did dismiss much of Mr. Hall's suit but left standing his claims of defamation and wrongful termination. Meanwhile, Micro Power, in its countersuit in the state court, accused him of stealing trade secrets—a charge that he denies. Micro Power also said he used company funds to support his wife. He says the company permitted the expenditures and deducted them from his salary.

John Hadluck, Seiko's chief litigator in the case, concedes that the court record reads a bit like "Rashomon," the film classic in which villagers and a samurai in old Japan recount wildly differing versions of the same event. Seiko tells a different tale from essentially the same set of facts.

Mr. Hadluck says one of Mr. Hall's main deficiencies was his inability to produce consistent profits. "He would come up with an occasional product which would produce a burst of revenue, but that's not running a company," he says. "He just loved to tinker with new ideas."

Seiko contends that "poor management" justified the 1985–86 crackdown on Mr. Hall. But those were bad years for the entire semiconductor industry: Advanced Micro Devices Inc., a leading producer of analog devices, lost $8.9 million in 1985 and $95.2 million in 1986. And Mr. Hall insists that Micro Power did reasonably well under his leadership. He says that its sales increased an average of 25% a year to nearly $30 million in 1986 and that it reported profits of up to $1.6 million for eight consecutive years before he was fired.

Seiko also declines full responsibility for the actions of Micro Power's board. At the time of Mr. Hall's ouster, Seiko voted only 50%

of the company's stock, although it was supported by other shareholders, including Mr. Trueger.

"I'm sorry for John," says Mr. Sakaniwa, the former Seiko Instruments official and a close friend of both Mr. Hall and the Hattori family. "Micro Power was his baby: so, I can understand why he couldn't take it." Mr. Sakaniwa says he respects Mr. Hall's "creative genius" but attributes much of the trouble at Micro Power to what he sees as his lack of "common sense or business sense." He denies there was any Seiko conspiracy to oust Mr. Hall and prevent Micro Power from going public. "I know deep in my heart that Seiko never intended to deceive him," he says.

The Missile Issue

Still being debated are whether Seiko transferred some of his technology without the necessary license and whether that data subsequently was reshipped to China, where it might have wound up in the missile program. The Commerce Department's initial investigation found nothing to substantiate that complaint. Seiko says it did look over some of Micro Power's data for manufacturing high-speed flash converters but didn't find the information good enough to use. Seiko Instruments' Mr. Enami says the company also was cleared of Mr. Hall's charges by Japan's Ministry of International Trade and Industry.

But the Pentagon's technology-watchers believe that some data transferred to Japan may have been of military significance. And Mr. Hall says the Commerce Department's investigators heard Seiko's side of the story but never called him back. Rep. Helen Bentley, a Japan-bashing Maryland Republican, has asked both the Commerce Department and the U.S. Customs Service to reopen the investigation.

Now, as Mr. Hall contemplates a disappointing settlement of the dispute, his former wife is little better off. "It's a very hard time for me. Seiko can't help me. John can't help me," Ms. Endo says in a Tokyo telephone call. "I was very miserable last year. I felt so sorry for John."

Mr. Sakaniwa, the former Seiko executive, says this sad dispute shows that "we have to be more careful about personalities when we choose our partners." He adds: "In the U.S. system, it is very easy to sue for trifling reasons."

Oddly, Mr. Hall comes to much the same conclusion. American entrepreneurs, he advises, should look beyond the individuals with whom they strike agreements and consider when they might deal with in the future. "If Shoji were still alive, this probably wouldn't have happened," he says, invoking the name of Seiko's patriarch. "If Ichiro didn't die, this case would've been settled long ago."

HOW PROMISE TURNED BITTER
FOR RELUCTANT CASE SUPERSTAR

by Nell Margolis

Among the many start-ups spawned by the computer-aided software engineering boom of the mid-1980s, Optima Development, Inc. looked like a strong contender.

Co-founded by Ken Orr, a CASE methodology pioneer, funded with venture capital and headed by a dynamic young executive with roots in software marketing, the Schaumburg, Ill.-based company appeared poised for flight.

In reality, however, it may have been headed for a crash even before takeoff. Accounts that emerged in the wake of Optima's November 1989 insolvency show a company generally cursed with the ability to be in the right place at the wrong time and by the incompatibility of its founder and its hired-gun chief executive, Patricia Palmer.

"It was the classic 'founder vs. new leader' problem," said William Bryant, former Optima marketing vice-president and the estranged husband of Palmer. "Somebody should have left. It wouldn't have mattered which one."

In 1987, Orr, a respected software engineering methodologist and consultant, made a fairly aggressive—although not necessarily happy—move "from educator to product vendor," recalled Vaughan Merlyn, chairman of Bellevue, Wash.-based CASE Research, Inc.

Several sources who have worked for and with Orr over the years recalled a successful consultant turned reluctant executive.

"He never wanted to leave Topeka in the first place," said Leon Stucki, himself the president of a CASE tool vendor firm and a long-time Orr business associate.

But the daily uncertainties of consulting, he said, left Orr open to friends' urging that he parlay his successful CASE consulting and training practice into a company offering front-end software design automation tools.

Largely at the urging of James Whitely, the venture capitalist and a longtime Orr friend and business associate who co-founded and

Originally published in Computerworld, *Jan. 15, 1990. Used with permission. Copyright 1990 by Computerworld, Inc., Framingham, MA 01701.*

helped fund Optima, Orr brought in Palmer, whose roots were in software marketing and consulting, as the first chief executive officer. However, things did not go smoothly.

"It became pretty clear almost right away that she and I didn't see eye to eye on almost anything," Orr said.

"There was clearly a values collision," Palmer said.

They agreed on little else, starting with where to base the company. Palmer, convinced that only an urban center offered the resources necessary to launch a successful company, opted for a suburban Chicago headquarters. Orr manned his post of chairman and chief scientist from his Topeka base.

"When Ken said, 'Let's just leave the development group in Kansas,'" Palmer recalled, "that was probably the beginning of the end. That was the road to nowhere." Orr said Optima was able to last as long as it did because of his decision to shield Optima's technology arm from the urban, fast-track, venture capital culture that he said was Palmer's undoing.

In recognizing his own potential limits as a CEO, Orr avoided a pitfall that has tripped many a thinker on his way into the world of commerce. Ironically, it was apparently the last pitfall the fledgling Optima did avoid.

In short order, according to the accounts of numerous sources, practically everything that could go wrong did.

The original, homegrown Optima tool, said a technical consultant who worked closely with the company, "was not well engineered; it was very slow, and the data dictionary was incomplete."

In addition, said the technical consultant, the Orr methodology, which had—and still has—its devout adherents, met with resistance when it entered the commercial mainstream. "Orr wasn't the household name that Gane and Sarson, or Yourdon and DeMarco, were," the consultant said.

Optima's long-term relationship with Pacific Bell ("our major client, almost a silent partner," according to Palmer) fell victim to Pacific Bell's own internal reorganization and decision to focus on core businesses.

Of all the problems that came cannonballing at Optima, however, none was more ultimately destructive than the dissent that permeated its management team from day one.

Orr paints a picture of Palmer as having been lured—as are so many start-up executives—by seemingly ready venture funding and then driven into a spate of overexpansion by its demands for an early return on investment. "Venture capital is a lot like steroids," he said. "You get pumped up artificially; then you get overly aggressive; then you get paranoid."

Orr claimed that Palmer squandered hard-won capital on glitzy offices and trappings and invested in an expensive sales force before there were sufficient products to sell.

True on bare facts, said Palmer—but wrong and wrong again on interpretation. By her own account, her expertise produced generous discounts and clever deals that enabled her to create the "look and feel" of a successful company on a virtual shoestring. "Offices" that she opened in New York, Texas and San Francisco, she said, were merely mailing addresses or, in one case, a budget-wise space-sharing arrangement.

In the mid-1980s, Palmer noted, CASE was a relatively new concept and a distinctly difficult sell. "You can't just drop a product like that in distributors' laps," she said. "They won't understand it. This means you're looking at the most expensive sales setup in the industry: direct sales to the Fortune 500."

"That's fine," Stucki said, "if you have the resources." Optima did not.

An approximately $800,000 first round of venture capital quickly disappeared and a hoped-for second round never materialized. Optima's money began running out just in time to send its executives scurrying for capital "at the end of 1987—just around Wall Street's Black Monday," said the technical consultant.

Even with this litany of woes, Merlyn said, Optima might have been able to bootstrap itself into a new and stronger start had it been in an industry niche that was not itself going through a wrenching transition.

Optima's customers are unlikely to find themselves left in the lurch, however. Although the company is gone, at least two firms are currently claiming rights to market its tools.

Orr, still head of the Topeka-based Ken Orr Institute, is again happily immersed in a combination of academics: He holds an associate professorship at Washington University in St. Louis and is involved in corporate consulting, including work with IBM "doing AD/Cycle explaining conferences around the world."

Palmer still laments Optima's crash on takeoff. "We could have made a difference," she said.

BLOWUP: The Saga of a Partnership Gone Bad

By Edward O. Welles

When Jim Eme walked into the building on a Monday morning in July 1987, he was met by a roomful of empty desks and a pile of res-ignation letters thrust through the mail slot and fallen to the floor. Over the weekend, six of his eight salesmen had stolen into the com-pany and cleaned out their desks while co-workers mingled at the company picnic. Gone, Eme says, were customers lists, price lists, and valuable parts diagrams that Illinois Computer Cable (ICC) had painstakingly assembled in five years of business. Even calculators and staplers had been swept off desks. The place was barren, as empty as the feeling in Eme's gut. The company he had founded was dead.

John Berst, ICC's president, was over in the administrative offices, in a one-story brick building on what had been in more innocent times a rolling stretch of midwestern prairie, since transposed into suburban Chicago industrial parkland. When Berst's phone rang that morning, Eme was on the other end saying, "John, you'd better get over here right away." Then he told him what had happened. Berst thought he had exorcised this demon earlier in the year when one of ICC's four partners, Bob Ohlson, angrily left the company, unable to gain the con-trol he felt he needed to run it. Eme, Berst, and ICC's fourth partner, Ralph Dote (pronounced DO-tee), had come to see Ohlson as a man on an increasingly vicious power trip. They wanted him out.

In March 1987, when Bob Ohlson left ICC, he did not go gently. Rather, he kept reappearing like the ghost of Hamlet's father, warning darkly of thing to come. One day in April he showed up at ICC at 7:00 a.m. to tell bleary-eyed factory workers that he had not resigned, he had been *fired*. In June he barged into an operations meeting at a local restaurant, haranguing Berst for "sticking a knife in my back." He next arrived on the doorstep of Ralph Dote, who was about to move into a new house nearby. When Dote's wife came to the door, Ohlson warned her that bankruptcy court would be the couple's next address; the company would fail if he and Ralph did not wrest control of ICC.

Originally published in INC., *May, 1989. Reprinted with permission, Goldhirsh Group, Inc., 38 Commercial Wharf, Boston, MA 02110, via Copyright Clearance Center, Inc.*

About the only thing left in the sales office that day in July was a business card for a nearby company that Berst had never heard of: Cable Comm Technologies Inc. When Berst called Dun & Bradstreet that afternoon, his worst fear was confirmed: Cable Comm's president was one Robert Ohlson. The renegade company, as it turned out, had formed amidst the fear and loathing that swirled around ICC in the spring of 1987, well before the mass defection of July 20. Unbeknownst to Berst, Ohlson had been planning this coup for the past four months, summoning his loyalists inside ICC to evening meetings at his house.

Ohlson had taken 18 of ICC's 80-odd employees with him, including three-fourths of the sales staff in a sales-driven business. He beheaded ICC and, not pausing at that, proudly displayed his prize on a pike. "I could have wiped out the whole organization if I had had the money," he recently boasted, sitting in his new office. This was sweet revenge for the betrayal Ohlson felt he had suffered at the hands of Berst.

It was Berst, however, who had felt betrayed as he closed his office door that July morning and tried to center his thoughts. His first call went to his banker, who, after listening to his plight, said, "Tell me, John, what sort of forecast do you have for July?"

Berst replied, "Look, I don't even know what I have left here."

The Founding

Illinois Computer Cable Inc. began life five years earlier in Downers Grove, Ill., with an act almost as startling as the coup of July 20, 1987. Jim Eme, fresh from vacation, returned to the cable company he worked for at the time, Tel Com Products, Inc., to find someone else sitting at his desk. Eme, 36, had been Tel Com's sales manager; now, he was being demoted to salesman. Eme had worried that it would come to this. As Tel Com had grown, its founder's ego had kept pace. The running joke around the office was that every time the ashtray in the boss's car filled up, he bought a new car. Morale was in free-fall. Tel Com was in the process of phasing out its in-house sales staff and going to outside sales reps. Eme knew he had to get out, and in August 1982 he did, founding Illinois Computer Cable in the basement of his house.

On his way out at Tel Com, Eme had tried to get Ralph Dote to join him. Eme had faith in himself as a marketer, but he needed a younger man's energy to hook his talent to. Dote was 31, Tel Com's star sales-man. For two years he had sold more than $1 million worth of cable. He was making 50 grand a year, not bad for a young guy without a college degree. Eme had warned Dote that even he would get his comeuppance at Tel Com. Dote scoffed at the thought. "I told him, 'Jim, you're crazy. What can they do to me? I'm their best salesman.' He said, 'Ralph, you wait. You'll see.'"

Eme's warning proved prophetic. At Dote's next salary review, it was proposed that his base pay be lowered and his commission percentage cut. By January a disillusioned Dote had joined Eme.

Dote's mentor at Tel Com had been Bob Ohlson, 20 years his senior. Ohlson joined ICC in February and then persuaded his partners to hire John Berst, 41, away from Tel Com as ICC's chief financial officer. Eme, Dote, and Ohlson made a 10% share of ICC available to Berst. Four men, embittered by life at one company, left to form a new one. This time, they vowed, things would be different.

The 'Weak Link'

Jim Eme had started over at a vulnerable time in his life: children and mortgage, the ego-bruising experience at Tel Com. Now, he was presi-dent and founder of a new company, but he opted for humility. He saw himself as a partner in a business devoid of hierarchy—an entrepreneur among equals.

By early 1985 Bob Ohlson believed that that kind of sentiment was nice, but it wouldn't grow the company. He told the other three they needed to structure ICC more like a corporation, less like a partner-ship. He proposed a change in job titles and duties. He would assume Eme's: president. Eme, whom Ohlson pegged as an ideas man, would become head of R&D. Eme was ambivalent about the switch. "It took me three or four months to get over it, yet it was also a relief," he recalls. "Those responsibilities were now on his shoulders." And Ohlson gladly inherited them.

Ohlson had a steel-trap mind. He had always been good with num-bers; he spoke well. In later years, when life had become increasingly bitter, his powers of persuasion only grew. His partners took to calling him "the man with the golden tongue."

In ICC, Ohlson saw a golden business he was loath to entrust to others he thought less worthy or capable. By its fourth year ICC's sales had climbed to $4.7 million; net profit approached 15%. Yet Ohlson demeaned his partners, labeling Dote "a lucky SOB, a guy in the right spot at the right time." As for Eme, Ohlson says: "He was the worst sales guy I ever saw in my life."

In his zeal to mold the company in an image he deemed worthy, Ohlson hired a management-consulting firm in mid-1985 to assess the partners' effectiveness. The consultants came in and asked each partner about the weaknesses of the other three. When it came Ralph Dote's turn he spoke up: "Well, I think I have some weaknesses, too." Dote felt blindsided when the consultants' report came back naming him the "weak link" in the partnership. He claims he was the only one of the four to level with the consultants about his own shortcomings.

Ralph Dote had always been the top salesman in the company. It was his accounts—85% of which he brought over the first year from Tel Com—that formed ICC's underpinnings. But now his honesty had given Bob Ohlson an opening. In sales meetings Ohlson would rip into Dote, saying he was a lousy sales manager and that he could never produce enough. What really stung was that Eme, Dote's presumed ally, was chiming in and criticizing him as a "weak player."

"God, I don't believe it. He's got Jim believing this," Dote recalls thinking. He asked Eme to meet him for breakfast one day. "Don't you see what he's trying to do, Jim? He's trying to divide us," Dote said to Eme, who responded with a blank look.

With Dote on the ropes, Ohlson subsequently turned his fire on Eme. Dote recalls Ohlson berating Eme, "You don't bring in sales. I ask you a question and I get a dissertation." Wounded, Eme next sought out Dote. "Ralph, I see what you were saying," he said. "You were right, and I was wrong."

Keeping Score

John Berst grew up in a household where hard work was a given. His father was a wagon jobber: he bought popcorn, peanuts, and pretzels in bulk and rebagged them for sale to neighborhood bars and convenience stores. He worked seven days a week; his son began helping him at the age of six.

Berst's workaholic tendencies jibed with Ohlson's. This was a bond between the two, a bond strengthened by Ohlson's initial advocacy of Berst's cause. It was Ohlson who had brought Berst to ICC. The two shared other things as well. Temperamentally, they were a lot alike; they were close in age. Their children were grown or in college, they had time on their hands, unlike Eme and Dote, who were starting families, doing their best to juggle work and home life.

If Bob Ohlson was fire, Jim Eme was air. Eme was soft-spoken, unflappable. Ohlson misread Eme's subdued nature. He saw him as a guy with his feet on the desk, his nose buried in technical journals—a man of inaction.

That impression was wrong. In his twenties Eme had been a Chicago police officer assigned to a quiet section of the city. Bored by writing traffic tickets, he volunteered for duty in one of Chicago's roughest neighborhoods. Eme's first marriage ended in divorce, fostered in part by the disjunction between the commonplace cares at home and the ready presence of death on the street. Distracted by his personal affairs, Eme started walking, unthinking, into dangerous situations on the job. He knew it was time to quit being a cop.

Bob Ohlson, likewise, carried private burdens. His wife had cancer. Ohlson would linger at the office until 6:00 or 7:00 at night. He often came in on Saturday mornings. Ohlson saw the time he put in as evidence of his superior commitment to ICC. Eme and Dote saw in it a need to escape the reminders of death that awaited him at home.

"I fell into Bob's trap," concedes Berst. "By now he had me wondering what were they doing over there when we were over here busting our cans. He made a pretty good case." Ohlson and Berst started discussing how to gain control of the company when they held only 40%. One strategy they settled on was to hire a salesman, with the secret intent of elevating him to sales manager, displacing Dote.

To turn up the heat on Dote and Eme, Ohlson came into a meeting at the end of the fiscal year in October 1985 proposing salary increases for himself and Berst. In his mind, they were the workers, Dote and Eme the drones. "We knew what it takes to run an entrepreneurial venture," Ohlson says. "The better things got, the more Ralph and Jim decided they were going to retire without extending us the courtesy of getting off the payroll."

Berst sat quietly by as Dote objected. "We're partners," Dote said.

"This is a corporation, and I'm the president," Ohlson rejoined. Ohlson had come to the meeting armed with magazine articles on typical salary ranges among top managers. Other presidents made more than their subordinates, he asserted.

After some heated debate it was agreed Ohlson would make $90,000, Berst $80,000, Eme $75,000, and Dote $65,000. The hierarchy was now in place. Dote knew Ohlson didn't need the money and Ohlson admitted as much. "This is just a way to keep score, Ralph," he said.

Power Play

Bob Ohlson was an "excellence" freak. In addition to hiring consultants, he was always trying to get his partners to read books on management. He interpreted their relative lack of interest as a sign of their business ineptitude. In early 1986, in his ongoing compulsion to systemize the business, Ohlson planned a weekend retreat for the four partners at Berst's vacation house in Wisconsin. Ohlson typed up daily agendas for the team to follow, hour by hour, including when they would break for lunch. On the way up in Berst's van he played Tom Peters and Lee Iacocca tapes.

Late on Saturday afternoon Ohlson dropped a bombshell. Some weeks earlier, Berst recalls, Ohlson had ordered $40,000 worth of communications devices to sell to the IBM market. Berst, Eme, and Dote were incredulous. ICC had never gone close to IBM products. It was mainly a DEC house. Why all of a sudden get into something they knew virtually nothing about? Ohlson sat back with a broad smile. "Don't worry," he assured them. "I'll take care of it."

The decision resulted in one sale with a low margin and an overly generous warranty backed by ICC. A dispute over what had been actually delivered resulted in an investigation by ICC's lawyers to get the company its due. (Much of that $40,000 inventory still sits in ICC's warehouse.)

Berst believes the decision signaled a move by Ohlson to take the company in a direction that would put it more under his control. Ohlson maintains the company needed to evolve from its existing markets to the sale of electronic "boxes," such as modems and multiplexers, rather than just cable. In effect, ICC had to offer "systems solutions." His partners argued the exact opposite: ICC was cutting its own throat by getting away from what it did best—selling cable.

To sell these boxes, Ohlson persuaded his partners he needed to hire and mold a new breed: briefcase-toting, college-educated salesmen in three-piece suits who would spend a lot of time on the road. They would be true professionals, salesmen who could penetrate new markets and put ICC on the map. Again Ohlson's partners fought the move. The overhead these new hires would create was greater than that of the existing sales force—trained in house, skilled at selling computer cable to all takers over the phone.

When Ohlson interviewed these prospective hires he openly bad-mouthed ICC, telling them how unprofessional the sales operation was. Ohlson assured one candidate that he would be made sales manager within six months. Berst claims that Ohlson paid the moving expenses of another without telling the partners. Ohlson had ICC provide that salesman with a data link for his personal computer, giving him better access to a vendor. When other salesmen complained, Ohlson replied: "Well, he's an entrepreneur."

This entrepreneur wanted to use the computer to hack his way into a vendor's cost database. When Eme found out about it he approached Ohlson: "What if the vendor finds out? What sort of liability does ICC have?"

Ohlson waved him off with his usual reply. "Don't worry about it," he said. "I'll handle it."

Suspicions and Delusions

John Berst had always been loyal to Bob Ohlson, doubtful of the other two partners. But he was the company's CFO, the man who kept the books. And by mid-1986 it was apparent that the books didn't lie.

Berst recalls his shock when he discovered that Ohlson had paid a headhunter $5,000 to find a salesman without telling his partners. "I nearly fell off my chair. I said, 'What's this for? We haven't done anything like this before.'" Ohlson's decisions were driving Dote and Eme nuts—when they knew about them. They owned 60% of the company, yet Ohlson was committing them to decisions they knew nothing about.

Berst admits he "was really close to Bob." Blowing the whistle didn't feel right. The two men worked together six days a week. Their Saturdays had become a ritual. In at 8:00 a.m. to strategize about the business, out for a leisurely breakfast at 10:00 for more company talk, back to the office till 1:00. The bond strengthened in August 1986 when the company expanded into a second building, physically separating sales from administration. Ohlson started prowling the halls, stewing over the image that loomed ever more vivid in his mind of Dote and Eme over in the other building, feet on their desks, eyes fixed firmly on the clock. These were suspicions that Berst also bought into.

Berst began to see those suspicions as distorted delusion as summer turned to fall. His break with Ohlson came at October's end, when ICC closed the fiscal year. For the second year in a row Ohlson came into the year-end meeting with examples from the business press of salary ranges for corporate managers. Now, he wanted $125,000 for himself, $90,000 for Berst, $72,000 each for Dote and Eme. Eme's proposed salary amounted to a $3,000 cut.

Berst, who had started three years earlier at $36,000, was stunned. He was flattered that Ohlson thought he was worth so much, but he knew the company couldn't afford to pay him that much money. He also knew that Ohlson didn't deserve that kind of money. "That was the first time the veil dropped from my eyes. Bob Ohlson couldn't compromise."

Ohlson now saw Berst in a different light as well—as a traitor to the cause. Anger rose in Ohlson as he reasserted that he was the president of this corporation.

"I'm a managing partner of this corporation, too," interjected Ralph Dote, "and don't you forget it."

The next week the partners met again to hash out the salary dispute. Dote came in and said, "Here's my plan. You get $100,000, and the rest of us get $85,000. We're going back to equality in this company."

Dote knew he could make his plan stick. In half a year he had moved from being the odd man out to having the support of Eme—and now, at last, Berst. Ohlson had succeeded in allying his partners against him. Stymied and angry, Ohlson said: "Fine, I'm going to sit back like Ralph and Jim, put my feet up on the desk, and not do any work. Then we'll see what happens."

'Buy Me Out, John'

His partners had spent a year trying to stem Ohlson's unilateral actions, but somehow, like water working on a leaky dike, his will had always found the opening it sought. "This guy has a determination factor you wouldn't believe," Eme recalls. "He'll wear you down."

By the time Berst and Ohlson met on January 31, 1987, Ohlson's determination had driven him to the edge—and brought him back to his former ally. He told Berst the stress was threatening his health. "Buy me out, John," he said.

Berst softened. He knew no business was worth a man's health, but he also knew by now it was all but over between him and Ohlson. Two weeks earlier, with sales slumping, Berst had attended a sales meeting to buck up the troops. Before Berst returned to the administrative offices, word had gotten back to Ohlson. Berst claims that when he entered the building Ohlson confronted him, demanding to know what right he had to meddle with sales.

On February 3 the four men met. Eme asked Ohlson pointedly what made him think that one of them could simply buy another out when the buy-sell agreement stipulated that any shares sold would go to the corporation, not an individual. That provoked a half-hour monologue by Ohlson about how poorly run ICC was. By now perceptions were so skewed that a meeting of the minds was impossible. The first quarter of the fiscal year had been bad. Ohlson blamed it on excessive spending by the others. They countered that these were justifiable capital expenses, agreed to by a majority of the group, which would yield benefits down the road. As Ohlson got up to leave the meeting his exasperation boiled over into threat. "I can take four or five people out of here and start a company," he warned.

The Breakup

In that last utterance lay the seed of truth, the spark of action. Bob Ohlson was a visible figure around ICC. Production workers saw nothing of the angry, driven man squaring off with his partners behind closed doors. They saw the kindly, caring president, the man with his finger on the corporate pulse. The man was credible. His partners knew he could tear the company apart with a few reckless statements. They knew it was time to separate Ohlson from ICC.

On March 9, 1987, the four met again, but this time the arena had shifted; the stakes had been raised to match emotions. Ohlson maintains that when they sat down in the office of ICC's attorney, the other three owners fired him and that a buyout offer—for 60% of stock value—came only later. Berst, Eme, and Dote recall offering that day to buy Ohlson out for $150,000—more than 100% of stock value. They offered Ohlson a company car, a consulting contract, and health insurance. Then they told Ohlson they wanted a noncompete clause.

That stunned him. Eme recalls Ohlson sitting expressionless in his seat as though he had just been hit full force in the chest. "I think he truly felt that we would make him a hell of an offer," Eme says. "His delusion was that everything was going to be OK." Offended by the offer Ohlson balked at signing. He wasn't about to do that when he had his signature on a $700,000 line of company credit. Suddenly, Ohlson was not in control.

His partners then said they had no choice but to accept his resignation, since under the agreement a majority stake could vote a minority holder out. Berst and Dote approached to limply shake their former partner's hand. Dote recalls extending his hand and saying, "Bob, I'm sorry. I never thought it would come to this." Dote assumed this was good-bye.

The next day Dote's phone rang. Ohlson was on the line, asking Dote to meet him for breakfast. Dote, incredulous, acquiesced.

Over breakfast, Ohlson did the talking. "You and I could control the company," Dote recalls him saying. "We could get rid of Jim and John."

When Ohlson started criticizing Eme, Dote cut him short. "Wait a minute, Bob. Two years ago it was me you were jumping on."

Ohlson rejoined: "And Ralph, you're better for it. I made an entrepreneur out of you."

Ohlson's Svengali nature had been evident with people like Ralph Dote. Despite his salesman's bravado, Dote had his vulnerable side. He had married at 22. Eight months later his wife was diagnosed as having cancer. Within two years she died. Soon after that, he started a small business, a grocery store, and it foundered. Two or three weeks after Dote closed the doors of that business, his father died.

When Dote started at ICC he was a young man with few assets. Ohlson lent him $10,000 so he could pick up his stock options. Ohlson interpreted such a gesture as an emblem of the future faith he had in Dote. Others saw his motives differently. Through gestures like that, Ohlson gained control over those around him.

The breakfast meeting was merely the opening salvo in Ohlson's campaign to regain Dote's heart and mind—and so the company into which he had invested so much of himself. The campaign gathered steam when Ohlson began sending off impassioned, overwrought letters to Dote, commenting on how ICC was about to go down and it wasn't too late for Dote to jump ship. A letter came from a Michigan corporation offering to buy Dote's stake in ICC. This was strange. ICC had never before received an unsolicited offer like this. Moreover, what was the point in buying a minority share? Dote claims that Ohlson's attorney was working through the corporation.

Asked about this, Ohlson replies obliquely that he had found a generous buyer for ICC, and his partners were too dumb to know a good deal when they saw one.

Dote sent copies of the letters to his lawyer. For a month he would not answer his phone. One day when Dote was at work, Ohlson knocked on his door at home and warned his second wife, Jackie, that ICC would go down the tubes if he wasn't let back in. In a few months the Dotes were to move into a new house. Ohlson told Jackie they'd never move into the house. When Dote learned of Ohlson's visit he told his lawyer, "I would have killed the son of a bitch if I had been there."

Working on Dote proved to be one front of a two-front war Ohlson was gearing up to wage against ICC. His rebuff at the March meeting had only quickened his appetite for revenge. That month Ohlson and those most loyal to him started meeting after-hours to plan their shadow company. Salespeople formed the core of a constituency Ohlson knew he needed to broaden if he were to pull this off. That called for a bold strike.

Early one April morning he strode unannounced into the cafeteria, where production workers were gulping coffee before the start of the day shift. His sources had told him that Eme was at a trade show, Berst on vacation, and Dote in the other building. He announced to the stunned workers that he had not resigned, he had been fired. The production manager phoned over to the other building: "Ralph, you won't believe who's over here." By the time Dote got over to the administrative building, Ohlson was gone.

The guerrilla theater continued in June and July when Ohlson twice showed up at sales meetings in which he berated Berst, who had since been elected ICC's new president, for betraying him. In July Ohlson swept past the receptionist and into Berst's office, demanding they settle their dispute. When Berst told Ohlson the attorneys were working on just that, Ohlson summarily vowed that Best's fortunes, like Dote's, would fall with ICC's. Berst recalls him saying: "John, one day I'll live in your house and play with your toys."

Attrition

Ohlson's outbursts were surface flares signaling deeper tensions at ICC, where in the spring of 1987 an eerie and exhausted calm prevailed. In May and June John Berst started losing employees one by one. The office manager left. The inventory supervisor, a quality-control supervisor, a production manager, and a couple of production people followed. The attrition made Berst edgy. He wondered if this were Ohlson's doing.

Berst's suspicion deepened at the beginning of July when ICC's purchasing agent came into Berst's office and handed him his resignation. This was an employee Berst had courted for months. Berst considered himself the younger man's mentor. Now, he too was leaving. Berst looked him in the eye and said, "Just be man enough to tell me this: does this have anything to do with Bob Ohlson?" The employee took offense at the inference and angrily denied it.

In June an abnormally large amount of inventory came in the door at ICC and a lot of product went out. Commission checks would go out on July 15 for product shipped in June. In the meantime, Berst got notice from more people who said they were leaving, not in two weeks, but on July 15, the same day his salespeople drew their hefty June commission checks. Ohlson was after Berst to settle their case by July 15 and was willing to accept substantially less money than first offered. July 15. Berst kept hearing that date as though he was Caesar and a voice in his head was urging him to beware. He called up ICC's lawyer: "Tell Bob Ohlson we've got a deal—but not till after the 15 of July."

The Coup

The deal was blown away by the mass resignation that greeted Berst on Monday, July 20, 1987, an event that he labels simply "the coup." After getting the news from Eme, Berst closed his office door and stared at the wall. He had been in business 25 years, and now all of that had been destroyed by a single act. "Everything I had done in my professional career was about to come crashing down," he recalls. "This was the end of the world."

The self-pity soon passed, hardening into anger. Berst knew that with his experience and education, he would survive. But what about others? "I have 65 people working for me. A lot of them are not worried about paying for college educations. They're worried about next week's paycheck."

First he called his banker and gave him the news. Then he sat down with Eme and Dote and agreed that ICC had to get back to its core business in order to survive. Ohlson had been trying to move them away from selling cable over the phone to more comprehensive "systems solutions" peddled by high-priced salesmen on the road. The three men agreed to promote a number of customer-service people to sales. Berst next stepped onto the factory floor.

What he felt in the room was fear. "We had a number of husband-and-wife combinations on the floor, single parents, people who had been with the company four or five years," recalls Berst. "These people don't make a lot of money; they've always relied on their paychecks." Tension had been growing for months among the partners, and they had done their best to build an emotional firewall between their disputes and the rest of the company. In a small shop like ICC, that didn't work. Rumors inevitably started, fed by the high-profile, high-energy persona of Bob Ohlson. Berst spoke.

"We've had a lot of resignations, and we're angry about it," Berst said to his workers. "But we're not going to lie down and die. If you have confidence in us, and if we stay angry enough, we'll pull this out."

In the coup's aftermath the plot began to come to light. In July one of ICC's salespeople, working on deals that would close in the future, had said he worked for Cable Comm, Ohlson's company-to-be, but claimed it was a subsidiary of ICC. Hence he could offer customers the usual comfort level provided by an established company, but future payment would go to Cable Comm, not ICC. Another salesman, again claiming to represent ICC, had subcontracted with another cable manufacturer to supply cable to an ICC customer, thus pocketing the profit. This was revealed one day in July when Berst got a call from a customer wanting to know where the cable was that he had ordered. Berst had no record of it.

The large amount of product shipped in June—for which the salesmen were compensated on July 15—now also made sense. Some of it had originally been promised for the future. Some of it had never even been ordered. In the latter part of July, a lot of it came back. That month John Berst wrote $60,000 worth of credits to customers for product they had not ordered. That month he also received calls from headhunters who had heard from former ICC employees that the company was going into Chapter 11.

Bob Ohlson's shadow company was indeed hungry for start-up money. He had lured many people from ICC with the promise of equity ownership in the company, provided they were willing to invest. This issue came to be fraught with symbolism, evidence of how enlightened the new company would be in contrast to ICC. Bruce

Swoboda, ICC's systems manager, calls Bob Ohlson "the world's greatest salesperson. He could talk you into anything. It's very scary." Swoboda asserts that a lot of these salespeople were not unduly unhappy at ICC, but they fell under Bob Ohlson's persuasive power. Swoboda points to the Cable Comm business card one salesman left behind. "I take that as a sign that he feels guilty about what he did."

Ohlson's Story

"If I had had enough money, I probably could have cleaned the whole organization out. This was a super move on our part." Bob Ohlson's smile broadens as he leans back on the couch in his office, lights a cigarette, rests a foot on the arm of his desk chair, and launches into a vigorous self-defense of what went down at ICC. The bravado—the obvious lack of remorse—overlays a bitterness that rises when the subjects turns to how this experience has marked him. "Obviously I'm more cynical about personal relationships. At one time I would have considered John Berst my best friend in the whole world. And then he went and stuck a knife in my back."

Ohlson is a tall, affable, slightly stoop-shouldered man. His new company, Cable Comm, has 36 employees and by his account is doing "very well." In its first year he had hoped Cable Comm would do $3 million in sales but fell "a little short of that." He won't say how short. In conversation Ohlson's demeanor ranges from courtly to profane, with one oft-recurring word being "vision." Bob Ohlson claims that he had it and his partners did not.

Ohlson's former partners claim the vision he implanted in many impressionable minds at ICC—chiefly the sales staff—had little to do with the company's central mission as agreed to by the partners. Ohlson's idea was to sell whole systems solutions instead of just cable. Equity ownership also became a part of the emergent and renegade vision. Again, it had never been raised as a point of contention, claims Berst; yet when people defected with Ohlson, it was flung back in Berst's face as evidence of how retrograde ICC was.

Ohlson denies any wrongdoing in setting up his company, claiming that he consulted a lawyer. Asked about some of his salespeople taking ICC customer lists, he replies: "A customer list doesn't mean a damn thing. We know where the customers are." He labels "entirely false" charges that before July 15 ICC salespeople loyal to him misrepresented themselves to gain commissions for Cable Comm. He concedes that the pressure he put on Ralph Dote amounted to harassment, "but I had heard Ralph was sitting on the fence." As for the secrecy and timing surrounding the coup, Ohlson defends them as necessary. "I know John Berst well enough to know that if this had been done any other way, he would have stopped payment on those [June commission] checks." He adds: "This was carefully planned. People stayed on two or three days after getting paid so those checks would clear." Finally, Ohlson asserts that his former partners' insistence on a non-compete clause drove him to extreme measures: "It was bull. Why should I sign my life away for a measly $150,000? You know, if this had been handled cleanly none of this would have happened. These guys threw me a challenge. And"—again he offers a confiding smile—"the more I thought about it, the more I said, 'Screw them.'"

The Revival

"I'm still angry at Bob. I may never get over that," says John Berst as he wheels his Lincoln Continental out of the ICC parking lot and heads across the prairie cum-industrial-parkland for lunch at a nearby restaurant. "But Bob and I were also friends," he continues. "I miss that. I'd like to see him again, but if I said, 'Hey, let's have lunch,' I can hear his tone already. He's so arrogant." The easy ride of the big car seems to buffer us from a raw winter day and the larger shocks beyond that life inevitably provides.

It is almost a year and a half after the coup, and ICC is back from the dead. The company now employs 95 people, up from 60 in July 1987. In 1988 it opened 875 new accounts. Sales were $5.8 million, up $1 million from the year before. By June the company will move into a new building.

We have just come from ICC's factory floor, walking through a maze of workers bending over cable-handling equipment and stacking inventory toward the ceiling. Berst had shown me a carton full of identical die-cast parts and picked one up. The part is called an Ethernet hood, and it fits over the coupling on the end of a computer cable. It also serves as emblem to a larger issue. When Jim Eme wanted ICC to make the Ethernet hood, Bob Ohlson had scoffed at the idea. "The piece was researched by Jim," Berst says. "We can't bring it in fast enough. I could sell twice as many of these. Bob said it would never sell. It's not a winner."

The Ethernet hood is one of about 20 identifiable contributions, technical and otherwise, that mark Eme in Berst's mind as a true "resource." These are contributions, he adds, that Bob Ohlson was either unable or unwilling to acknowledge.

Berst believes that Ohlson ultimately did him a favor. Ohlson's fanaticism forced Berst to see Ohlson for what he was. It moved him as well to refocus the business and reflect on his partners as people. Berst, under Ohlson's sway, could not appreciate the subtleties of Eme's character. He, too, saw Dote as the weak link.

In the ICC meetings, which used to turn inevitably stormy, Ohlson would often enter with a schedule for how long people would speak on a given subject. Now, if the partners need to chew over an issue, they do just that, no matter how long it takes. And once a year, Berst submits his resignation to Eme and Dote. He gives up control to get back his partners' respect.

But trust, in the deeper sense, may never be regained at Illinois Computer Cable. Berst admits that candor was once the norm at ICC, but the coup changed all that. He confesses now to a "loneliness," adding: "I tend to hold my thoughts in. I feel I have to be guarded about what I say and whom I say it to now. You're not sure who may be passing information to the other company or entertaining thoughts of doing something like this again."

John Berst these days may be running a revived company, but he is also looking over his shoulder. And he has lost a friend and confidant. "With Bob Ohlson I bared my soul," he says. "Now, I'm reluctant to totally confide in anyone."

3.5   GRASPING FAILURE FROM THE JAWS OF SUCCESS

From the earlier stories in this book, you may think that computing failure is associated mainly with the optimistic unknowns, the misbegotten mergees, those who go out on a limb with the wrong technology, and the strange people. Think again.

In this section, we'll look at some extremely successful computing firms that simply failed to keep their success alive. These stories are particularly sad. Early product success and tremendous customer loyalty aren't enough, we will see here, to keep a computer company booming. And when corporate death eventually and inevitably happens, there are plenty of mourners left to look one another in the eyes and say, "How'd that happen?" There are usually plenty of answers available; being sure those answers are the right and true ones is a harder problem.

One of the fascinating things about the history of computing is that yesterday's successes are so quickly forgotten. The companies whose stories we present in this section have what once were well-known names—Wang Labs, Commodore, and Atari. Many of the readers of this book will not have heard of them; yet in their heyday, these were the Apples and Microsofts of their time. (I suppose it is inevitable that a book-browsing young reader in the 21st century will come across this passage in a dusty library copy of this book, and say "Apple? Microsoft? Who were they?"!)

One of the interesting things about the stories in this section of the book is that they are nicely organized into "lessons learned." Two of the stories make quite a point of capturing not just the whats and the hows, but the possible whys for these corporate calamities. If failure is the strongest learning experience—and many experts in learning say that it is—then who better can we learn from than these early-day successes who let success slip away?

First, there is An Wang, and Wang Labs. We present two stories of the temporary demise of Wang (it was to bounce back later, but in a dramatically changed form). There is a crucial six month gap between the two stories. In the first, written as the review of a book about Wang (*Riding the Runaway Horse*), the reviewer comments not just on the book but on the earlier book by An Wang, brilliant founder of the firm, which presented his life's "Lessons" learned. The reviewer, anticipating the imminent death of the company, presents a supplementary set of "lessons" that Wang might better have followed if he hoped to save the firm. In the second story, Wang has just gone Chapter 11, the "largest company ever to file for protection" in that way. Here, you see a reinforcement of those unfortunate lessons learned from the first story, the lessons that might have allowed Wang to avoid the bankruptcy that followed.

I spoke earlier of sad stories and mourners. The third story of this section recounts the imminent and unfortunate demise of Commodore, one of the true pioneers of the computing field. What makes this story particularly sad, and what generated the larger number of mourners who lamented the company's passing, is that Commodore's Amiga computer was, at the time of the company's death, the head and shoulders best computer in the business. That's an arguable viewpoint, of course, but most objective observers of the scene at the time would put the Amiga ahead of any Apple it competed with, and far ahead of anything Intel was offering. Why did Commodore go under? According to this story, it was a corporate president who could not see the value of advertising the Amiga's obvious benefits—he believed that a "better mousetrap" would attract its own customers—and instead spent the money that might have saved the company on an exaggeratedly high salary for himself.

As that article comes to an end—it was written a number of years ago—its author speculates that Commodore might survive in spite of the trouble in which it is immersed. It did not.

Another ancient story of another early success in the field closes this section of the book. Here we present a fascinating and nearly complete history of that once well-known games company, Atari. Atari, the article begins, "created an industry where none had existed before." The story then poses the question "How did the company that was the only game in town [at its peak, it held 80% of the games market], start losing the game?"

The answer that follows is fascinating for its insight and its carefully collected lessons learned. According to this story, once again we have a president who failed to grasp and work with what he had. (Should we have called this section of the book "Off with their [corporate] heads"?!) The long-term president, who presided over Atari's dwindling successes, ran the company like an empire. All decisions had to be made by him, according to the authors of the story, and those decisions were not made based on any consistent and well-understood corporate goals.

Furthermore, in a business where software talent and creativity was the difference between product "hits" and lackluster "misses," the president placed no value on the talented engineers and games programmers who were truly the company's backbone, insulting them and driving them to leave the company. (Many of the best left to form quite successful competitors to Atari). When the president finally realized what he had done, he over-reacted and lavished money on the programmers who remained with the company, resulting in what one personnel consultant called "the wealthiest and most unhappy group of people I've ever met."

At the same time as the talent drain, the company—basking in its former glory—turned conservative, becoming "risk averse" and suffering from "perfection paralysis." There were "no new ideas, no innovations, and no brainstorming sessions," according to one Atari observer.

There, the story ends. It was written in 1983, and closes with some questions about whether Atari will slip quietly away, or survive in some transmogrified form. With the hindsight of 15 years, we can now see that the expectations established by the authors have largely come true. The successful Atari of yore is no more.

WHAT WENT WRONG AT WANG

by Joseph Nocera

In 1986, four years before his death of esophageal cancer, An Wang, the founder and presiding genius of Wang Laboratories, published his memoirs. Rather smugly (I remember thinking at the time), he entitled them "Lessons"—the idea apparently being that the masses could learn much from the example of a great man like, well, like the author. Alas, Mr. Wang's timing was a bit off. Around the time his book began appearing in bookstores, his company was announcing a huge quarterly loss. It was laying off workers by the thousands and its stock price was falling precipitously.

It occurred to me then that perhaps there were a few lessons in the story of Wang Laboratories that the Doctor (as he was often called) had somehow overlooked in his triumphant recounting. Such as what happens when an aggressive company founder finds such astonishing success that he begins to believe in his own infallibility.

Now comes Charles C. Kenney, a reporter for the Boston Globe, to detail the lessons the Doctor left out—the real lessons, as it turns out, in "the rise and decline of Wang Laboratories," to borrow from his book's subtitle. "Riding the Runaway Horse" (Little, Brown, 323 pages, $22.95) is a kind of Tom Peters tome in reverse, a painful primer in how to turn a once great company into a laughing-stock.

Make no mistake: Wang Laboratories was absolutely a great company in its prime—the virtual creator of the market for computerized office products, the employer of 32,000 people, mostly in Massachusetts, the generator of 30 straight years of increased profit, and most inspiring of all, a wonderful example of what an immigrant with ambition and ideas can accomplish in America. (Mr. Wang was born in China.)

There was a time not that long ago when every secretary in America swore by Wang products, a time when the company was growing so fast that it really must have felt like a runaway horse. How could a franchise this strong be piddled away in a few short years? Although Mr. Kenney's book is shaped as a narrative, you won't have much trouble finding the answers. Or should I say the lessons?

Originally published in the Wall Street Journal, *Feb. 26, 1992. Reprinted by permission,* © *1992 Dow Jones & Co., Inc. All rights reserved worldwide.*

Lesson No. 1: Genius is not genetically transmitted. Everyone now agrees that many of the problems at Wang Laboratories began and ended with An Wang's decision to groom his oldest son, Fred, to be his successor. "He was driven not by money or power, but by a desire to pass along his empire to his sons," writes Mr. Kenney, who adds that Mr. Wang was adhering to a value system he had learned in China, where family comes before all else. But sometimes it makes more sense to be driven by money, especially when you supposedly owe a fiduciary responsibility to the people who own shares in your company.

Mr. Wang's solution to this problem was to establish two classes of stock, thus ensuring that shareholders could not stand in his way, no matter how much he put his personal interests ahead of theirs. Mr. Kenney describes Fred Wang as a nice enough fellow, but plainly ill-equipped to manage a multibillion-dollar company. But when Wang's directors objected to Mr. Wang's plan to install number one son as company president in 1986—after the son had made a botch of the company's product development—the founder would brook no dissent. "He is my son," Mr. Wang insisted. "He can do it."

Lesson No. 2: Arrogance is bad for business. And heavens knows, Wang Laboratories was one arrogant place after its great triumphs of the late 1970s and early 1980s. Its key product was its revolutionary word processor, a forerunner to the personal computer, a machine in such incredible demand that customers would wait months to get their hands on one. Unfortunately, Wang started to believe that its products were so good that customers would always wait months for them. In this it was mistaken. As for Mr. Wang, his arrogance took a somewhat different form.

So convinced was he that his instincts were unerring that he simply refused the entreaties of his staff to develop a personal computer. It is quite possible that had Wang developed such a machine, it would have owned the PC market, since its word processor had given it a huge head start in penetrating the office market.

Lesson No. 3: When you make product announcements, it helps to have products. That product-development botch I mentioned earlier? It was a doozy. In 1983, realizing that the company had missed the personal computer revolution, Fred Wang needed to find a way to keep Wang's customers loyal until it could develop its own competitive machines. So one day, he simply announced a series of 14 products, many of which were dazzlingly innovative. It turned out, however, that many of them existed only on paper. "The event," writes Mr. Kenney, "was madness." Eventually customers began catching on, which is around the time they also began switching to IBM in droves.

Lesson No. 4: When the chief executive officer, who has always avoided the slightest hint of pomp and circumstance, begins hiring security guards, buying corporate jets and moving into a 3,000-square-foot office with a marble fireplace and a whirlpool bath, it is not a good sign. Mr. Wang had become, in the words of former Wang President John Cunningham, "a humble egomaniac."

Lesson No. 5: Firing your son will usually generate some negative publicity. This is the moment people still remember about the decline of Wang Laboratories; that August day in 1989 when a desperately ill An Wang finally fired his son as president of Wang in a last-ditch effort to revive the company. The moment, widely publicized, seemed so poignant and truly sad, though as Mr. Kenney reports, it was all transacted in a fairly businesslike fashion, with both father and son knowing that the son was going to have to take the fall, and Fred Wang for once in his life rising to the occasion, accepting his public humiliation with grace and dignity.

As to whether this action will turn out to have saved the company Mr. Wang both built and nearly destroyed is difficult to know, even now. But at least it has a chance. There aren't any Wangs at Wang anymore.

WANG WILTS

By Marianne Kolbasuk McGee

Earlier this year, Wang Laboratories Inc. CEO Richard Miller embarked on a worldwide tour of the beleaguered computer maker's principal customers. Wang, he reassured them, had matters in hand and exciting new products in the pipeline. There was no cause for alarm.

Last week Miller was forced to eat those words. After struggling for years to refocus its product strategy, revitalize its sales, and return to profitability, Wang surrendered to the ultimate restructuring, becoming the largest computer company ever to file for protection from its creditors under Chapter 11 bankruptcy laws.

It wasn't a surprise, but the reality of the filing crashed like a body blow to New England's punch-drunk computer industry, staggering the region's already reeling economy. The impact of 5,000 more job cuts and a huge loss of business for the local companies that supplied Wang and its employees could be felt throughout the area and as far away as Houston, where political pundits on the floor of the Republican National Convention immediately characterized it as yet another blow to President Bush's reelection chances.

But the blame for Wang's downfall goes well beyond the protracted recession. Once a stellar success story, ranking 146 among the *Fortune 500*, the company's resistance to bold changes when its revenue and clientele first began to wane in the mid-1980s left it mired in debt, unable to play technological catch-up with the rest of the industry. As of last week, Wang owed more than $500 million in long- and short-term debt, while incurring a loss of $139.2 million on revenue of $1.9 billion for fiscal 1992, ended June 30. The loss left the company with a negative net worth estimated at $70 million, which would have allowed many of its lenders to call in their loans had Wang not filed for protection.

Missing the Revolution

Change hadn't always been a dirty word at Wang. In the 1970s, the vendor successfully transformed itself from a maker of desktop calculators to an innovative leader in electronic word processing and office

Originally published in Information Week, *August 24, 1992. Used with permission.*
Copyright 1992 by CMP Publications, Inc., 600 Community Dr., Manhasset, NY 11030.

automation. Later it assumed a strong position in the booming mini-computer scene of the early 1980s.

But the PC revolution proved its undoing. Despite his pioneering role in the industry, the company's founder, the late An Wang, failed to understand how severely the general-purpose PC would ultimately cut his company's specialized line of word processors. Then, throughout the late '80s, the computer maker continued to resist the trend toward industry standards. In the process, Wang fumbled its last, best hope: the commanding early lead it held in electronic document imaging technology.

Unfortunately, the corner into which Wang has wedged itself has also snared the vendor's few remaining loyal customers, who are now between the sharpest rock and hardest place ever.

"For the last 12 years, we've been almost exclusively a Wang shop, and I'd like to continue working with them," says Harold Crane, manager of information services at MPC Products Corp., a $40 million aerospace components manufacturer in Skokie, Ill. "However, I see this Chapter 11 as either a step toward liquidation or toward something else that might force us to reconsider where we're headed with our own operations."

"These developments definitely accelerate our plans to look at other vendors' products," concurs Duane Davis, director of IS at Kent Electronics Inc. The Houston-based distributor, which spent about $1 million last year on Wang products and services, recently upgraded its VS 1000 system to a VS 12000. Laments Davis, "Obviously, you can't make a break in a week or a month, but we will need to do something soon."

Of the 35,000 installed customers Wang says it has worldwide, the vendor admitted last week that only about 1,000 accounted for 85% of the company's 1992 revenue. The majority of Wang's customers over the last several years have migrated to computer platforms from vendors with more open, standards-based strategies and seemingly more stable balance sheets.

"Three years ago, we began moving our operations off our 10 Wang minicomputers and onto PC LANS," says Joseph Rasmussen, director of GTE Service Corp. in Stamford, Conn. "PCs were not part of Wang's strategy, but we decided back then that PCs and industry standards would be a big part of our strategy."

Indeed, John Reynolds, national manager for information services at Intelogic Trace Inc., a San Antonio, Texas, computer services firm that helps VS users migrate to PC LANS, says Wang-related business has increased eightfold in the last four years.

Too Rich to Switch

Amid this mass VS exodus, a small constituency of users has stayed put, unable to justify the cost of jettisoning their investment in Wang's proprietary VS software.

"Although we use some DEC and NCR products in our operations, the backbone of our claims processing and applications development is Wang," relates Richard Benashski, an information systems consultant at ITT Hartford, the Stamford, Conn., insurance firm. "If we have to migrate, we will move to a Unix-based environment," he says. "But we haven't till now because we've had a good relationship with Wang and because our investment in their products is so great."

Like the insurer, some other Wang customers are holdouts to the now shattered belief that former RCA executive Miller, who became Wang's chief executive in 1989, would be the company's miracle worker. Although he was a newcomer to the computer industry when he took the helm at the Lowell, Mass.-based company, many of Wang's customers hoped that Miller's previous accomplishments as a turnaround wizard would also mean magic at Wang.

Miller did help trim Wang's work force by about 18,000 from a peak of 31,500 (another 5,000 of Wang's current 13,500 workers will be eliminated in the newest restructuring); he also cut Wang's debt by about half from its high of $1.05 billion in 1989. During his tenure, however, product development continued to stagnate, while deals were cut that undermined the company's greatest asset—its installed base.

In return for a $25 million investment from IBM, last year Miller committed Wang to resell IBM's AS/400 midrange systems and RS/6000 workstations and server line. An additional $75 million infusion from IBM was pegged to product sales; but the day before the bankruptcy filing, Big Blue said Wang's sales were disappointingly low and did not warrant the additional investment.

Some observers say Wang's decision to resell the AS/400, which competes directly with the VS, was another fatal mistake in the first place, sending signals to its customers as early as June 1991 that Wang's minicomputer days were numbered. "It was a suicidal move," says Edson de Castro, founder and former president of Data General Corp., another New England computer firm that saw both its best and worst days in the mid-to-late 1980s.

"Even if Wang hasn't pushed the IBM line as hard as IBM would've liked, Wang has been acting as an extension of IBM's sales force during this last year, and nobody benefits more from all this than IBM," agrees Rikki Kirzner, an analyst with market researcher Dataquest Inc. in San Jose.

And although Wang has finished porting its image technology onto the RS/6000 platform—a key objective of the alliance with IBM—those products are not slated to ship until next month, more than a year after the deal was inked.

Still, as Miller reiterated last week, whatever lies ahead for Wang rests heavily on the porting of its Office 2000 software, which include its imaging products, to the RS/6000 platform. Office 2000, which Wang announced in March 1991, is the banner under which the vendor is offering software and services supporting industry standards and a variety of platforms.

Wang officials say other plans for its restructuring have not yet been worked out. Although Miller maintains that Wang will continue to enhance its VS product line, making good on its promise to introduce the last seven of the 37 new VS products it planned for this year, he admits that its manufacturing operations will now be drastically reduced. Meanwhile, most observers believe last week's bankruptcy filing is a prelude to the firm closing down its manufacturing operations for good.

As to whether Wang decides to farm out the production of any future VS systems, it's unlikely that new lines will ever be developed, observers say. "There won't be a VS 14000," says Mike Howard, a Gartner Group Inc. analyst, referring to the potential for a successor to the VS 12000.

Adds Roger Sullivan, an analyst with Norwell, Mass.-based BIS Strategic Decisions, Wang's contradictory statements about its plans to develop future VS products could be another tactic to stall a mass desertion by its remaining VS users.

Smaller is Better

For Wang to emerge intact from Chapter 11, it must transform itself into a drastically smaller firm specializing in software and services that can compete with the likes of EDS, TRW, DEC, and IBM, suggest analysts. That won't be easy: "Everyone has some kind of imaging product these days, and services have become key to just about everyone," says Kirzner of Dataquest.

As for Miller's stated goal of sustaining $1.4 billion in revenue within two years, he has yet to find a believer. "This company will be much, much smaller than that—by millions," argues Gartner's Howard.

But the likelihood that Wang will be sold off in pieces is also very low; there doesn't appear to be any interested buyer. That leaves the ball in Miller's court: He either succeeds in his bid to become a niche software player, or Wang closes up shop for good.

The odds are against him. But if, despite the odds, Wang does magically emerge from Chapter 11 as a healthy competitor in software and professional services, there will truly have been a "Massachusetts Miracle." Few technology companies have survived far milder transformations.

THE RISE AND FALL OF COMMODORE:
Amiga Came, Saw, But Failed To Conquer

By Anthony Gnoffo Jr.

It was a wake in cyberspace.

Minutes after Commodore International Ltd., the company that helped launch the personal-computer revolution 15 years ago, said it was going out of business last month, the Commodore faithful tapped into the Internet, CompuServe, GEnie, and a host of other on-line services and computer bulletin boards.

They came from their bedrooms and dens, from offices and college dormitories, from America and Europe and Australia and Asia, from everywhere people keep desktop computers. Software engineers, videographers, techno-artists, hackers—they eulogized Commodore's Amiga computer as far better than those pitiful Macintoshes and IBM-compatibles.

Their Amigas can handle streams of video that would choke a Mac or an IBM. Their Amigas can produce eye-popping graphics and dazzling sound at a lower cost than the competition. Yet their Amiga was so unappreciated in the personal-computer marketplace dominated by Macs and IBMs.

Didn't Try Harder

Why didn't Commodore try harder, they wondered.

"They really seemed to believe," said Brian Jackson, a former Commodore engineer, "that if you build a better mousetrap, the world will beat a path to your door."

Why didn't chairman Irving Gould, who routinely was paid more in a month than most people make in a year, spend more to market the Amiga? Why was their beloved computer left to wither and die?

They may never know.

As is its habit, Commodore, which is incorporated in the Bahamas but keeps much of its corporate offices in West Chester, announced its bad news after the close of the stock market on April 29. As has also

Originally published in such Knight-Ridder newspapers as the State College (PA) Centre Daily Times, *May 15, 1994. Reprinted with permission of Knight-Ridder/Tribune Information Services.*

been their habit, Commodore officials have not returned repeated phone calls to answer any of the questions.

Drowning in debt from its recent losses, Commodore did say that it would voluntarily sell off its assets for the benefit of its creditors. Among the creditors is Gould, who lent the company $17 million in 1993, when the company erased its shareholders' equity with a $356.5 million loss for the year that ended June 30.

Commodore's overseas subsidiaries were not included in the announcement. What is to become of them, including operations in Europe and Asia, is not known.

The company said it will turn its assets over to an unidentified trustee who will oversee their sale under Bahamian law.

Uncertainty

There have been assumptions and rumors among the Commodore cult that Commodore's technology, so adored for its ability to process video images and multimedia applications, will live on. Such theories hold that some other company—perhaps a big Japanese consumer electronics house—will buy the rights to Commodore's proprietary chips. But no one knows for sure, and no companies have made any offers.

At least not in public.

There is also a movement afoot among the small companies and individuals who develop software and peripheral hardware for Commodore products to assemble a consortium to buy the technology rights. It is being organized on the Internet, just as a move to gain control of the company's board of directors was pursued this year; that effort failed.

"No one knows what's going on or what will happen," said one Commodore dealer. "There's nothing but guesses and speculation."

Commodore was a leader. As early as 1979, Commodore shipped 80,000 small computers, 14 percent of all the PCs sold that year, according to the market-research firm, Dataquest, of San Jose, Calif.

Fueled by the popular Commodore 64 computer, which was introduced in 1982, the company hit its peak in 1984, shipping 3.4 million desktop computers and controlling nearly a quarter of the market.

Of course, 1984 was the year that Apple introduced Macintosh. And it was also about that time that computer firms from the Silicon Valley to Singapore began marketing inexpensive clones of the IBM PC.

Since 1979, Commodore has sold more than 20 million personal computers worldwide, according to Dataquest. Compare that, however, with the universe of IBM-compatible personal computers, of which nearly 30 million were sold in 1992 alone.

Isolated Foundation

Instead of recognizing the pervasiveness of IBM's operating system, Commodore continued to bet on its own system, and upon that isolated foundation, built its Amiga computer. And just as Sony's Betamax video format failed to capture the market, even though it was judged superior to VHS, Commodore's Amiga operations system failed to wrest customers from IBM's MS-DOS.

Commodore's marketing efforts on behalf of Amiga were spotty. Ad campaigns were launched, then dropped before they could be effective, analysts said.

Eventually, Commodore made an effort to sell IBM-compatible systems in Europe. But the effort, said Dataquest analyst Phillippe de Marcillac, was too little and too late.

"If they had just been more wholehearted about things," de Marcillac said, "a lot would have been different."

Many analysts, company insiders, shareholders and other Commodore stakeholders lay the blame squarely at the feet of Gould and his lieutenant, Mehdi R. Ali, the president of the company.

In 1993, when the company lost $356.5 million, Gould drew a salary and benefits of $708,333; Ali's salary and benefits amounted to $1,038,098.

Neither was awarded bonuses that year, according to the company's proxy statement. And for the current fiscal year, Ali had his base salary reduced from $1 million to $750,000, and Gould's was reduced from $750,000 to $250,000.

"There is only one answer for what happened to Commodore, and that's Irving Gould," said Tim Bajarin, president of Creative Strategies International, a computer-marketing consulting firm in San Jose.

"He lived by quarterly numbers," Bajarin said of the Commodore chairman. "I don't think he ever understood the computer revolution and what it took to take part in the infrastructure of the computer revolution."

WHAT WENT WRONG AT ATARI?

By John Hubner and William F. Kistner Jr.

There has always been a certain innocence about Silicon Valley. Yes, high tech is deeply involved in the arms race; we have chemicals in the underground water supply that were never there before; and you have to go back to the '69 Chicago Cubs to find a collapse that rivals Osborne Computer's. But for all that, there is a "We're different, we're fresh, this is not business as usual" attitude here. Think of Corporate America and if a face pops into your mind at all, it's someone like ITT's old Mr. Mean, Harold Geneen. Think of the valley and a very different kind of person comes to mind: Sandy Kurtzig, who started Ask Computer systems in her apartment; the two Steves, Jobs and Wozniak, who started Apple Computer in a garage; Robert Noyce, inventor of the integrated circuit, vice-chairman of Intel Corp., high-tech's unofficial philosopher.

For most Americans, no company represented the essence of Silicon Valley better than Atari. That is because the alley's most important product is not microprocessors or computers, robots or video games. It is the entrepreneurial spirit. Atari is not just another successful company. Atari created an industry where none had existed before.

Back in '72 when Atari was called Syzygy, Nolan Bushnell took a computer designed to do dull things like process bills for PG&E and made it play games. Bushnell's first game, *Computer Space,* was a turkey that sold only 2,000 units. People in the coin-operated game business said "I told you so" and went back to figuring out new ways to put girls in bikinis on pinball machines. Bushnell went back to the lab and came out with *Pong*—and the rest is history.

Pong was followed by *Tank* and a string of hit coin-op games. In '77, Atari introduced the VCS (Video Computer System) 2600, the amazing little game machine that plugs into your TV. More than anything else, the VCS was responsible for the success of home video games.

Atari grew faster than a baby whale. In '76, the year Bushnell sold the company to Warner Communications Inc., Atari had $39 million in sales. By '82, Atari's sales were more than $2 billion. Not even the

Originally published in WEST, *the magazine section of the* San Jose Mercury News, *Nov. 6, 1983. Used with permission. Copyright 1983 San Jose Mercury News. All rights reserved.*

Defense Department grew that fast. People surveyed an American business landscape littered with the wreckage of old industries like steel and autos, thought about Atari and felt better. That is why smart young congressmen who sought to make the restoration of American business their issue were tagged "Atari Democrats." That is why Ray Kassar, who took over from Bushnell and presided over the growth, looked like a high-tech version of Alfred Sloan, the man who built General Motors.

And then came Dec. 8, 1982, the day that Atari—and Silicon Valley—lost its innocence. With no advance warning, Warner announced that sales of Atari's home video games had taken a sharp dive, contributing mightily to a projected 50 percent drop in Warner's earnings. Wall Street panicked: Warner's stock fell from $54 a share to below $30 in seven days, and now it hovers around $23.

In February, Atari announced that it was closing its domestic manufacturing plants and laying off 1,700 workers. In the first quarter of '83, the company lost $45.6 million. In the second quarter, it posted a whopping $310.5 million loss. Insiders expect a third quarter loss of $80 to $100 million.

"It's inconceivable that you could lose $300 million in one quarter," says Gene Lipkin, an Atari founder who is now president of ByVideo. "You can't blow it all in 90 days. Those losses are the cumulative effect of a number of years."

They are indeed. What happened? How did the company that was "the only game in town" start losing the game? How did Ray Kassar, in the words of one high-tech analyst, "blow the most attractive consumer franchise ever created"? For the answer, you have to go back to the beginning.

Gene Lipkin is one of Atari's four founding stockholders (the others are Nolan Bushnell, Joe Keenan, and Al Alcorn). Walking into the Lexington House restaurant in Los Gatos, feeling rocky afer a big party, Lipkin looks so scruffy in his washed-out jeans and perpetual three-day beard, you forget he has a reputation as an excellent administrator with one of the finest marketing minds in Silicon Valley.

Lipkin dropped out of Ball State in Indiana to work in the coin-op game business in South Florida, and when he first saw *Computer Space,* he knew he was looking at the future. "The distributors didn't realize they were looking at the greatest novelty of all-time, even though they were in a novelty-driven business." Lipkin says, "Instead, they came up with reasons why it would fail—They'll break in and steal the TV screen, the X-rays will hurt their eyes.'" Lipkin got in touch with Bushnell and came west to join the fledgling company. In '75, he signed the retailing agreement with Sears that put Atari on the map in the consumer business.

"A large part of our success was because we never took ourselves too seriously," Lipkin says. "Nolan's position was to fund engineering and game design. Our coin-op games utilized a lot of the early technology that was developed in the valley—processors, memory devices. That attracted a lot of talent, because engineers always want to work with the newest stuff. I'd say the formula was 75 percent luck, 20 percent sheer balls and 5 percent skill. We made a conscious decision to go for the whole banana. We had a lot of opportunities to stay small, but that wouldn't have been a lot of fun."

Nolan Bushnell is as big as an NBA guard, 6-foot-4, and his mind is quicker than the fastest guard's hands. He knows how to read a bottom line as well as any MBA—you don't accumulate a net worth of more than $70 million by being an absent-minded genius. The rap on him—"brilliant ideas, poor execution"—comes from the fact that he is more interested in "neat" products than in managing a company. (Engineers use "neat" the way valley girls use "bitchen.") The key to his success, to his entire personality, is his curiosity. Bushnell is an extremely busy man today, involved in a dozen companies ranging from personal robots ("slaves without guilt") to Pizza Time Theatre, but when he heard about an invitation-only haunted house up in Marin that was really scary, he dropped everything and drove up the next day.

"The exciting thing about Atari was taking a clean chalkboard and getting down on the floor with a group of guys you respected," Bushnell says, taking a pipe out of his mouth to smile his broadest smile. "You'd start with nothing and six hours later, you'd walk out knowing you'd created a product that was really going to be neat."

Between '73 and '76, engineers created the products that were the foundation of the company's amazing growth—the VCS, cartridge games, the 400 home computer. The company had a great future, but there was one very significant problem: Atari was not making enough profit to fund its growth.

Enter Emanuel "Manny" Gerard, co-president of Warner Communications Inc. Gerard knew Atari's future was bright as a June morning in Sunnyvale. In '76, he talked his boss, Warner Chairman Steven J. Ross, into buying Atari for $27 million.

WCI consists of Warner Bros.–Seven Arts movies, Warner Amex Cable, Atlantic, Elektra and Asylum records, the Franklin Mint, Malibu Grand Prix, the New York Cosmos soccer team, 48 percent of the Pittsburgh Pirates and more. The company is no sterile conglomerate—Warner is Steve Ross's creation, and he controls it by the sheer force of his personality. The rich and powerful are often described as "magnetic" or "fascinating" because they are rich and powerful; Ross would be captivating if he were broke. One ex-Atari executive describes him as "the only man I'd fly across country just to have dinner with."

Ross gives the people who run his subsidiaries total autonomy. He has little or no interest in overseeing daily operations. Though he operates out of New York, he is really the ultimate Hollywood deal maker, bringing creative people together in very creative ways.

He gets excited about deals where there is a chance to turn a 40 or 50 percent profit—the kind of bonanza a hit movie brings. Businesses that turn a 10 to 15 percent profit year after year bore him. It costs $4.50 to $6 to produce a game cartridge for the VCS; advertising adds $1 to $2 more per cartridge. The average wholesale selling price in '82—and this includes reduced or "distressed" merchandise—was $18.95.

Furthermore, industry wisdom has always had it that Atari never made money on the video computer system—it was supposed to be the razor that's all but given away so people will buy razor blades. In fact, it costs about $40 to manufacture a VCS. The average selling price last year was $125.

And that is why Steve Ross bought Atari.

Warner left Atari's management in place, but sent Manny Gerard west to oversee the company. Gerard, an engaging former securities analyst, was amazed at how informally the company was structured. "When we took over," Gerard has said, "it was amateur night in Dixie."

"By New York standards, it was amateur night," Bushnell agrees. "We didn't have the money to put in management structures and data processing. We sold because we couldn't fund the growth we were looking at. A growing company requires more money than an established company. And after five years, I was tired. We all were."

To give the company a corporate structure, Gerard hired Ray Kassar, then 50, a marketing executive who had spent his career at Burlington Industries, the huge textile company. Gerard and Kassar share the same passport to power, a Harvard MBA. Kassar came to Burlington in '48, and left in '74 when he finished second in the race for the top job. He then started a company that made long-staple cotton shirts in Egypt. Long-staple cotton shirts feel like silk; he marketed them under the "Kassar" label.

Bushnell remained chairman, but he was spending a great deal of time away from the company, pursuing the dreams that money can buy. So much time, Gerard fired him.

"Manny told me he was going to make Kassar chairman and said, "'Why not take the vice-chairmanship?'" Bushnell recalls. "I thought vice-chairman was a horseshit title. I didn't want it. I want to be in the thick of things. I was getting more and more involved in Pizza Time, which they saw as a separate business. There were no hard feelings. I still relish the times with Manny. My ideal business scenario would be I cook the deals, Manny negotiates them, Ross does the finances."

Bushnell took his big stuffed bear and his bar with on-tap beer with him when he moved out of the executive suite. Kassar re-did the office in earth tones and modern, less-is-more furniture.

Ray Kassar in his early days epitomized the dedicated executive. He is an articulate, elegant, impeccably dressed man who has refined tastes in wine, food and the art. "Kassar is smart, he's a good marketer. He has tremendous organizational abilities, and he works long hours," Bushnell says.

At a time when sales were down—the VCS hadn't caught on and consumers had developed an "if you've played one, you've played them all" attitude about *Pong*-like games—Kassar dramatically increased Atari's advertising budget. Gerard decided the future was in hand-held games, not arcade games or programmable cartridges for the VCS, but not long after Atari brought out the hand-held *Super-Breakout,* the bottom fell out of that market. The company was losing money; in New York, Ross was starting to think buying it had been a disaster. Kassar just worked harder.

The breakthrough came in '79, when *Space Invaders* arrived from Japan. People who had never before stuffed a quarter in a game machine couldn't destroy enough of the itchy-looking aliens. Atari bought the home game license, and programmer Rick Mauer stayed up for four days and nights converting *Invaders* to the VCS. The game converted beautifully, and soon kids all over the country were begging to play it at home.

And then came *Pac-Man,* the ravenous yellow dot that did for video games what *Monopoly* did for board games. Arcades sprang up like taverns after Prohibition. Atari took the early lead in the coin-op market, cashing in on the Pac-Man phenomenon with classic games like *Asteroids* and *Missile Command.* Kassar had his emissaries aggressively court executives of Namco, the Japanese company that had created *Pac-Man.* After a series of dinners in the finest restaurants in Tokyo and San Francisco, the Atari people wrested the home game rights away from Bally Midway Manufacturing, the Chicago company that manufactured the arcade version.

Largely due to the home version of *Pac-Man,* sales of the VCS rose from 800,000 units in '78 to around 12 million in '82. Atari had more than an 80 percent share of the home game hardware and software market. Despite George Plimpton's earnest commercials, Mattel's *Intellivision,* the company's nearest competitor, had only a 15 percent market share. Atari's 400 and 800 computers led the home computer market.

But beneath all the excitement over sales figures that kept rising faster than top scores on *Pac-Man,* Atari was a deeply troubled company. The seeds of destruction had been sown.

There is a simple reason why Ray Kassar gets so much of the blame for Atari's downfall. He ran Atari like an emperor. Instead of building a tight organization, appointing people he trusted and giving them the support they needed to make important decisions, Kassar kept power to himself. Instead of moving around the giant company and discovering what people were doing and what their problems were, he stayed in his office, writing memos and making phone calls. Everything had to flow through him: he insisted on being in on every decision.

As a result, Atari never developed a corporate structure. An Atari executive's standing depended not on how well he performed; it depended on whether he was in or out of Kassar's favor. If he liked you, anything was possible; one of his chauffeurs ended up as director of sales for Southern France. If Kassar decided he didn't like somebody, or if an executive began acting too independently and Kassar thought he might be building a power base, he got rid of him. There were, according to one former executive's count, some 17 different presidents of the coin-operated, consumer and computer divisions in less than three years.

"Somebody would make a presentation in a meeting and Ray would nod and smile," the former executive says. "Then the guy would leave the room and Ray would say, 'This is stupid, this is intolerable, get rid of him.' The frustrating thing was, he never said what he expected and what he thought we should be doing. You ended up trying to guess what Ray wanted."

Former executives say that Kassar was fond of pitting people against one another, then sitting back while they fought it out. "Ray has terrible people skills," Gene Lipkin says. "Numbers were more important than people, it was profit at any expense. He had no compassion." The way to win battles at Atari was to go behind a superior's back and appeal directly to Kassar. He would approve a project that a division head had already canceled, then fail to call the division head and tell him he had been overruled, and why. Decisions were made on the basis of who had talked to Kassar last, which lead to considerable uneasiness, not to say paranoia, among executives.

"It became a monarchy, and that didn't have to happen," Bushnell says. "Look at G.E.: it's not a monarchy. There were not enough 'no men.' The strong people tended to leave, the weak stayed."

Those who stayed lived well, for Kassar appreciated the best money can buy—nobody had to guess that. The Atari dining room was famous for its superb nouvelle cuisine. Kassar's company car was a Rolls-Royce, though he rarely used it. Usually he rode back and forth from his San Francisco home in his personal car, a Mercedes. While a chauffeur drove, Kassar sat in the back seat, dictating memos. Some days, he flew down in a helicopter Warner had put at his disposal. When he had to go to New York or to some corner of the Warner empire, Kassar flew on a corporate jet, a G-3 Gulfstream, "the Rolls-Royce of the air." One of the perks for Atari executives was flying with him, but it didn't always work out that way. On at lest one flight to New York, Kassar bumped the executives who were supposed to go along and took his friends instead.

The perks were nice, the money was better. The salaries for upper-echelon Atari executives were in the six-figure range, with fat bonuses. It was a real carrot-and-stick situation: You were in constant danger of being fired, but if you stayed, you were rewarded with a nice bonus. The biggest bonuses of all went to Kassar. One executive who worked closely with him for a number of years puts Kassar's annual earnings in the vicinity of $3 million. Which makes it hard to understand why he risked a Securities and Exchange Commission investigation by selling some 5,000 shares of Warner stock, for approximately $260,000, just 23 minutes before Warner announced its drastically reduced projected earnings last December. The SEC charged Kassar with trading on the basis of insider information; Kassar denied any impropriety, but signed a consent decree requiring him to "disgorge" $81,875 in alleged profits. That is walking-around money when you are making $3 million a year.

"The atmosphere became real stuffy, real political," Lipkin says. "Ray suffered from the arrogance of success. He got caught up in thinking that he was responsible for the success, for every good thing that happened. The company was a phenomenon, a once-in-a-lifetime thing. It wasn't any one person who did it. But Ray never understood that. Ray understands politics. That's what allowed him to live as long as he did."

The atmosphere Kassar created at Atari was destructive in itself, but it is more important as a frame of reference for the business mistakes he made. These mistakes are crucial to understanding what happened to Atari; they're even more important for the broader lessons they teach. For here again, Atari may be the vanguard for Silicon Valley.

Lesson I: The Engineers Drive the Bus

From his earliest days at Atari, Ray Kassar thought that running a high-tech business was just like running a textile company. Textiles are a mature, stable industry. Because the market neither grows nor shrinks much in any one year, textiles is a "marketing game"—competitors slug it out for a share of the market, coming up with fresh advertising strategies and new designs for old products like towels.

High-tech is an engineering-driven industry where you must invent and re-invent, or die. (The term "engineer" here includes both the hardware wizards who invent machines like the VCS and the software designers who bring the machines to life with programming.) Kassar did not understand what engineers did, or how important a role they played at Atari. He made no effort to get to know his engineers.

"When he made Kassar chairman," Bushnell says, "I told Manny he was the wrong man. I didn't think Kassar could get along with engineers. He couldn't get down on the floor with them. Unless you can do that, you're not going to get along with them. An engineer doesn't always come in a body that can talk. But they're not shitheads. You've got to have enough faith in them to say, 'I don't know what you're talking about; here's some money, go show me.'"

"Nolan is one extreme, Kassar is the other," says Larry Kaplan, one of the original Atari game designers. Kaplan is in an interesting judge of Atari under Bushnell and Atari under Ray Kassar, because after leaving the company in '79 to join Activision, he returned in '82 for a brief stint as vice-president of product design. "Bushnell had thousands of ideas—some good, some not so good," Kaplan says. "He loves games. If you did a good game, Nolan would come down and say, 'God, I really enjoyed your new game.' Nolan understand engineers; they like working for him."

"Ray had no feeling for the products, no feeling for engineers, and he really didn't have a feeling for the market. Ray didn't play video games. He didn't even have the equipment in his office."

Computers are like words or paint or music: Most people who work in any of those media are craftsmen; a few are artists. Atari in its early days had programmers whose work was so good measured on the two scales that count—graphics and playability—that they qualify as artists. "Dave Crane, Al Miller and Bob Whitehead are the best designers for the VCS in the world," Kaplan says.

Kaplan designed *Kaboom!,* an early Activision hit. Thanks to his Activision stock and his high-salaried days at Atari, he is well-off financially. At ease in the backyard of his home in Los Altos, he isn't hard to picture as a political science professor who has already written his big book. Lighting another Marlboro, he recalls the day in May 1979, that he and the three "best designers in the world" had a meeting with Ray Kassar.

The designers found Kassar at his desk, wearing a well-tailored suit. They were, as usual, in jeans. The four had a lot on their minds. They wanted Atari to treat them the way Warner treats recording artists. They felt their games had played a large role in the company's success, and they asked Kassar for royalties on them. They wanted recognition, too. Musicians got their names and pictures on record albums; why couldn't theirs be put on game cartridges?

"Kassar called us towel designers," Kaplan recalls. "He said, 'I've dealt with your kind before. You're a dime a dozen. You're not unique. Anybody can do a cartridge.'"

Crane, Miller and Whitehead left to form Activision in October of the same year. Kaplan joined them a short time later. "Activision," Kaplan says, "was started to prove that Kassar was wrong."

In '81, another group of game designers left Atari to form Imagic. It appears that neither incident taught Kasar much about engineers, because instead of trying to improve relations with them, he called them "high-strung prima donnas." The remark made its way around Atari, and people began wearing T-shirts with a picture of an opera singer and the words "I'm another high-strung prima donna from Atari."

"If he was smart, Kassar would have put on a T-shirt and gone over to the engineering building and talked to those guys," says a former high-ranking Atari executive. "He didn't. In all the years I was there, I can't remember him going over to engineering more than two or three times."

Lesson II: Don't Throw Money at Morale Problems

The VCS programmers still working for Atari were very unhappy. The fun of being a game designer is in creating original, playable games—why else be one? But instead of turning his designers loose to do original games that were great to play, Kassar's marketing sense told him the big money was in licensing movie titles like *Raiders of the Lost Ark* and *E.T.*, and coin-op conversions like *Pac-Man*. The games based on movies turned out to be dull and have bad graphics, despite its enormous sales, the home version of *Pac-Man* is a very pale imitation of the arcade game. The designers were also unhappy about their lack of recognition, both inside and outside the company. Nobody in management played their games, so nobody complimented them on their work. Activision's designers had become well-known in the game world because their names and pictures appeared on the games they created. And it bothered the Atari people no end that the designers who had gone off to found Activision became rich when the company went public.

In February 1982, when another group of VCS programmers threatened to leave, Kassar panicked. If they quit, Atari would have had no VCS programmers left. "Kassar was desperate. He was running scared," Kaplan says. He responded by throwing money at the designers. Salaries were increased and a hastily-created bonus plan was instituted.

But because the bonus plan rewarded sales and not quality or originality, it created more problems than it solved. The big question became, "Who gets to do the hot coin-op and movie titles?" Tod Frye, who did the *Pac-Man* conversion, earned between $1 and $1.2 million for his efforts. The other designers felt any one of them could have done it. They became secretive, not talking to each other or to marketing people because they did not want to share their royalties. When the company brought in a New York compensation analyst to find out why the designers weren't producing, the analyst called them "the wealthiest, most unhappy group of people I've ever met."

"What's amazing is that all that money didn't get people to be more productive," Kaplan says. "Programmers just sat around worrying about how to get more money. They'd approach a project with a 'how much am I gonna make off this game?' attitude. There was blackmail. A guy would say, "I'm not gonna finish this game unless you give me X amount of money right now,' and he'd get it."

The morale problem wasn't confined to the VCS designers. "There was tons of animosity," Kaplan says. "Coin-op and consumer hated each other, the marketing groups hated engineering. It was empire builders fighting empire builders. None of them had any idea what was going on. It was all knee-jerk. They wanted sports games because Mattel had sports games, even though the VCS doesn't do them well. Somebody would say, 'Let's do a new game system.' Somebody else would say, 'Let's do a new computer,' or 'Maybe we should go with AtariTel' (a new system that connects the phone with a computer so you can do things like call home and turn on the lights). All the good people were gone. The people who were left had no idea what it takes to do a quality piece of work. It was really depressing."

Kassar was as liberal with contracts as he was with the programmers' bonus plan. He would sign a long-term contract with an executive, and then fire him a few months later. A number of people who have left Atari agreed to talk about the company only on the condition their names not be used. The reason is that their long-term contracts are still in effect. Instead of simply saying "You're fired," one of Kassar's people would tell a high-echelon executive to take a month off while he was reassigned. A month later, the executive would call and be told his new assignment hadn't been worked out. The condition became known as "being at the Beach Club." From Atari's point of view, it makes sense. Instead of firing people and facing court battles over breach of contract, the company counts on former executives—all of whom are high-achievers, or they wouldn't have made it to Atari in the first place—to tire of their Beach Club status and find other jobs.

"I want to help, this is an important story," one former executive said. "But if you use my name, it'll cost me my contract. Atari is vindictive, they've got lawyers, they'll find a way to get out of it. They've got us all by the wallet."

Lesson III: Never Underestimate Consumers, Even If They Are Kids

Not all of Atari's inferior games can be blamed on the designers. Some of what Bushnell calls "cramped executions" resulted from designers not being given enough time to do the job properly.

"Kassar called me one day and said he'd bought the right to *E.T.* for $22 million," a former Atari executive says. "I said, 'OK, we'll take our time and really do it right.' Ray said he'd guarantee the game would be out at Christmas. I said, 'Ray, that gives us about seven weeks to program the game.' It usually takes nine months to do a really good game. Ray said, 'This is such a hot property, whatever we put out will sell.' We ended up putting out a piece of junk that sold far below Kassar's expectations."

Meanwhile, Activision's success had led to others entering the video game software market—Parker Bros., 20th Century Fox, Fisher-Price, CBS. With more than 200 titles to chose from, kids no longer bought a game just because it was new. They became more selective, waiting for a friend or a magazine article to tell them which games were good. The market, which had grown in great spurts like an adolescent, leveled off. The projected growth for 1983 is about 50 percent, instead of the 200 to 300 percent rate of past years. Video games are not a fad. They are here to stay, like records. But like the record business, video games have become a hit-driven industry. *Dragon's Lair,* the first laserdisc video game, was last summer's hit; who knows what next year's will be?

Kassar thought the industry was still booming, and that any game with the word "Atari" on it would sell. So many *Raiders* and *E.T.s* were produced that even if they'd been hits there would have been excess inventory. *Berserk, Defender* and *Ms. Pac-Man* were hits, but they too were overproduced. Atari was churning out games as if it still had better than a 60 percent market share. Actually, its share of the home game market had dropped to 40 percent. Suddenly, retailers' shelves were full of Atari games, and so were Atari warehouses.

"Atari overstuffed the pipeline," says one competitor. "We're all suffering from that. There are so many unsold games out there, retailers aren't ordering any new ones. When Atari gets drunk, we all wake up with a hangover."

Lesson IV: Take Care with Your Distributors or They'll Take Care of You

When things were going well at Atari, nobody paid much attention to the distributors. There was little reason to: every game the company shipped sold. Distributors were little more than sophisticated truckers, moving cartridges from the warehouse to the retail shelf.

But over the years, while nobody was looking, some nasty problems developed. Atari had between 130 and 140 distributors across the country, far too many. Territories overlapped, distributors got into price wars competing for customers. When business was booming, Atari couldn't churn out games fast enough, and retailers' orders were allocated. So, figuring they wouldn't get all the games they needed from one distributor, retailers would place identical orders with a second distributor, hoping that between the two, they would get the games they wanted. When business slowed down, the double orders were still on the books.

"You looked at the backlog of orders and you thought business was still booming," a former Atari executive says. "Then you looked closer, saw all the duplicates, and realized how much water there was in the inventory. The orders for some titles were larger than the installed base of VCSs."

Things really got messy early last winter when Atari decided to restructure its distribution. The company sent a letter to distributors on Nov. 1, informing them their contracts were canceled. The letter said that on Dec. 12, a small number of exclusive distributorships would be awarded. Theoretically, Atari should have grabbed the top 40 distributors and sent other manufacturers scrambling for what was left.

"The biggest error was that the original distributors didn't have exclusive contracts," says a former Atari official. "They weren't preempted from carrying other manufacturers' products. So when Activision, Coleco and Imagic came along, they went to the same distributors. Atari put everybody else in business.

"And when the company cut the number, they failed to audit the distributors they dropped. You know what happens when you don't audit distributors? If I'm a distributor and I just lost my district, I'm going to ship everything back. I'm going to call on my accounts and say, 'I want you to carry this new line of products I've got. As an incentive, you see all that Atari inventory that's not moving? I'll take it back and give you full credit.' Because Atari didn't keep track of what was out there, they bought back lots of merchandise they didn't have to. A big chunk of the $300 million they had to write off was because they failed to audit distributors when they canceled them."

Atari is still trying to dig its way out from under the inventory avalanche. Late in September of this year, people around Alamogordo, N.M., were amazed when 20 trucks filled with Atari games, VCSs and home computers ended up in the local dump, where they were crushed by a bulldozer. Atari says they were defectives, but kids who scavenged the dump said the games were playable.

Lesson V: Don't Sit on Your Hands When You're Ahead

During the past six years, Atari has spent millions on engineering, but the company has few new products to show for the money. This isn't because "neat" new products weren't being developed. Atari co-founder Al Alcorn, for example, developed an innovative holography game called *Cosmos*. But the game was never released. The reason, according to Bushnell, is that the company became "risk averse" and suffered from "the paralysis of perfection."Gene Lipkin is more blunt: "Ray Kassar wouldn't know a good product if it hit him in the ass."

"They've probably got more good products gathering dust on shelves than any 10 companies," Bushnell says. "Why not release them? You never know what a product is going to do until you get out there and mix it up in the marketplace."

Most of the money Atari spend in engineering, however, did not go into developing new products. That's one reason why the hardware engineers were as unhappy as the game designers.

"Engineers were doing revisions of the VCS motherboard to save 3 cents a board on the next run," Kaplan says. "Things like that are maintenance engineering, they're fire-fighting. There were no new ideas at Atari, no innovations, no brainstorming sessions, no 'Let's tackle this new technology.' The attitude was, 'Let's cut back. Let's keep the profit margin high and the costs reduced.' The company became very conservative. It retrenched. It lost its bias to action, its ability to take innovation and run with it."

Because Atari didn't release products that were better than its old ones, other companies did. For five years Atari sat on the 5200, the "Super Game System." The 5200 is a sophisticated version of the VCS; it has bigger chips, so games played on it have more action and better graphics. At $189, the 5200 would have been the first and only high-priced game machine on the market. But while Kassar debated releasing the system, Coleco, a floundering swimming pool and electro-mechanical game company in Hartford, Conn., beat Atari to the punch. ColecoVision, a high-priced, high-resolution machine, was an immediate hit; the company shipped more than 500,000 units in 1982.

Coleco's success caused a panic at Atari. Playing catch-up ball, the company rushed the 5200 into production. The haste hurt. The controls are very sloppy and do not self-center. The 5200 is not compatible with VCS software, so people who own the cheaper system have to buy the same game twice if they upgrade to the 5200.

Lesson VI: Don't Play the Game Without a Game Plan

There is something sad about the Atari 400 home computer. It is a great little machine, but it never grew up. The 400 and its cousins the 800 could have grown into a personal computer that would have challenged the Apple II. But that would have meant developing a long-range plan, and long-range strategic thinking was never Ray Kassar's strength. He was good at what Bushnell calls "harvesting."

"When Kassar thought about home computers, he didn't ask himself, 'What will the market be in two years and how can I dominate it?'" says a former executive. "He said, 'Forget tomorrow. How can I sell as many of these machines as I can today?' Everything was today, totally today."

To sell as many machines as quickly as possible, Kassar put the 400 and 8000 in K-marts and Toys-Я-Us. The result is that they are perceived as sophisticated game machines, not computers. Nobody who gets serious about computers and wants to upgrade is going to shop for disk drives or printers in a toy store.

Atari is jumping back into the compact market with its new XL line, but it might be too late. Commodore has become the Beetle of low-price computers. IBM is coming out with the Peanut, Apple the Macintosh, Coleco the Adam.

"Atari has an uphill battle to regain the consumer's confidence that its new line will offer competitive value for the money," says Clive Smith, research director for advanced consumer electronics at the Yankee Group, a Boston consulting firm. "The new line of computers has been consistently plagued by late deliveries. Despite some attractive features, the line is still not price competitive in a market that is going to get even more price competitive. Whether they stay in the market or not in large part depends on whether management has the stomach to continue the struggle."

Lesson VII: Watch a Successful Subsidiary as Closely as a Turkey

It is one thing for Kassar to let his best programmers escape; it is quite another for Warner to let it happen. The company is famous for treating talent like royalty. When David Geffen, the superb record producer, threatened to go off on his own, Warner gave him his own company, a studio on its Hollywood lot and a ton of money, and told him to go make records. Geffen's label is now the most prestigious in the business.

"Atari should have set up a company for Crane and Miller and those other guys," Bushnell says. "Why they didn't do that, I don't know."

"It just shows how much power Warner gave Kassar," adds a former Atari executive. "They had no idea what was going on out here. The numbers were so good, Kassar looked like a genius and they never questioned him. It's easy not to question success. I guess the lesson for Warner is, ask as many questions when things are going well as when they are going bad."

Just how out of touch Warner officials were with Atari is shown in a letter to Warner shareholders signed by Ross and dated March 3, 1982. Ross wrote that "the long-term outlook of WCI has never been better," and predicted that Atari would have a "further dramatic increase in revenues and operating income in . . . 1982."

There was instead, of course, a dramatic *decrease* in Atari revenues. Warner has not recovered: Wall Street is full of rumors of a possible takeover, and Ross, according to a close associate, "is trying to hold up walls that are falling in on him."

In February of '83, the chairman flew to Sunnyvale in a Warner G-3, and he was not his usual charming self. He spent three days here attending business review meetings, and "really took Manny and Ray apart, berating them in front of everybody," a former executive says. "That's not his style. Usually he never raises his voice."

Ross got back aboard the G-3 and was in the air, headed for San Diego, when he turned around and radioed Atari that he was coming back to Sunnyvale. "My God, now what!" went through the mind of every Atari executive, but Ross had returned only to apologize. He was afraid that he had demoralized the entire company, and he didn't want to leave things that way.

Despite the gesture, Ross had Kassar's resignation by spring. He replaced him with James J. Morgan, 41, a former executive vice president of marketing at Phillip Morris U.S.A. Ross made the decision in an incredibly short time, given how important the job is. He met Morris on a Wednesday and hired him that Friday.

Despite repeated requests, Atari, Warner and Ray Kassar chose not to cooperate with this article. Bruce Entin, vice president for corporate relations, said that "Atari now has a new chairman and chief executive officer, and the key management team is relatively new. In short, Atari is setting its sights on the future—not the past." But there is no clear line of demarcation between present and past. Morgan must deal with the problem left by his predecessor. How well he performs this Herculean task will determine what kind of future Atari has.

Almost everything about Atari, including whether it will survive, is in doubt. There are rumors that Warner will sell the company. Only one can be substantiated: Last winter, Nolan Bushnell tried to buy back his old firm. Warner rejected the offer. Bushnell is taciturn about why he made the offer, and will not say if he is going to make another.

"I saw it as an opportunity," Bushnell says. "The company represents an interesting set of capabilities, even now. It has a future if they can stop the flow of red ink. There's some good engineering going on. It's a do-able task."

Atari has some definite strengths. Everyone, inside and outside the company, thinks that John Farrand, 39, president of coin-op, is a superb manager. Software and hardware engineering have recently been placed in Farrand's division. The company has some excellent coin-op games out: *Kangaroo, Star Wars* and *Dig Dug.* The best racing game ever, *Pole Position,* is licensed from Namco.

If Atari does drop out of home computers, it will still be a force in software. The company has an excellent line of educational software it is now beginning to sell to schools. Ted Hoff, who invented the microprocessor at Intel, and Alan Kay, Atari's chief scientist, are two of the most inventive minds in electronics.

"I think we have a good future," says one Atari official. "People have been holding their breaths, going around asking each other, 'Are we going to stay in business?' We still have a lot of market presence. People are proving to be surprisingly loyal, despite all that's happened."

There are those who have exactly the opposite view, those who think the company's future isn't much better than Osborne Computer's.

"I think that Atari's future is very, very bleak," Kaplan says. "They're too late on the laser disc, and there's no doubt in my mind laser games like *Dragon's Lair* are the future. They're too late on personal computers, they missed portable computers, they're too late on a high-end game machine. My guess is that the only things that are going to be left are coin-op and software."

Pole Position is a perfect metaphor for the high-tech industry. It moves at a race car pace; there are plenty of dangerous corners; it is easy to crash; and once you've crashed, you've lost your innocence. You don't drive with the abandon you once did.

The trick is to *use* the crash, to *use* the loss of innocence. If you hit the wall and survive, you are wiser and take more calculated risks when you get back on the track. The problem is, cigarette executives don't make the best race car drivers. Like textiles, tobacco is an old industry that moves at a cautious pace. Changing the colors on the Marlboro package is a major decision that every department from marketing to product design gets involved in. Introducing a new product like Players in the distinctive black pack—when all that's new is the package—is considered revolutionary. One wonders if Warner hasn't repeated the mistake it made with Kassar. Can a man who is used to a market as steady as the traffic on a suburban street make the right decisions in a market as fluid and ever-changing as a Grand Prix race?

"They have an opportunity to stay in business, but they have to come up with a new plan," says Ted Costello, an investment specialist who is a vice-president at Dean Witter Reynolds in Palo Alto. "Conventional wisdom says it takes three years to make a major management change. They could do it in a year and a half, but my guess is, it will be closer to a three-year process. It will take Morgan six months to get the damage report and access the marketplace. To come up with a game plan will take another six to 12 months. It will take another 12 months to get the new methods into operation. We're in for another three to six quarters before we begin to get an indication of what the company is capable of doing."

That is an awfully long time in an industry where last year was 100 years ago.

Mission Impossible's Dirty Little Secrets: Stories of Project and Product Failure

All too often, computing failure stories are about *companies* that failed. That's what the stories in the preceding chapter of this book were about.

But in this chapter, we deal with a smaller scale of computing calamity. Here, we present stories of projects and products that failed. The failure may not have pulled down an entire enterprise, as was true in the previous section, but it was just as painful to those who were on board when the crash occurred. As a result of these failures, a project was canceled or a product never materialized in the marketplace. If you've ever worked on such a project or product, you know that the emotional—if not the financial—devastation of this kind of calamity is just as serious as if the whole company had gone under.

I well remember just such a project on which I participated. Like so many other computing calamities, this one started with high hopes. My team and I thought we were going to be world-beaters, solving a computing problem that had never been solved before. (We were producing a translation system that would convert software from a computing system that was becoming obsolescent to a brand, spanking new one.)

It wasn't until the end of the project that we realized there was a serious flaw in our apparently brilliant plan. The flaw, as is typical of such situations, did not lie in the technology we had chosen to use. It lay, instead, in the fact that the application programmers whose software was to be translated had failed to follow a set of standard practices that their management had told them to. We had been told by their management that our translation problem was limited in scope to that set of standard practices. The actual application software was perhaps 10 times as complicated as we had expected it to be, and suddenly what had been technically feasible was becoming economically and technically infeasible. There wasn't much I could do, at the end, except to excuse my team with my deep thanks and apologies, lick my wounds for awhile (this included writing what I thought at the time was an epic poem about the failed system!), and move on to the next (hopefully, successful) project.

In the sections that follow, we look at several varieties of project/product failure. There is a collection of projects where the project turned out to be larger than the expectations established for it beforehand. (That would describe my own project in the previous paragraph, for example.) I call these the problems of the "eyes–stomach tradeoff," and what I mean by that is that the eyes of the project planners were larger than the stomachs of the project problem-solvers who would need to digest the problem and produce a solution. ("My eyes were bigger than my stomach," says the child who took a huge helping of food but couldn't finish eating it). That's what the stories in section 4.1 are about.

In 4.2, we present a different kind of project/product failure. What characterizes the story in this section is that the project problem gets solved, all right, but that solution doesn't match the solution that its users really needed.

In 4.3, we present a somewhat similar scenario. In this story, the project apparently succeeds, but the problem to be solved by the project remains unsolved at the end. In the medical profession, this is sometimes described by the tongue-in-cheek expression, "the operation was a success but the patient died."

And in section 4.4, there is yet another variation on this project/product failure theme. Here, in the face of a failure so massive that it isn't terribly clear what all should have been done differently, we simply throw up our hands in despair with "it just wasn't meant to be." There was no clear path, even in retrospect, from the problem to be solved, via the project set up to solve the problem, to the product that was to provide that solution.

There are some interesting themes cutting across all of these stories, you are about to see. Let me highlight, here, a couple of them for you.

One of the most common themes resides in the project leader who is so optimistic about the anticipated results that he or she won't listen to the calm voice of reason that tries to tell them that they are about to fail. "We were afraid to tell the CEO" who had defined the project, say the participants in one of the stories. "I wrote three separate whistle-blower memos," says another project participant, "but none of the Vice Presidents that I sent them to would listen to me." "My project leader didn't want to hear any bad news," says yet a third such project team member.

A second interesting failure theme lies in communication with the potential customers and especially the users of the proposed new system. In one story: "We failed to understand the user requirements." In another, a bank tried to pass on to its home-banking customers the extra costs of a system that was actually designed to save, not cost, them money! And in a third story, the proposed customers never did get on board the project—they simply didn't feel that they needed the proposed product—and yet the project continued on with the thinking that at least it was valuable as "research and development."

And now, on to those project/product failure stories.

4.1   THE EYES–STOMACH TRADEOFF

Perhaps the most fascinating thing about this group of failure stories is that it was the very success of the companies in question that led to the project failures. In our first story, one which is all-too-common in the computing field, the CEO of a company whose growth is so rapid as to risk getting out of control, is sold a bill of goods by a vendor representative who promises that the technology he is selling can harness that growth. (This phenomenon is sometimes referred to as the "CEO and the airline magazine" story, because so often a CEO reads about a half-baked new technology in the magazine of the airline which he has flown most recently, returns to his home base, and imposes the technology on his Information Technology area without their advice or consent. In this story, however, the seduction of the CEO takes place on a golf course!) In fact, nearly all of the problems of this project are classic elements of a computing calamity story—the technical decision is imposed top-down, the cost and schedule estimates are established (also top-down) before the project team is even assembled, the customers and users aren't convinced they need the product, and the project participants are afraid to tell the CEO that he is embarking on and (later) rapidly approaching a failure.

In the third story (we'll deal with the second in a moment), growth is again a major culprit. Here, enterprise growth is so rapid that a quickly-planned system is obsolete before it can be built. It was "outdated and outmanned," one project participant said, in retrospect. And, to make matters disastrous, no alternative or backup methodology was planned in case the main project failed to produce its intended product.

In the second story, it wasn't so much growth as it was a whole new problem area that created the dilemma that caused the project to (partially) fail. In this story, the company is IBM, the site is the Atlanta Olympics, and the project is the information technology system built to support the Olympics. As you may remember, IBM got a black eye for that project, in that the press-oriented system outputs, which were to provide news information to press representatives covering the Olympics, were an abysmal failure, and that failure was rapidly reported by its potential press customers to the world! (Some failure stories eventually have happy endings. IBM learned from its Atlanta Olympic failures, and at the Nagano Winter Olympics a few years later, the headlines said "IBM is crowing about its performance at the Winter Olympics—unlike the black eye it got at the Atlanta summer games two years ago. . ."

Enough introduction. Let's get on to the eyes/stomach tradeoff stories.

ANATOMY OF A FAILURE: The Inside Story of a Fatally Flawed Data Warehouse Project

by Lauren Gibbons Paul

Wasted time. Squandered money. Lost jobs. Ruined reputations. Jeopardized careers.

Project failures are the dirty little secret of data warehousing. Anyone who has spent time around data warehouse projects is likely to have chalked up a failure or two. The majority of those debacles can be attributed not to technology snafus but to lack of strong executive sponsorship and to poor management.

For many, being part of an abysmal data warehouse project is a rite of passage. But that doesn't make it any easier. The project manager and consultant who were central figures in the data warehousing effort at the company we'll call Close Call Corp. deserve credit for candidly sharing their experiences here. Through a spokesman, the CEO of Close Call—who pushed for the warehouse in the first place—declined to comment.

Because it's so hard to do data warehousing well, the kinds of things that went awry in this case study could afflict any implementation in any industry. Do not, therefore, assume your company is safe from a failure of this magnitude. If you look closely—and are honest about it—chances are, you'll recognize some of the red flags raised here.

The road to hell is paved with golf games. For the CEO of Close Call Corp., his trip netherward began with a day on the links in the fall of 1995 with a software vendor. At the time, the CEO was particularly vulnerable to a "business-transforming" pitch. He knew he needed to make technology changes—and fast. His teleservices company, which he'd founded with $200 in the 1970s and had grown into a modest empire worth $100 million, was at a crossroads. Intent on choosing the straightest path through a double-digit growth period, he was searching for technological help. So when the vendor tempted him with visions of integrated data flow and information on demand, the CEO couldn't resist.

Editor's Note: All names in this case study have been changed.

Originally published in CIO Enterprise, November 15, 1997. Used with permission.

By Definition

DATA WAREHOUSE:
A relational
database filled
with large volumes
of cross-indexed
historical business
information that
users access with
desktop-based
query tools. The
warehouse resides
on its own server
and is separate
from the transac-
tion-processing or
run-the-business
systems.

Historically, Close Call's outbound (tele-marketing) and inbound (catalog sales) business units had operated as totally separate companies. The company had recently gone public, and rapid growth was putting major pressure on its antiquated and proprietary systems. The vendor made a convincing case that a data warehouse was the answer to Close Call's prayers. Nothing to it, went the siren call, you can be up and running on a fully functional data warehouse in three to four months. The CEO began salivating at the thought of providing a unified view of Close Call's business data to its autonomous business units.

But with 1996 already shaping up to be a banner year for Close Call, the timing for a data warehouse project could hardly have been worse. The company was planning to expand from six call centers to 116, implementing new, open switching systems in the new centers to enable automatic dialing and call routing. In addition, information systems (IS) was updating all of Close Call's internal management systems by deploying new human resources and general ledger software.

When the CEO returned from his fateful golf game and sounded the call for a data warehouse, he ensured that 1996 would be a year to remember—but not for the reasons he'd hoped.

Unrealistic Expectations

The CEO expected the can-do culture that he'd nurtured from the early days of the company to carry it through this period of exponential growth and technological change. He believed that making all the systems changes—including building the data warehouse—in a very short time frame was just a matter of getting the right people for the job, according to a consultant we'll call Michael Farraday, cofounder of the data warehousing and decision support consulting firm that was called in to do the warehouse design and data modeling. "He put

Red Flags
Signs the Close Call data warehouse was destined to fail

❋ No pre-launch objectives or metrics

❋ Many major systems projects underway simultaneously

❋ The CEO set budgets and deadlines before project team was on board

❋ No insider presence on data warehouse project team

❋ An overburdened project manager

❋ Source data availability unconfirmed at the outset

❋ No user demand for sophisticated data analysis

❋ No routine meetings of executive sponsors and project manager

❋ No initial involvement of business managers

decisions in place and said, 'Go make this happen.' That approach had always worked in the past. Not this time," says Farraday.

Based on the few technology tidbits he had obtained from the software vendor on the fairway, the CEO was convinced he could have a 500GB production data warehouse up and running in four months despite the fact the existing IS staff was already stretched to the limit. Before the project team was on board he set the project deadlines and a budget of $250,000, the ultimate no-no, says Farrady, who has 12 years' data warehousing experience.

Because no one in-house had data warehousing experience or time to devote to the project, five outside people were hired. The outsiders included Manager of MIS Jackie Pemberton (not her real name), who was brought on in part to manage the data warehousing project, and a director of MIS, both of whom had proven data warehousing track records and a combined total of nearly three decades of experience in the field. Pemberton was also put in charge of the general-business systems software rollout.

Unrealistic time and resource allocations alone might not have grounded Close Call's data warehouse had the business ranks been clamoring for the information it could provide. But because they'd never been exposed to an analytical environment before, the users didn't know what they were missing. Indeed, the business unit managers were quite content with the canned reports they could get from a DOS-based Reflex database. The few who needed more analysis entered the report numbers into a spreadsheet and did rudimentary manipulations.

The lack of demand for a new reporting system foreshadowed a virtually insurmountable problem, says Farraday: Down the road, the users would not be willing to commit the time and effort required to make the warehouse a success. "The challenges go up dramatically if the data warehouse represents the first analytical environment," says Farraday. "[The users] never really understood what a data warehouse could do."

The Project Launch

The new director of MIS assembled the initial project team, consisting of Pemberton, two senior managers from sales and telemarketing and a database administrator as well as Farraday and another consultant from his firm. Pemberton, the director of MIS and the consultants pushed back on the scope of the project, the present deadlines and budget, but the CEO stuck to his guns. Ultimately, he grudgingly accepted the idea of a pilot in five months rather than insisting on the full-blown production warehouse. But he never seemed to understand the magnitude of the undertaking, says Farraday.

From the start, the data warehouse lacked a clearly defined business objective, mostly because the users had never asked for greater analytical abilities. Pemberton believed she would be able to articulate the business case herself after gathering detailed user requirements.

Early on, Pemberton met weekly with the director of MIS, who in turn met separately with the executive sponsors (the CEO and the CFO) every week. Only when things began to fall apart several months later did the four begin to meet face to face each week. Also, the general managers of the business units said they were too busy to get involved in the requirements assessment stage of the project. "The feeling was, 'Go talk to my guys. They'll tell you what they need,'" says Pemberton. In retrospect, she says the director of MIS didn't reach out to the business users as much as perhaps he should have.

Despite the early uncertainties, optimism prevailed at the project launch. "[The director of MIS] had so much positive energy. I really thought together we could make this happen," says Pemberton.

Collecting User Requirements

Farraday and his consulting colleague saw the process of gathering user requirements for the warehouse as critical. Along with Pemberton, they embarked on three painstaking months of interviewing the key users as 1996 began. Instead of merely asking users what data they needed from a data warehouse, they invited them to talk in general terms about their jobs, homing in on how their job performance was evaluated and how they managed people.

Although the users complained the interviews took too much time, everyone felt this stage had been a resounding success. In spite of the very separate business units, the team was beginning to build the consolidated picture of the business they'd need to begin constructing the warehouse.

Building the Business Model

As they collected user requirements, Pemberton and Farraday set about creating a business model that would capture the business professionals' requirements in their own terms. Independent of technology, this model would define the business dimensions (for example, looking at the business in terms of products, locations or time periods), attributes, relationships, facts and logical navigation paths, all of which would translate to the design of the warehouse. The challenge was to get the distinct and autonomous business units to settle on these critical definitions.

This, too, went much more smoothly than anticipated. "People from different groups were agreeing on things they had never agreed on before," says Farraday.

The bad news was that the model revealed a highly complex set of business requirements and an inconsistent group of data "facts" that would populate the warehouse. Unlike a retail data warehouse in which the quantity of a particular SKU sold at a particular time

Post Mortem
Lessons from the Close Call data warehousing disaster

* Executive sponsorship and partnership with IS are the most critical success factors for a warehouse. If possible, establish dual leadership by business and IS executives for the project or pick a project manager from the business side of the house, says Jane Griffin, president and CEO of Systems Techniques Inc., an Atlanta data warehousing consulting and software company.

* Don't let the project proceed without a clear understanding of the business objectives and how they will be measured. "The warehouse must have a strong business imperative," says Stephen Graham, vice president of software research for International Data Corp. Canada in Toronto.

* Do an incremental pilot project to determine if you can realize the projected benefit.

* Expect to make a major investment in ongoing management of the data warehouse. "Any parent knows birth pales in comparison to taking care of the kid every day," says Wayne Eckerson, director of the Business Intelligence and Data Warehouse Service of the Patricia Seybold Group in Boston.

* When all else fails, cut and run. Data warehousing consultant Barbara Gaskin gives Close Call credit for making a clean break with the project once it was clear the pilot had failed. "It was a smart decision to abandon that project. Companies often hemorrhage money serving one small user group," says Gaskin, principal at Decision Support Technology Inc., a consulting firm in Wellesley, Mass.

becomes an unalterable "fact," performance of customer service representatives—what Close Call was trying to measure—was much more subjective and obscure. Business managers had created their own customized spreadsheets into which they reentered the data they wanted to examine from the Reflex database reports. Because the managers looked at things differently (for example, some defined "revenues" as actual revenues, others considered them estimated revenues), defining the fact groups therefore became a hellish ordeal that required sorting through literally hundreds of calculations based on subjective assumptions. This process alone took nearly a month, says Farraday, which meant the team couldn't start building the relational format and user interface. It was a delay the executive sponsors were not inclined to forgive.

Source Data Crisis

Then came the biggest blow to date. With the pilot deadline at hand, Close Call's IS veterans, who believed their jobs were threatened by the data warehousing project, finally admitted to the project team that there was no way to populate the warehouse. The only data available was basic customer and transaction information that had been captured by Close Call's proprietary telecommunications switching systems as a byproduct of call routing. Writing a program to extract that data for the warehouse would be too expensive and time-consuming even to consider. Clearly, the old switching systems in the original six call centers would have to be updated with open technology to capture the data for the warehouse electronically, says Farraday.

Panicked at the thought of breaking that news to the executive sponsors, the team jury-rigged a way to populate the pilot by parsing the DOS-based Reflex reports and manipulating the report data into a relational database format. But the handwriting was on the wall—without replacing the proprietary switching systems, there would be no data warehouse.

By this point, Pemberton and her team were in overdrive, working 15-hour days, six days a week. Twice-weekly trips to Close Call's other major corporate office in the next state also took their toll. "I was trying so hard, but it was an emotional nightmare," says Pemberton.

The Pilot

The pilot contained a small summary-level set of data that the team had manipulated and manually loaded into the database. After the pilot was complete in August, the team faced an unpleasant revelation. Even if there had been pristine source data, the users weren't having any of it. "They said, 'You're giving me what I already had, and it's harder for me to get it and the data doesn't even match my hard copy,'" recalls Farraday. "We lost the users at that point."

The anger began to build and hit a crescendo in the executive suite. "They had wanted their production warehouse in place in four months and at the end of eight months we said, 'Here's your itsy-bitsy little one-page pilot, and guess what, you're not even getting your warehouse,'" says Pemberton.

It was all over but the shouting.

Crashing Down

A few weeks after the pilot debacle, Pemberton found herself with a new boss. The director of MIS, who had been promised the CIO spot, ended up with two new bosses, who shared the responsibilities of IS management as vice presidents of technology. To no one's surprise, the director of MIS elected to leave the company shortly thereafter.

Undaunted, Pemberton assembled a team of 57 IS staff and business users and in a few weeks created a detailed plan for reengineering the outbound business processes and updating their systems. With her heart in her mouth and passion still unspent, she presented her plan to the executives in October 1996, telling them it would take two years to reengineer before they could even begin the data warehouse. She said she believed nothing less than the survival of the company was at stake. Her words fell on deaf ears. "They said, 'Thanks for your work, but no thanks,'" says Pemberton. No one spoke in favor of her proposal at the meeting.

The Aftermath

Close Call's CEO canceled the data warehousing project in October 1996. Though it was hardly a shock, Pemberton was shattered. "I had never been involved in a situation where I failed at my job. I had gone in with such high hopes. I really wanted to give them a data warehouse," says Pemberton. In February 1997, she quit without a new job nor any prospects of one and took three weeks off to recover. (Pemberton reports she is now a senior data warehousing manager for another company and has just delivered a pilot of a data warehouse.)

From the CEO's point of view, the entire project had been a fiasco, says Pemberton. The anemic pilot was delivered four months later than the initial (highly unrealistic) deadline for the fully functional warehouse. Although the CEO had budgeted a paltry $250,000 for the project, the team had spent nearly $750,000 on hardware, software and services.

"Management finally said, "'We have spent a lot of money, and we have gotten no value,'" says Pemberton. "It was devastating."

Besides wasting money and time, the project cost Close Call 50 percent of its IS staff, about half of whom quit, according to Farraday. Today, Farraday reports that the company is reengineering its outbound business processes with an eye toward another data warehousing attempt. But in the meantime, Close Call's stock price has taken a beating, losing more than two thirds of its value between October 1996 and September 1997. Farraday attributes the company's change of fortune to attempting too many technology projects at once. "They bit off more than they could chew," he says.

So much for believing everything you hear on the golf course.

NO MANAGEMENT MEDALS

by Bruce Caldwell

IBM's travails at the Atlanta Olympics provide evidence that project management is often as important to pulling off large IT projects as the underlying hardware and software.

After pouring nearly three years and $40 million into its Olympic integration effort, IBM carried off a nearly flawless performance on most technical fronts. Its 100 custom applications managed staffing, budgeting, event calendaring, materials, logistics, medical services, and ticketing. IBM's Olympics Web site took nearly 189 million hits and helped sell $5.3 million in tickets over the Internet.

But high-profile glitches sullied IBM's record. In particular, the 12 news wire services that had contracted with the Atlanta Olympics committee had trouble obtaining complete, accurate competition results. Some of those problems are still unresolved today—well after the closing ceremonies.

The results system for the World New Press Association (WNPA) was written in Visual Gen and C and resided on an IBM System/390 mainframe running MVS, CICS, and DB2, says Luis Estrada, IBM's games competitions systems program manager. The mainframe fed results into an RS/6000 for distribution to the 12 news agencies, as well as to the Olympiad's Internet site. The systems themselves worked perfectly, Estrada says. But the process broke down because user requirements were not understood, he concedes.

On the morning of July 20, the first full day of the Games, distribution of results data hit a transmission bottleneck: phone-line bandwidth and the news agencies' 9.6-Kbps modems.

Changing the transmission protocol from synchronous, which requires a considerable wait for a response from the receiving modem, to asynchronous, which does not wait for a response, solved the speed problem by July 22, Estrada says. But then a more troublesome bottleneck appeared.

Although the results distribution system was capable of prioritizing data, the people in charge hadn't set priorities. Stats about gold-medal winners were buried within streams of data of little interest to anyone.

Originally published in Information Week, *Aug. 19, 1996. Used with permission. Copyright 1996 by CMP Publications, Inc., 600 Community Dr., Manhasset, NY 11030.*

Even after priorities were programmed in on July 20, prioritization became an ongoing task because of constant changes in participants and schedules.

An effort to simplify results distribution led to chaos. At the 1994 Winter Games in Lillehammer, Norway, results had been distributed to the news agencies in the languages and formats they required, Estrada says. To simplify its task for Atlanta, the International Olympic Committee (IOC) and the WNPA established a standard, encoded format that could be translated by users at the Atlanta Games into the required language and format.

"The news agencies were to develop the means to decode it themselves, and as integrators, we were responsible for making sure it all happened," Estrada notes. But the users were not prepared for the task of customizing the data, and format changes made during the Games added to the confusion rather than alleviating it. Clearly, Estrada acknowledges, "a lot more rehearsing and testing were needed."

Despite IBM's stumbling, Debra Chrapaty, IT director for the National Basketball Association, says she isn't having second thoughts about the multimillion-dollar contract the league signed with IBM before the Olympics for an integrated statistics system. "Their stats collection and commentator systems are wonderfully designed," Chrapaty says. "It was the deployment and integration that killed them." Indeed, she says she hopes some of the veterans of the Atlanta Games are available for the NBA project, which entails delivery of real-time statistics to broadcast commentators, similar to the IBM commentator information system that performed well in Atlanta.

The IOC's computer department has called for a meeting in October with IBM and the news agencies to prepare for the 1998 Winter Games in Nagano, Japan, and the 2000 Summer Games in Sydney, Australia.

HOW NEW TECHNOLOGY WAS OXFORD'S NEMESIS

by Ron Winslow and George Anders

The annals of business are filled with Frankenstein stories—tales of technology run amok. But the computer-system horrors at Oxford Health Plans Inc. take the genre to a new level.

Only two months ago, Oxford was basking in Wall Street admiration for its blazing growth. This week, the health-maintenance organization disclosed that it will post a loss of $120 million or more for the current quarter, on top of a surprise third-quarter loss of $78.2 million—its first loss since going public in 1991.

Oxford's shares closed yesterday at $17.125, down $2.9375, or 15%, on the Nasdaq Stock Market. Yesterday's closing stock price was down 75% from its level just before the company first revealed its troubles in late October.

How did disaster strike so quickly? As Oxford's business was faltering, it never saw the warning signs. One reason was a long list of troubles with a computer system that went on-line last year: how it was designed, how it was installed and how Oxford executives managed it.

The computer problems left Oxford unable to send out monthly bills to thousands of customer accounts and rendered it incapable of tracking payments to hundreds of doctors and hospitals. In less than a year, uncollected payments from customers tripled to more than $400 million, while the sum Oxford owed care givers swelled more than 50%, to more than $650 million.

For any company grappling with new information systems, Oxford offers a lesson in how not to proceed—and in how hotshot technology can create even worse problems than the ones it was intended to solve.

Plan for Growth

Oxford's dazzling growth was both its distinction and its undoing. The HMO began planning the new computer system in 1993, when it had just 217,000 members. The system didn't rev up until October of last year, by which time the HMO's membership had swelled to about 1.5 million. Thus, the new system was already outdated and outmanned.

Problems popped up immediately. Processing a new member sign-up was supposed to take just six seconds but instead took 15 minutes (a lag that later was fixed). And even as Oxford's back-office infrastructure was overwhelmed, the company continued signing up hordes of new customers that its system couldn't handle—more than half a million new members in the past year.

"If you drive a train at 150 miles an hour without good tracks, you derail," says David Friend, a global director at Watson Wyatt & Co., Bethesda, Md.

Take Baby Steps, Not Big Ones

Build your new information highway from exit to exit, not coast to coast. Oxford locked into a design for the entire system in late 1993, which made it difficult to adjust to subsequent technological improvements as the project moved forward. Moreover, it tried to convert the bulk of its membership-billing database in one fell swoop—some 43,000 accounts covering 1.9 million members.

Computer specialists say that such a sweeping conversion is far too difficult; companies should switch just the records for, say, one county or one business group a time. "Put all of your small customers on the new system and see how it goes," suggests John Salek, of REL Consultancy in Purchase, N.Y.

Oxford's all-or-nothing approach misfired, making it all the harder to do further repairs without creating even bigger snags. Stephen F. Wiggins, Oxford's founder and chairman, acknowledges that a more incremental conversion would have been preferable.

Beware of "Dirty Data"

Oxford's old software was riddled with seemingly innocuous errors in member records that turned out to cause enormous problems in the new system. For instance, the old Pick Systems database tolerated errors that let a patient's Social Security number be entered in a box reserved for date of treatment. But the new database, from Oracle Corp., spit out such inconsistencies and refused to process the data until they were corrected.

The new software is "very unforgiving. If you don't get it right, you don't get it in," says Seth Lefferts, an information-systems manager at Oxford.

So when the program detected a single mistake in, for example, a 1,000-member account, it kicked out the entire group—delaying billing and claims processing for all 1,000 members. When technicians fixed the error and re-entered the account, the new software would spit it out yet again when it detected the next mistake in a member's record. And so on.

The volume of individual mistakes "wasn't huge," says Paul Ricker, Oxford's vice president of information systems. "But the effect was rather extreme."

Oracle says it continues to work with Oxford and the HMO's other vendors to get the system working optimally.

Don't Lose Track of Receivables

Once the Oracle software began balking at the old system's erroneous data, Oxford was forced to stop billing some customers for months at a time and often sent flawed invoices to many others. The HMO had no backup system, not even a platoon of pencil-wielding clerks, to fill the gap. Yet the company, following standard accounting practices, continued booking the unbilled income as quarterly revenue.

Then came the rub: When Oxford started to catch up on long-over-due accounts, contacting customers for the first time in months, many refused to pay and others said they had quit the HMO long ago. Hence, the company had to write off $111 million in uncollectible bills and admit it had overestimated its membership by 30,000.

Mr. Wiggins now says he should have "hired an army of temps, put them at a bank of IBM Selectrics, and had them type out bills. That would have made sure that everybody that owed us money had a slip of paper saying so."

Don't Forget the Little Guy

When the data overload swamped Oxford, the company focused first on trying to catch up with its biggest customer accounts and major providers. That seemed to make sense: Why not place top priority on fixing the biggest sources of your revenue and costs?

The risk of such logic, as Oxford now concedes, is that small customers are the ones most likely to disappear when service gets bad. The don't yelp; they simply stop paying and sign up elsewhere. As it turned out, the vast majority of the $111 million hit for uncollectible accounts came from small groups and individuals.

Don't Ignore Payables

Oxford's failure to process claims on time angered many of the star physicians and renowned teaching hospitals whose participation was a key selling point of the HMO. Some providers say they still haven't been paid for care they delivered well over six months ago. A big doctor group at Columbia University's respected College of Physicians and Surgeons was owed $16 million at one point; New York Cornell Medical Center was owed as much as $17 million earlier this year.

This meant more than mere embarrassment. Oxford lost track of its actual medical costs—critical information for reacting to surprise problems, setting reserves and projecting future liabilities. That last item, known as costs "incurred but not reported," or IBNR, is especially crucial in the insurance business. Oxford executives "weren't getting the statistics and data they needed to make accurate estimates on the IBNR," says Rob Levy of consulting firm William M. Mercer & Co. "So they were winging it. That's a disaster to any business."

Mr. Wiggins says that the company followed accepted practices in estimating such costs and that it thought it was making conservative projections. However, one particularly disturbing trend went undetected: a sharp 14% rise in Medicare costs at a time when Oxford's vaunted marketing machine was recruiting new elderly patients at a rate of more than 100 a day.

Fortify Ranks of Propeller Heads

Hire a data chief who knows how to manage a giant conversion. Many of Oxford's information-system managers cut their teeth when the company was tiny, but a wholly different pacing and organization are needed when a project involves 150 programmers instead of a dozen. Intermediate goals need to be spelled out precisely, and multiple projects need to be coordinated.

Oxford dealt with data crises by piling more people onto the trouble areas, but it didn't seem capable of anticipating the next snafu.

Mr. Wiggins says his company is now looking for seasoned managers for information systems, medical management and other crucial areas of the company.

4.2 HITTING THE WRONG BULLSEYE

What a fascinating story this one is. Just after the Automatic Teller Machine (ATM) had emerged as the greatest technology success of the banking industry in years, a number of forward-thinking bankers were busy anticipating the next great leap forward in the banking industry.

That forward leap, the industry generally agreed, was "home banking." If remote banking in a business location is goodness, the reasoning here went, why isn't remote banking from the home even better?

There was nothing wrong with that notion, most bank observers even today would agree, but there was plenty wrong with the operationalization of that notion in this story. Banks, you must remember, are fairly conservative institutions, and that conservatism contributed to the downfall in this story. For example, the bank in this story, at the outset, planned to use a technology (e.g., Atari computers) that was obsolete before they could begin putting their system on the air, and yet the bank decided to stick with that obsolete technology in their otherwise-leading-edge project and notion! In another classic case of bank conservatism, the bank had carefully scoped out home-banking as a money-saver, and yet they planned to charge their customers for the privilege of using the system! And finally, when it turned out to be difficult to manipulate some of the data behind the scenes in an automated fashion, the bank employed manual means of doing so, effectively negating the projected cost savings they were to have achieved on the project!

ANATOMY OF A TECHNOLOGICAL FAILURE:
Why Home Banking Did Not Succeed

by Hooman Mehran

All the goals that home banking set for itself in the early 1980s had been achieved by the close of 1992. Banking customers today can transfer funds, make bill payments, and download pertinent information to their home computer hard drives for detailed analysis. However, this is all being accomplished in a manner that the banking industry would hardly have imagined ten years ago. Third-party computer service suppliers and touch-tone services offered by the banks have largely filled in the void that the bank-owned systems had eyed in 1982 and 1983. How this came to pass in this unpredicted manner is a story of missed opportunities, miscalculations and short-sighted profit analyses by the banking industry throughout the decade. A home banking revolution controlled by the banks could have produced a new defining role for an industry that has seen significant portions of its market share eaten into by non-industry competitors. Instead, the banks had to content themselves with merely occupying a role on the periphery while other vendors slowly took center stage.

The technology to offer home banking systems was economically feasible by the mid-1970s, about the same time that the automated teller machines began to hit the market. Serious planning only appears to have begun, however, with the deregulation of the banking industry that began early in the administration of Ronald Reagan. Two basic regulatory barriers prevented the banks from plunging wholeheartedly into home banking: (1) regulations that restricted a bank's activities across state lines and (2) regulations that curtailed non-banking activities, which providing home banking computer services could technically be categorized as. The Federal Reserve ruled in 1982 that a terminal in a home in Connecticut tied to a New York bank "does not constitute an interstate bank"[1] thus clearing the first obstacle. The second hurdle was eliminated a year later when Regulation Y of the National Bank Act was modified to state explicitly that home banking activities are "closely related to banking"[2] and thus permissible.

Originally published in The Stern Information Systems Review, *New York University, Spring 1993. Used with permission.*

The reasons for the banks to push ahead with home banking plans were obvious. Primary in the bankers' minds was the high cost of check processing that could slowly be phased out as more customers became familiar with settling debts on-line. Developing a superior system could be a marketing tool in and of itself that could both attract new customers to the bank as well as encourage existing customers to consolidate all their activities there. There were also benefits to be derived from selling its software to other banks, a strategy Chemical made no secret about when it unveiled its Pronto system in 1983.

Most significantly, there were the intangible benefits that could be derived from being the hub of a customer's computer activity. Jane Bryant Quinn warned readers of her *Newsweek* column as early as 1983 that banks could build up sizable information repositories on their customers and that "courts can be casual about demanding information that the government wants,"[3] even if the banks had made up-front claims to the consumer about confidentiality. There seemed to be little resistance on the part of consumers, however, to the prospect of allowing banks to have such free access to their records. *American Banker* advised its readers early on that banks should look toward being "actively involved in every aspect of the product offering, not just the banking side."[4] The other gains to be made from home banking, it was argued, paled in comparison to the power that could be generated from serving in an administrative role. "The bank," warned the newsletter, "needs to be in total control of whatever it is their customer has in mind doing with that terminal."[5] This was a remarkably clairvoyant message for October 1982. Unfortunately, the American bankers were not paying attention to the *American Banker.*

Chemical Bank was the one of the first major banks to roll out a major home banking system, called Pronto, that was managed by a bank and not a third-party time-sharing system. They refused to divulge exactly how much they had spent at the time,[6] but later estimates put their outlay at that point at $20 million. Although that figure was to rise by nearly five-fold over the next six years, the cash flowed at a very slow and halting pace. From the outset, it was obvious that Chemical was interested in seeing the enterprise produce a positive cash flow as quickly as possible. To that end, they instituted a $10 "modest monthly fee," a feature that did not exist in the wildly successful Pronto test environments.

Pronto was designed for use on Atari 400 or 800 computers equipped with modems of 300 or 1200 baud. Citibank, which was developing a home banking system called HomeBase, also sets its sights on equipment at that level. These banks, and many others, completely ignored the PC revolution that was transforming the computer industry at that very time and making 80-column screens and 2400 baud modems universal standards. Pronto and Direct Access (which is what HomeBase eventually evolved into) never attempted to break the 40-column, 1200 baud restrictions of machines that were the standards of the 1970s. It is clear from this small example alone that the banks had predefined spending limits on home banking development, met them by the early 1980s, and refused to budge from them even as cheaper and more efficient technology appeared on the scene and established new standards.

If the banks were reluctant to stay on the leading edge with respect to development, industry-watchers were slow to notice it. *Time* magazine stated in November, 1983 that by 1995, "the home banking industry will have revenues of as much as $2.6 billion."[7] The magazine was more accurate in its prediction that customers would not accept dedicated banking terminals in their homes, which is what some banks were pushing at the time. *Esquire* did an analysis on home banking in its earliest days and besides noting the inability of the systems to dispense cash (which all critics hastened to point out meant that the ATM successes could not be duplicated on the home level), scoffed at the $5 to $10 monthly charge and stated that unless banks started to move toward providing a complete information package, the efforts would be doomed.[8] Words of criticism were hard to find, however, and the general consensus in the early 1980s was that home banking was well on its way to wide acceptance.

The first public cracks in the armor started appearing in 1984, not yet a year after the official introduction of Pronto and a full year before Direct Access market testing was complete. Banks were still pouring large amounts of capital into ATM development and enhancement and were beginning to be wary about spending anything further on home banking. One banking executive pointed out that "we don't want to be stuck with a very heavy investment if the whole thing fizzles and dies."[9] If the players already in the field were beginning to second guess their commitments to the project, surely those who had not yet entered the market had reason to hesitate. Additionally, there was some question about whether the boom in personal computer sales was in fact translating into terminals in the home study or in the office. Rumors of new computers stored away in closets concerned executives who were beginning to feel that sales figures that had been published were overstating their potential customer base. Home banking introduction dates were quietly postponed, if not missed entirely. "Last year's wave of the future," lamented *American Banker,* "is this year's neap tide."

By the time of the American Bankers Association annual convention in October 1984, the optimism had faded almost entirely. First Interstate Bank of California had been laboring for two and a half years on a home banking pilot. The bank's retail banking chief, Alex W. Hart, told the conventioneers that he was ready to throw in the towel. "We are less enamored by this with every passing month," Hart stated.[11] Hart estimated that 45% of all personal computers sold to individuals lay dormant. He also added that the test results for First Interstate's system were encouraging only up to the point of the introduction of the monthly fee.

Citibank's Direct Access hoped to reverse the tide in 1985 with a download feature that allowed customers to feed personal transaction data to spreadsheets or financial calculation programs. The feature was hastily added to the system between the testing phase and the actual roll out in an attempt to provide a point of distinction between Direct Access and its competitors, which the American Bankers Association numbered at 26 at the time. However, the download feature only heightened customer concerns about home banking security which had been present from the start.

Besides security and the monthly fee, the home banking feature that most irked customers was the elimination of the float period. When a check is written, the customer has use of the funds until the check is cashed. With an electronic transfer via a home banking system, the funds are gone the instant the payment is confirmed. Customers correctly suspected that the banks were using the new technology to retain the benefits of the float for themselves. The banks were also looking forward to the day, after widespread home banking acceptance, that they could charge merchants for being paid through the service, as had always been done in the credit card business.

In 1985, for the first time, banks began to notice the number of users shrinking rather than growing. They still could not accept that home banking had failed entirely, however. Manufacturers Hanover, for instance, attributed the drop in usage of its Excel system (no relation to the Microsoft spreadsheet program) to users who were "using their office computers to do their personal banking, and got orders to stop."[12] Chemical began hedging its bet by teaming up with Bank of America, AT&T and Time, Inc. to form a joint venture called Covidea that would offer Pronto's line of services in conjunction with discount stock brokerage and merchandise shopping. In attempting to reverse the ominous trends, Chemical had thus decided to share the controls with partners. Analysts who just a year or two earlier had warned the banks that they must retain control of the whole enterprise, now were indicating that this could be the move that would save home banking.

Nineteen eighty-five was home banking's year of widest availability, but by the end of the year, prospects for the industry were fading rapidly. Customers who used the system tended to be enthusiastic about it, but even computer trade magazines had to grudgingly admit that it was "still a long way from being as popular as the automated teller machine."[13] Chemical Bank was now claiming that a fully utilized home banking system could reduce merchant payment costs to as little as six cents per check. However, it was reluctant, even through the Covidea arm, to pass that savings on to the customer. Only the enthusiast who already had a computer for other purposes, or was willing to spend about $100 for a Covidea-supplied ASCII terminal, could tap into home banking. And even then, it was only after paying a stiff monthly fee that did not cover the saved postage costs for check mailing, in spite of what the banks were claiming.

American Banker called the impasse a classic example of a chicken-and-egg situation: the non-enthusiasts were unwilling to give home banking a try until costs came down and the banks were unwilling to lower costs until they could reach beyond the enthusiast base.[14] There was talk about abandoning the personal market and going after businesses instead, and the various software offerings were hastily overhauled and repackaged as "business banking" systems. The banks sensed a little less price sensitivity on the part of the businesses, and correspondingly raised the monthly fees from the $8 to $15 range to the $20 to $50 vicinity. As a result, these offerings did little to increase the number of on-line users, which held steady at 75,000 by early 1986. This was a far cry from the 10% total customer base penetration that had been predicted only two years earlier.

A complaint frequently voiced by customers from the start was that the number of merchants available on the service was too restrictive. Besides phone companies and utilities, a great number of payees each month, such as doctors or baby-sitters, had to be paid by traditional means. The banks chose to address this problem by offering to send a cashier's check to anyone designated for a payment that was not on the merchant directory list. This was purely a stop-gap measure intended to slow the rising number of home banking defections. Yet, whatever money that was saved by the bank by not having to manually read, encode and process a customer's handwritten check was lost in the postage fee for sending the automated check to the nonparticipating merchant.

Worse still, the back office infrastructure was not available in many banks to handle new enhancements such as this, so the "automated" processing was often a manual process. In the early days of the automated teller machine, customers used to peer jokingly around the terminals and wonder aloud who inside was handing out the cash. In the case of home banking, it was no joke: there really was someone on the other side of the terminal manually generating checks, transferring funds and performing a whole host of other tasks. In their panicked attempts to add services and make the systems more enticing to customers, the banks were raising unit costs to unacceptably high levels.

The dropouts soon began to outnumber the active participants: less than half of the 70 financial institutions that offered the service in 1985 were still active by early 1989. The most notable dropout was Chemical, which, in its new cost-conscious, capital-intensive environment refused to invest any more than the $90 million it had already spent on Pronto. "If it's not profitable," American Banker noted about the new philosophy at Chemical and other banks across the nation, "they get rid of it."[15] Videotex services, such as CheckFree, Princeton Telecom and, most notably, IBM's [and Sears'] Prodigy began seizing the initiative by nearly adding all the on-line services to their offerings that the banks could. Prodigy even offered advertising space to retailers to help reduce the end-user's cost for accessing the system. This was an innovation that the banks could certainly have used a couple of years earlier while they were struggling to grow their customer base.

Upon the demise of Pronto, *American Banker* stated that home banking still had a future, but that it would only be carried on through the third-party videotex services. Cable television companies and the regional Bells were interested in establishing videotex gateways, and willing to put up the cash to make them a success. The industry consensus was that such services would "make it more cost-effective to offer video banking services."[16]

Chemical's exit left Citibank, with a user base approaching 40,000, as the largest provider of home banking services. But Citibank had suspended further enhancements on Direct Access and was grooming its successor, the Enhanced Telephone, for a 1990 debut. Enhanced Telephone, basically a regular telephone with a built-in keyboard and monitor, solved what banks perceived to be the major stumbling block to home bank growth: the customer who was unwilling or unable to buy a home computer to hook into the service. Citibank sates that it was willing to sell Enhanced Telephone terminals to customers for about $100, which was a fraction of the cost to produce the devices.

The Enhanced Telephone never made it to the market. Certainly the short-term profit needs that affected Chemical's thinking had some role in Citibank's holding back on its introduction. What really made the device infeasible was the rapid growth of touch-tone banking services. The technology had really been in place for years for fund transfers and bill payments to be carried out by touch-tone, but banks had always shied away from it. Throughout the early 1980s, touch-tone systems were used to provide answers to balance inquiries only. It was believed that customers would be reluctant to transfer money and pay bills without any sort of tangible receipt that a teller, ATM, or a home computer could provide. However, the bankers soon learned that "consumers are pretty comfortable with technology"[17] and were willing to risk a paperless transaction in exchange for low-cost convenience with no installation charges.

Home banking is often cited in textbooks and articles that deal with technology in the financial services industry as the flip side of the coin of the ATM. Every argument about technology strategy that uses ATM development in the 1970s as its prime example uses as the counter example the failure of home banking in the 1980s. Certainly there was a great deal of loss of investment from the attempts of the banks to gain control of this new technology, but it is not appropriate to place the blame for the loss on the failure of home banking as a notion. Rather, as we have seen, it was the execution that was flawed.

If the banks realized that they had more to gain than the customers from a fully implemented, bank-controlled home banking operation, they never revealed it in their pricing structure. All the advantages that home banking offered to the customer are available from the combination of third-party videotex and touch-tone services in operation today. Most of the advantages that the banks would have reaped, particularly in the customer information area, have been divided among others. Most significantly, the banks are in a weaker position than ever because of their subordinate role as mere merchants on systems run by others. At a time when the banking industry is seeing its traditional activity being chipped away by competitors from outside the industry (witness the recent credit card offerings by General Motors and General Electric), the home banking systems could have defined a new role for them while at the same time consolidating their existing roles.

When the American Banking Association revised its predicted timetable of home banking profitability in 1984, terrified banks closed off the technological investments and scurried to cash in on what they had accomplished thus far. Unfortunately, this left them with products developed for 1970s-style Commodore and Atari computers with 40-column screens and 300 baud modems. The personal computer revolution started by the introduction of the IBM PC in 1981 simply passed them by. Home banking may have been a flawed notion, and perhaps it may not have ultimately spared the banking industry the crises they face in the early 1990s. But this cannot be stated for certain, because the banks' early experimentation with home banking was never fully developed or exploited.

REFERENCES

1. "Chemical Unveils Pronto System," *American Banker,* September 9, 1982, p. 28.

2. "Slow Progress in Home Banking," *American Banker,* April 2, 1984, p. 22.

3. "Banking by Computer," *Newsweek,* November 21, 1983, p. 85.

4. "Home Banking Reaches Critical Juncture," *American Banker,* October 19, 1982, p. 19.

5. Ibid.

6. "Chemical Unveils Pronto system," *American Banker,* September 9, 1982, p. 28.

7. "Armchair Banking and Investing," *Time,* November 14, 1983, p. 90.

8. "Playing with Money," *Esquire,* January, 1983, p. 42.

9. "Slow Process in Home Banking," *American Banker,* May 14, 1984, p. 22.

10. Ibid.

11. "Home Banking Won't Take Hold Until 1990's," American Banker, October 25, 1984, p. 14.

12. "Push-Button Banking From Your Easy Chair," *BusinessWeek,* October 7, 1985, p.126.

13. "Should You Try Banking By Computer?," *Personal Computing,* November, 1985, p.63.

14. "The Chicken, the Egg, and Video Banking's Unfulfilled Promise," *American Banker,* January 22, 1986, p.11.

15. "Chemical's Exit Not Fatal Blow to Home Banking," *American Banker,* December 7, 1988, p. 1.

16. Ibid.

17. "Home Banking Back in the Race," *American Banker,* May 18, 1992, p. 26A.

4.3 THE OPERATION WAS A SUCCESS, BUT THE PATIENT DIED

It is surprising how often a project that has clearly failed is referred to as a success in the literature surrounding the history of the project. There is a reason for that, I suppose—hardly anyone ever wants to admit, especially publicly, that they have failed. This is just such a story.

One of the great successes often cited in the literature on Expert Systems software is a system built by a leading computer vendor, the goal of which was to assist customers and salespeople in ordering and manufacturing the various parts needed to make up a computing system. In this story, the company and the project names are fictionalized, but if you think you know the identity of both from previous war stories encountered elsewhere, you are probably right!

In this story, as it turns out, that very "successful" system actually consisted of two major parts—the part used by manufacturing, which according to this story actually *was* the success the world thinks it to be—and the part to be used by the sales organization, which apparently was a miserable failure! The story that follows is about the failed portion of the project.

This is the classic story of a project that "took on a life of its own." It was fairly clear early on, according to our story, that the salespeople (to be the users of the system) really didn't need or want the system. But everyone at the company in question thought that the users were simply wrong, and they overrode that judgment and proceeded with the project. The sales "users" were fairly vocal in their opposition, and the history of the project is littered with quotes like "the project is a miserable failure, but nobody is willing to kill it." (The developers counter with "the sales force just doesn't understand. . .")

More than a decade and tens of millions of dollars later, the company finally accepted the judgment of its sales force, and canceled the project. Perhaps this story is an all-time winner for developer stubbornness, or perhaps it is an all-time winner for user stubbornness; it really doesn't matter, does it? This is simply a whale of a computing calamity story!

PULLING THE PLUG: Software Project Management and the Problem of Project Escalation[1]

by Mark Keil

Abstract

Information technology (IT) projects can fail for any number of reasons and in some cases can result in considerable financial losses for the organizations that undertake them. One pattern of failure that has been observed but seldom studied is the IT project that seems to take on a life of its own, continuing to absorb valuable resources without reaching its objective. A significant number of these projects will ultimately fail, potentially weakening a firm's competitive position while siphoning off resources that could be spent developing and implementing successful systems. The escalation literature provides a promising theoretical base for explaining this type of IT failure. Using a model of escalation based on the literature, a case study of IT project escalation is discussed and analyzed. The results suggest that escalation is promoted by a combination of project, psychological, social, and organizational factors. The managerial implications of these findings are discussed along with prescriptions for how to avoid the problem of escalation.

Introduction

By 1994, annual U.S. spending on the development of information technology (IT) applications reached $250 billion (Johnson, 1995). The strategic importance that IT now plays, coupled with the burgeoning costs of developing systems, has raised the stakes associated with project failure. Despite the costs involved, press reports suggest that such failures occur with alarming frequency (Betts, 1992; Cringely, 1994; Ellis, 1994; Gibbs, 1994; Kindel, 1992; Kull, 1986; McPartlin, 1992; Mehler, 1991; Neumann and Hoffman, 1988; Rothfeder, 1988). While it is difficult to obtain statistics on the actual frequency of IT failures, various sources suggest that at least half of all IT projects are not as successful as we would like them to be (Gladden, 1982; Lyytinen and Hirschheim, 1987).

Originally published in MIS Quarterly, *December 1995 (vol. 19, no. 4). Reprinted by special permission. Copyright 1995 by the Society for Information Management and the Management Information Systems Research Center at the University of Minnesota.*

While there are undoubtedly many different modes of IT failure, one pattern of failure that has been observed but seldom studied is the IT project that seems to "take on a life of its own," continuing to absorb valuable resources without ever reaching its objective (Keider, 1974; Lyytinen and Hirschheim, 1987; Meredith, 1988). Eventually, these projects are abandoned (or significantly redirected), but the cost of having funded them can represent a tremendous waste of organizational resources. Why are troubled projects allowed to continue for so long before they are ultimately abandoned or brought under control?

Traditional wisdom holds that information systems projects get "out of control" because of poor project management practices. It would be hard to argue otherwise. But what is meant by "poor project management?" This phrase has become a dumping ground for explanations of IT failure that range from a chronic tendency to underestimate the cost of scope of an IT project (Boehm, 1981; Brooks, 1975; Kemerer, 1987) to failure in managing the risks associated with IT projects (Alter and Ginzberg, 1978; Ginzberg, 1981; McFarlan, 1981). While there is merit behind these traditional views, they do not explain why projects that get out of control seem to stay that way.

Many IT projects that seem to take on a life of their own represent what can be described as escalation. Escalation has been defined as continued commitment in the face of negative information about prior resource allocations coupled with "uncertainty surrounding the likelihood of goal attainment" (Brockner, 1992). Project escalation can therefore be said to occur when there is *continued commitment and negative information.*[2]

In order to both explain this phenomenon and prevent its occurrence, it is necessary to look beyond traditional explanations of poor project management and to consider possible psychological, social, and organizational factors that may promote project escalation.

Background

One of the most difficult management issues that can arise in connection with IT projects is deciding whether to abandon or continue a project that is in trouble. Unfortunately, there is very little information available on the subject of IT project abandonment. One study found that 35 percent of these projects were not abandoned until the implementation stage of the life cycle (Ewusi-Mensah and Przasnyski, 1991). This suggests that IT managers are doing a poor job of identifying or terminating projects that are likely to fail. While there may be several reasons why such a high fraction of abandoned projects are not terminated earlier in the life cycle, one explanation may be that managers have a natural tendency toward escalation or continued commitment to a failing course of action (Brockner, 1992).

Factors That Can Promote Escalation

Previous research suggests that escalation is a complex phenomenon that may be influenced by many different factors. Based on a review of the literature, Staw and Ross (1987a) provide a useful taxonomy that groups these factors into four categories: project factors, psychological factors, social factors, and organizational factors.[3]

Project factors are the objective features of the project itself and how it is perceived by management (Ross and Staw, 1993). These factors include the costs and benefits associated with the project as well as the expected difficulty and duration of the project. Other things being equal, projects are more prone to escalation when they involve a large potential payoff, when they are viewed as requiring a long-term investment in order to receive any substantial gain, and when setbacks are perceived as temporary problems that can be overcome.

Psychological factors are those that cause managers to convince themselves that things do not look so bad and that continuation will eventually lead to success (Brockner, 1992). These factors include the manager's previous experience with similar projects, the degree to which the manager feels personally responsible for the outcome of the project, as well as psychological and cognitive biases that can affect the way in which information concerning the project is perceived or processed. Projects are more prone to escalation when there is a previous history of success and when there is a high level of personal responsibility.

Escalation is also more likely to occur when managers make errors in processing information. Previous research shows, for example, that human decision making is subject to numerous biases, many of which operate at a subconscious level (Kahneman and Tversky, 1982). One such bias can lead to "throwing good money after bad" in an effort to turn around a failing project (Garland, 1990). Prior research also suggests that managers may engage in a type of self-justification behavior in which they commit additional resources in order to turn a project around rather than terminating the project and admitting that their earlier decisions were incorrect. Self-justification can lead managers to "bias facts in the direction of previously accepted beliefs and preferences," resulting in project escalation (Ross and Staw, 1993, p. 716).

Social factors can also promote escalation. These factors include competitive rivalry with other social groups, the need for external justification, and norms for consistency (Ross and Staw, 1993). Projects are more prone to escalation when competitive rivalry exists between the decision-making group and another social group, when external stakeholders have been led to believe that the project is (or will be) successful, and when norms of behavior favor "staying the course."

Finally, organizational factors involve the structural and political environment surrounding a project. These factors include political support for the project and the degree to which the project becomes institutionalized with the goals and values of the organization. Projects are more prone to escalation when there is strong political support at the senior management level and when the project has become institutionalized.

Prior Research on Escalation

Prior research on escalation has been based almost exclusively on laboratory experiments that have focused on individual decision making. While these studies have generated useful information concerning factors that may promote or impede escalation at an individual level, there is a growing recognition of the need for more field-based studies that capture the organizational dynamics of the phenomenon (Garland, et al., 1990; Ross and Staw, 1993). To date, there have been only a handful of field-based studies of escalation (Newman and Sabherwal, 1994; Ross and Staw, 1986; 1993). For these reasons, this research focuses on three research questions: (1) Does escalation occur in actual IT projects? (2) What are the factors that seem to promote escalation? And (3) What are the course of events that can break a cycle of escalation?

Methods

Since the objectives of this research were to determine whether the escalation phenomenon could be observed in an actual IT project and, if so, to understand more about the reasons *why* it occurs, this research employed a longitudinal case study approach. Given the exploratory nature of the research, an in-depth case study of a single project named CONFIG[4] was conducted in a company called CompuSys.[5]

Three different kinds of data were collected: interview data (obtained from talking with users, developers, and managers), observations (recorded from meetings that took place involving users, developers, and managers), and historical documents (in the form of meeting minutes, memos, and reports concerning CONFIG).

A Brief History of the CONFIG Project and Why It Failed

In the early 1980s, CompuSys, a large computer company, began developing an expert system called CONFIG. CONFIG was designed to help the company's sales representatives produce error-free configurations prior to price quoting. The system was intended to reduce costly "allowances" in which the company had to supply hardware without charge to customers when price quotations were found to have been based on inaccurate product specifications. In addition to the tangible costs associated with "allowances," configuration errors caused several more significant, but less tangible, problems for CompuSys. These problems included delays in the order fulfillment process and disgruntled customers who threatened the reputation of the company.

From the very beginning, the CONFIG project faced serious challenges including a lack of sponsorship within the Sales organization, problems of software accuracy and performance, and an unrealistic project schedule. Later, many implementation difficulties were experienced as the system was deployed within the Sales organization. As a result, very few sales representatives actually used the system. While numerous attempts were made to improve the system, the level of usage among sales representatives remained disappointingly low. Nevertheless, the CONFIG projects was funded for a period of more than a decade during which it was continually adapted and refined, resulting in a series of redeployments to the field. During this period, both the size and composition of the project team varied, but the commitment to the project was unwavering. The last major effort to adapt and redeploy CONFIG took place during 1989–1990. Despite a long and troubled history, the CONFIG project was continually funded until the end of 1992 when financial support was withdrawn and all further development and support for the project was terminated. A brief description of the project's history and why it failed is provided below.

The Business Problem and the Origins of CONFIG

Throughout its history, CompuSys has prided itself on the almost limitless number of different configurations it offered to customers. This required putting together, or configuring, a group of components that were compatible with one another and that, when combined, would result in a complete and functioning system for the customer. By the 1970s, the growing size and complexity of CompuSys' product line made it increasingly difficult to insure that systems were properly configured when they left the factory. Despite manual efforts to verify that all the necessary components were present, incorrectly configured systems would frequently be shipped to the customer.

In 1975, CompuSys established a task force to study the problem and develop better solutions for verifying system configurations before shipping the goods. In 1978, CompuSys funded the development of an expert system known as VERIFIER that would be capable of verifying and correcting system configurations. As VERIFIER moved through the proof of concept stage, Tom Jones, who later became manager of the company's Artificial Intelligence Technology Center, was recognized as its champion. During the early 1980s, Jones recruited a growing number of individuals to help develop and maintain VERIFIER and to explore other business applications of expert systems. One of the key individuals he brought into the group was George Smith, who was appointed program manager for VERIFIER in 1982 and was heavily involved in managing its transition from a prototype into an evolving production system.

By the early 1980s, VERIFIER was in production use and reportedly saving the company millions of dollars per year, with performance that exceeded some of the company's best human configurers. As a result of both this project and his previous contributions, Jones had secured a high level of status and respect within CompuSys. Having gained some confidence in building VERIFIER, Jones and his group of managers and developers began to search for other opportunities where they could apply the technology. This was the beginning of a cascading sequence of events that set the stage for project failure in the case of CONFIG.

Prior History of Success Prompts Development of CONFIG

The very success of VERIFIER, which was developed and funded by the Manufacturing organization, led to the realization that the configuration problem originated in the sales offices and that, while VERIFIER helped Manufacturing, it did nothing to assist Sales.[6] With this realization, the idea for CONFIG was born. Unlike VERIFIER, which was a *batch-oriented tool* used by Manufacturing for configuration *validation,* CONFIG was to be an *interactive tool* that would aid sales representatives in *creating and validating* configurations prior to quotation.

By 1981, the group that developed VERIFIER had begun funding the initial prototype of CONFIG. The CONFIG program manager formed a "user design team" (UDT) composed of about a dozen representatives from the Sales organization. This group typically met twice annually with the developers; its charter was to provide guidance and feedback as additional features and functions were added to the evolving prototype. The UDT met with the developers on 13 occasions between November 1981, and August 1988, when the group ceased to meet regularly.

Initially, there were only a few developers who were assigned to work on CONFIG, but the resources devoted to the project increased substantially during the 1980s.[7] Although the composition of the project team assigned to CONFIG changed over time, both Jones and Smith maintained a high level of involvement.[8] The development activity was funded primarily out of Manufacturing, where the group was housed until the late 1980s.

A Flawed Design Concept

CONFIG's original design concept called for a standalone support tool for sales representatives. As the project unfolded, the need for integration between CONFIG and the company's quoting system became increasingly apparent, and the standalone design concept proved to be fatally flawed. Ironically, at the same time that the CONFIG project was getting underway, another group of developers that was more closely aligned with the Sales organization was just beginning to develop a new computerized price quotation system (PQS).

While the connection between the configuration process and the price quotation process seems obvious now, at the time, these two systems were being developed and managed as entirely separate processes. This was largely due to a company culture that promoted the creation of "stovepipe organizations," resulting in a lack of cross-functional coordination. As a result, two standalone systems that did not talk to one another were created—one for generating configurations and one for generating price quotations.

The basic design concept of CONFIG—as a standalone support tool for sales representatives—emerged and remained intact for several reasons. First, because the development group resided in Manufacturing, they had a limited understanding of the sales function. Their model of the sales process was one in which configuring and quoting were seen as two separate processes (Keil, et al., 1995a; Markus and Keil, 1994); this model led them to believe that it was not necessary to have accurate price information during the configuration process. The sales force did not operate this way, however; most representatives found that pricing information often drove the configuration process. Thus, it was necessary to work back and forth between the system's technical configuration and what the customer was willing to pay.

As early as 1982, some of the more vocal sales representatives on the UDT had begun to argue that CONFIG and PQS had to be integrated. The developers, however, contended that this would be too challenging technically and made integration a "non-goal" for CONFIG's first release. Since the UDT served only in an advisory capacity, the sales representatives were not in a position to drive the development process. Consequently, the integration of CONFIG and PQS remained a low priority until 1984 when it became more obvious that there would have to be at least some level of integration between these two systems.

By that time, however, the composition of the UDT had shifted and the group was no longer representative of the salesforce at large; as more novice sales representatives lost interest in the process and left the group, the UDT had become dominated by a relatively small number of experienced, technically oriented sales representatives. As a group, they tended to be more forgiving of the software and were willing to compromise on such items as "ease of use" in exchange for a system that was accurate and functional. Rather than arguing for complete integration between CONFIG and PQS, the UDT was willing to settle for a non-interactive one-way linkage. The establishment of such a crude linkage was predicated on a model of the sales process in which CONFIG was still seen as a viable standalone system so long as its output could be passed on to PQS.

While this linkage was made operational in 1985, it was not enough to drive significant usage of CONFIG. In fact, those who used the system found it more time consuming to produce price quotes than those who did not. In the words of one sales representative:

> When you get done with CONFIG and want to print a quote, you create a file, transfer a file, you go into PQS, you import it. It's very cumbersome. The turnaround time is way too long, so I've started not to use the system [CONFIG] because when I need to do a quote, generally the customer is waiting. They've asked for something, and you can't wait a day or two to get stuff back.

System Fails to Gain Acceptance among Sales Reps

In addition to the fact that the tool was based on a flawed design concept, there were other reasons why CONFIG failed to gain acceptance among sales representatives. One reason was a lack of organizational incentives to use CONFIG. Quite simply, sales reps were not motivated to produce error-free configurations; they were rewarded on the basis of sales volume, not configuration accuracy. In the words of one sales rep:

> It's not that anyone wants to be inaccurate and make a lot of errors. It's just not something we are measured on, and we will work toward what we are measured on.

A sales manager who was asked to explain how reps' performance was evaluated said:

> You won't see anything [in the performance appraisal form] about quote accuracy. I'm not managed, nor is my manager managed, to "dirty" orders. So it doesn't really matter. It's not one of my metrics. It's not a critical success factor for me or for the sales reps. There are no kudos if they get it right, no scolding if they get it wrong.

Under this type of reward system, the costs associated with inaccurate configurations were never factored into the sales reps' compensation. Therefore, most of the people in sales (from district managers on down) thought that the configuration error problem was too minor to justify the effort of using CONFIG (Markus and Keil, 1994):

> We never miss the big stuff . . . CPU, etc . . . . only cables. Who cares about a $50 cable? It's not worth the time it takes to run it through CONFIG. Ninety percent of the time, the customer will authorize a modification anyway.

Was CONFIG an Example of Project Escalation?

As stated before, escalation can be defined as *continued commitment* of resources in the face of *negative information* (Brockner, 1992). In order to investigate whether these conditions actually existed, a detailed chronology of the project was reconstructed using the UDT meeting minutes and, in some cases, actual transcripts of UDT meetings as a foundation. The 13 UDT meetings that took place during the life of the project, along with the decisions to initiate and terminate the project, were chosen as natural decision points for analysis.[9] Where possible, the information from the UDT meeting minutes was supplemented by examination of agenda items, priority lists, and presentation slides associated with each meeting. Interview and historical data were then used to reconstruct events that occurred between UDT meetings. The resulting chronology was then validated by several individuals who were familiar with the project's history.

Using this chronology of events, two independent raters were then asked to assess the character of the information that was available to decision makers during the course of the CONFIG project. Based on their assessment, project information was coded as positive, negative, or ambiguous. The CONFIG project continued for a period of more than a decade despite the fact that information concerning the project was predominantly negative during this period of time. Therefore, the CONFIG project satisfies the definition of project escalation.

Objective usage data as well as the subjective opinions of individuals closely associated with the project offer confirmatory evidence of escalation. There was a pattern of declining use during the last several years of the project's history.

The fact that CONFIG was used for a very small percentage of system quotations and that its usage declined steadily during a four-year period represents significant negative information concerning the project. This information was readily available to decision makers within the company.

Qualitative interview data gathered during 1990 provides additional evidence. As one manager observed: "I think the thing may have taken on a life of its own." By 1990, many sales representatives who were interviewed expressed a belief that the CONFIG project should be abandoned. The following remarks were typical:

> Based on the usage patterns, I don't think anybody would miss [CONFIG] very much if we turned it off tomorrow.

> If [CompuSys] has spent millions on this product we have really missed [the boat]. [We should] pull the plug on this effort immediately.

> The people responsible for developing [CONFIG] are trying to breathe life into something that should be allowed to die . . . We have proof today that [CONFIG] is not successful. It has failed miserably. The problem is nobody is willing to kill it.

Given what appears to be such a clear pattern of negative information one would have expected the project to be terminated or redirected much earlier than 1992, the year in which the project was finally halted. How, then, can the escalation that occurred be explained?

Discussion of Factors That Promoted Escalation

As suggested by the model presented earlier, there were four different types of factors that seemed to contribute to the escalation of the CONFIG project: project factors, psychological factors, social factors, and organizational factors.

Project Factors

Some factors associated with the characteristics of the project and how it was viewed by management were: (1) there was evidence that continued investment could produce a large payoff, (2) the project was regarded as an investment in research and development, and (3) project setbacks appeared to be temporary problems.

Evidence That Continued Investment Could Produce Large Payoff

Three separate financial analyses of the CONFIG project conducted in 1982, 1985, and again in 1987 provided evidence that a successfully developed and deployed system could have yielded a positive and significant net present value for the company.

The 1982 analysis indicated a net present value of $43.9 million (20 percent discount factor) for the five-year period FY82–FY86. Operating and development costs for the project were projected at $10.4 million between FY82 and FY86. A second financial analysis conducted in 1985 projected a net present value of $55.7 million (20 percent discount factor) for the five-year period FY85–FY89. A third financial analysis conducted in 1987 indicated a net present value of at least $41.1 million (20 percent discount factor) for the five-year period FY87–FY91.

In each of the analyses, it was argued that under virtually all scenarios, CONFIG had a very large potential value. Since all three financial analyses revealed a positive and significant NPV, the potential payoff associated with successful completion of the project may have served as a strong justification for continuation. It is important to note that there were other intangible benefits that were thought to be attainable as well and that these may have had an effect on escalation that was equal or greater than the tangible economic benefits that could be obtained.

Project Regarded as an Investment in Research and Development

Within CompuSys, there was a strong belief that artificial intelligence held great promise as a technology that could be used to solve complicated problems both within the company and for the company's customers as well. One manager who was closely associated with the project explained the escalation in these terms:

> I think it was a combination of optimism which you could call undue or not and a sense that this was a new technology that we were applying to this problem and that experimenting with

it could yield the results that we wanted even if we couldn't see them in front of us at the moment. So there was a kind of technological optimism . . .

There was always a sense that [Jones] would find a way to keep the project going. I think that [Jones] took for granted that the problem was real and that the technology held promise to solve it. He never wavered on that. Even though we sometimes got a cold reception from Sales, it continued to be funded anyway as an R&D project.

In the words of one executive:

Senior management had developed so much faith in the technology that they continued to fund it regardless of what the data said.

Project Setbacks That Appeared to be Temporary Problems

The limited acceptance among sales representatives was always regarded as a temporary problem that could be overcome with additional resources. Several user surveys that were conducted (in 1984, 1985, and 1986) seemed to suggest that the sales representatives did have need for better configuration support tools in the field and that they might use CONFIG more if issues such as lack of availability, lack of training, poor ease-of-use, and poor response time were resolved (CompuSys internal memorandum, 1987).

To the development team, this feedback implied that the tool could be made acceptable to the sales force with some additional development work and more emphasis on providing the availability, training, and support needed for a successful implementation. This led not only to the continuation of the project but to a massive effort in 1989 to improve the tool's user interface (Keil, et al., 1995a) and to redeploy it with "the necessary infrastructure to ensure optimization of the configuration creation process" (CompuSys internal memorandum, 1989). But despite introducing a far more usable tool with a near textbook implementation program, this multimillion-dollar redeployment effort failed to have a significant impact on sales reps' willingness to use CONFIG (Keil, et al., 1995a; Markus and Keil, 1994).

Psychological Factors

Some psychological factors apparently caused the key decision makers, Jones and Smith, to convince themselves that continuation would eventually lead to success (Brockner, 1992). These factors included the following: (1) prior history of success, (2) high degree of personal responsibility for the outcome of the project, (3) errors in information processing, and (4) emotional attachment to the project.

Prior History of Success

The success or failure of previous projects is a psychological factor that can influence a manager's decision frame for identifying, interpreting, and acting on project information. Prior history of success was evident in the case of CONFIG. The prior success of VERIFIER naturally caused the managers responsible for CONFIG [Jones and Smith] to be confident about its prospects for success. As one individual who was close to the project observed:

> What I saw were [Jones and Smith] building upon a previous success with [VERIFIER] and saying we can hit that home run again.

Staw and Ross' (1987a) model of the psychological determinants of commitment suggests that a prior success may inhibit a decision maker's willingness to re-examine the current course of action, thus promoting escalation. Psychological literature on selective perception (e.g., Allen and Marquis, 1964; Hastorf and Cantril, 1954; Hogarth, 1979) provides additional support for this notion. One would expect decision makers to ignore negative information or to downplay its significance when there is a prior history of success.

High Degree of Personal Responsibility for the Outcome of the Project

Based on interviews conducted with a wide range of individuals throughout the company, it was clear that Jones and Smith were perceived to be the managers most responsible for the continuation of the CONFIG project. Historical data gleaned from company memos and reports confirmed that both Jones and Smith were closely associated with the CONFIG project for a decade or more. Furthermore, many

interviewees were quick to point out that CONFIG was Jones' "baby,"
implying that he was the individual responsible for having initiated
the project.

According to escalation theory, individuals with a high degree of
personal responsibility will have a tendency to engage in self-justification; they will convince themselves that it is better to continue than
abandon because they want to show that their original decision to
pursue the project was "correct." The need to self-justify is heightened
when prior expenditures are irrevocable, public, freely chosen, and
repeated—all conditions that existed in the case of CONFIG. The net
effect of self-justification is to lower the probability that questionable
projects will be reconsidered.

Errors in Information Processing

Managers who reported to Jones and Smith suggested that neither one
of these two individuals wanted to hear negative information. Instead,
Jones and Smith apparently sought out positive information about the
project. As one manager who was closely involved recalled:

> I don't think they [Jones and Smith] ever perceived any
> problem with the product. If they did, they never shared it
> with me or as far as I know anybody in the group. They cer-
> tainly never wanted to hear that there was any problem.

Another individual explained how Jones and Smith would react
when presented with negative information:

> When we did surveys of people in the field the information
> we got wasn't what they [Jones and Smith] wanted, but you
> know denial is so powerful. . . Their response was: "Wrong
> answer, we don't like that answer." They never listened to
> [negative] feedback.

> When I approached [Smith] with negative feedback from
> the field, he would get defensive about it. He would always
> say: "Well, that's hearsay." And we would have to go out and
> conduct additional surveys.

He seemed to be exercising denial. [He'd say] "There must be something wrong with your survey process. Talk to these people individually." Sometimes we would be asked to go back and survey the same individuals again . . . and even if the information was still negative, [Jones and Smith] would find some way to put a positive spin on it.

The type of behavior described above is consistent with escalation theory. As Staw and Ross (1987a, p. 54) observe: "If the objective facts disconfirm one's opinion, the individual will work hard to find reasons to discredit the source of information or the quality of the data itself."

Emotional Attachment to the Project

Several key members of the development team expressed a strong bond with the project. In the words of one manager:

I'm trying to be very objective and pull myself away from being so *attached* to [CONFIG]. After you've had blood, sweat, and tears over it for the last three years, you get *very attached* to [CONFIG] and very defensive of it (emphasis added).

Another individual who had been one of the original CONFIG developers explained his reluctance to abandon CONFIG:

I don't think we want to get rid of [CONFIG]. I don't want to just throw out 10 years of work . . .

Given the level of emotional attachment displayed by various members of the development organization, it is reasonable to assume that Jones and Smith were also emotionally attached to the project. Several sales managers who were in a position to observe the development process commented on the emotional attachment that existed on the part of the development organization in general. As one manager observed:

Some of these guys had five or six years of their life in that project. Their life was in that . . . the emotional baggage of hanging on to it . . . not being able to say: "this isn't going to work" and walking away from it . . .

Social Factors

There also appeared to be some social factors that contributed to escalation: (1) competitive rivalry between Sales and Manufacturing, (2) need for external justification, and (3) norms for consistency.

Competitive Rivalry Between Sales and Manufacturing

Within CompuSys, the competitive rivalry that existed between Sales and Manufacturing was legendary. It is in the context of such rivalry that CONFIG's developers never seemed to consider that their basic design concept might be flawed. While many in Sales viewed CONFIG as a "turkey" of a system, Jones and Smith repeatedly attempted to blame the Sales organization for CONFIG's low acceptance. As two different managers observed:

> They [Jones and Smith] kept saying: "the sales force doesn't understand the tool. They don't want to take the time to learn it."

> The spin that they [Jones and Smith] would always put on the project was that the field just didn't understand . . . that the field just didn't support it.

As research on self-serving biases has shown, individuals are much more likely to attribute negative outcomes to external rather than internal causes (Staw and Ross, 1978). In the case of CONFIG, there is considerable evidence that decision makers saw the failing outcome as the result of ignorant or obstructionist behavior on the part of the sales force. Seen in this light, continuation of the project may have been viewed as the only way for Manufacturing to justify its investment and at the same time exert its will over Sales. For Manufacturing, the alternative of terminating the project would have been tantamount to admitting that Sales was "right" and that manufacturing was "wrong."

Need for External Justification

The need to justify a course of action can be heightened when a decision maker seeks to rationalize his/her behavior to other parties. In the case of CONFIG, there were external constituencies—such as customers and shareholders—that were led to believe that CompuSys was successfully pursuing artificial intelligence both to improve internal processes and as the basis for new service offerings to its customer base.

As early as 1982, journal articles and books began to appear describing the efforts that were underway at CompuSys to build expert systems such as CONFIG. In these writings, CONFIG was typically portrayed as a successful example of how CompuSys had embraced new technology to develop a leading-edge system that would improve customer service. Ironically, there were some sales representatives who never embraced the tool but saw the value in it from a public relations standpoint and referred to it in discussions with customers.

Norms for Consistency

Norms for consistency represent another social variable that may have promoted escalation. In the U.S., for example, substantial rewards are often given to managers "who can turn things around or convert a losing project into a winner" (Staw and Ross, 1987a, p. 58). Prior research has shown that managers who exhibit consistent commitment to a course of action are perceived as strong leaders, suggesting that "persistence is a socially valued style of leadership" (Staw and Ross, 1987a, p. 59). This combination of social norms suggests that there may be a kind of "hero effect" in which society reserves special praise and admiration for leaders who "stick to their guns" and are able to turn things around even when there is a low likelihood of success.

In addition to societal norms that may have favored persistence, there were also strong social norms *within* CompuSys that favored continuation. During the 1980s, it was not part of the company culture at CompuSys to kill projects; instead, failing projects were allowed to die from natural causes. In the words of one manager:

> Part of the culture then was that it was okay to let things linger before someone actually went out and killed them. That was not unusual.

In the case of CONFIG, this meant that managers were unwilling to terminate the project. As another manager observed:

> Nobody wanted to kill it. We're a humanitarian organization. Nobody wanted to shoot it in the head.

Organizational Factors

The fourth and final set of factors that may have promoted escalation were organizational (or political) in nature and included the following: (1) strong advocates who provided continued funding and protection, (2) empire building, and (3) slack resources and loose management controls.

Strong Champions Who Provided Continued Funding and Protection

According to one senior manager:

> There were always signals that CONFIG wasn't being embraced [by the field], but there were some very strong champions inside Manufacturing—largely [Vigilant] and [Jones]. [Vigilant, who was the Manufacturing VP] kept funding it out of his discretionary funds . . . This was a classic example of how [CompuSys] would continue to invest in a project when there were strong advocates—regardless of whether or not it made financial or market sense to do so.

Because of these strong advocates and their high position within the organization, other senior managers within Manufacturing who were critical of CONFIG had only a weak voice. In the words of one senior manager in Manufacturing:

> As long as [Vigilant] and [Jones] had control over it, there was nothing that I or anyone else could do.

While some senior managers outside of Manufacturing argued that CONFIG should be terminated, these arguments seem to have fallen on deaf ears. As one manager recalled:

> I wrote three whistle-blowing memos to three vice presidents . . . I couldn't stop it. It was a sacred cow project.

The presence of such strong advocates clearly promoted escalation. This is consistent with Staw's observation, "If advocates of a project are represented on governing bodies and budget committees charged with the fate of a venture, one may expect substantial persistence in the course of action" (Staw and Ross, 1987a, p. 61).

Empire Building

During the 1980s, Jones and Smith had created and staffed an entire organization whose existence was at least partially dependent on the CONFIG project. Many felt that Jones and Smith had a disincentive to abandon CONFIG because such an action would have threatened the growth of their "empire," thus diminishing their status. The following remarks from three different individuals were typical:

> They [Jones and Smith] were always trying to grow. The staffing level for [CONFIG] never went down. It only went up . . . [CompuSys was] in a period of relative growth and building empires was the thing to do because that was an indicator of how powerful you were . . . It was like: 'Hey, we're going to have our own building.'

> It was kingdom building—people preserving their kingdom and building their power base in order to sustain what they wanted to do in order to make themselves important.

> CompuSys is real good at creating fiefdoms. It's pretty typical throughout the corporation. And I think this was a classic case.

A reasonable interpretation of the above evidence would suggest that Jones and Smith may have had reason to believe that terminating the CONFIG project would diminish their status within CompuSys.

Slack Resources and Loose Management Controls

During the early 1980s, when CONFIG was being developed, CompuSys had plenty of cash, and project justification mechanisms were loose or non-existent. One manager offered the following explanation of how projects were initiated at CompuSys:

> In the early 1980s you'd sort of go tin-cupping to different parts of the organization. When you got enough money raised you went into development. Hopefully while you were tin-cupping you were still in some sort of needs analysis and design. But at some point you reached a critical mass of support and you built it. Oddly enough, you probably

never asked the people who were going to use it if they wanted it . . . you went to people who you thought would want to see this nice thing made. You didn't have to go to any board or council or group or management committee.

In addition to the unusually loose way in which projects were initiated and justified, once a project was started, formal reviews were seldom performed. In the words of one manager who was closely associated with the CONFIG project:

[CONFIG] was subject to review in a somewhat haphazard way. Sometimes it seemed to me that decisions about this kind of thing were made almost in an off-hand way.

Another senior manager explained how the CONFIG project continued to be funded out of discretionary R&D funds without undergoing any type of formal review process:

[As long as Tom Jones was in charge] it never got reviewed. It didn't get into the official budget review process until 1992.

The combination of slack resources and loose management controls that existed at CompuSys during the 1980s led to an environment that actually promoted escalation.

Summary Model of Factors That Promoted Escalation

Figure 1 represents a summary model of the factors that promoted escalation in the case of CONFIG. Consistent with theory, the escalation appeared to be promoted by a wide variety of variables including project, psychological, social, and organizational factors. While most of these factors have been discussed in the escalation literature, the case study revealed several additional factors that have not been widely discussed in previous studies. These factors include: emotional attachment to the project, empire building, and slack resources and loose management controls.

Project Factors

- Evidence that continued investment could produce large payoff
- Project regarded as an investment in research and development
- Project setbacks appeared to be temporary problems

Psychological Factors

- Prior history of success
- High degree of personal responsibility for the outcome of the project
- Errors in information processing
- Emotional attachment to the project*

Social Factors

- Competitive rivalry between Sales and Manufacturing
- Need for external justification
- Norms for consistency

Organizational Factors

- Strong advocates who provided continued funding and protection
- Empire building*
- Slack Resources and loose management controls*

Project Escalation

* Indicates factor that has not been widely discussed in the escalation literature

Figure 1. Summary Model of Factors That Promoted Escalation

Reasons for the Eventual Termination of CONFIG

After more than a decade of development and tens of millions of dollars, the CONFIG project was eventually terminated at the end of 1992. The pattern of escalation was ultimately broken by two factors: (1) the passing away of the project's primary champion, and (2) an external shock to the company.

Project's Primary Champion Dies

In 1992, Tom Jones, the project's primary champion, died abruptly of cancer. As one senior manager recalled: "When [Jones] died, there ceased to be enough support to keep it going." Another manager reflected:

> [Jones] could always find a way to pull the money that he needed to keep it alive. Because he believed in the thing. It was the thing he had staked his career on. After [Jones] died he wasn't around to protect it. He wasn't there to influence the funding.

External Shock to the Company

By the end of the 1980s, CompuSys was confronted with a downturn in the U.S. computer market. Faced with mounting losses during the early 1990s, the company was forced to begin laying off employees and restructuring its operations. Suddenly, a company that was used to operating in a growth mode found itself fighting to regain profitability. This chain of events represented an external shock to the company that appears to have contributed to the cancellation of the CONFIG project. In the words of one manager:

> After [Jones] passed away, there were a lot of organizational changes and [several of] the Manufacturing VPs who had supported [CONFIG] left the company. Then a new guy came in to a situation where resources were scarce because we were in a cost-cutting and down-sizing mode . . . He's like: 'What am I doing? We're spending this on something that nobody really wants. Stop.' He wasn't invested personally in it . . .

Other managers offered similar views, suggesting that the external shock to the organization was a contributing factor in the eventual termination of the project. The following remarks from three different individuals were typical:

> I firmly believe that if we had not run into the financial problems that we ran into as a corporation that [CONFIG] would still be alive and well.

> At this point in our history we are killing projects left and right unless they start producing fairly quickly. I think this is due to the cash constraints that we now face. . .

> Management and controls placed on everything are much more stringent now. There are better established program guidelines now. Projects and programs are much tighter defined.

Summary Model of Organizational Exit from Escalation

Consistent with an earlier model (Ross and Staw, 1993), changes in top management were judged to be an important factor in breaking the pattern of escalation. In the case of CONFIG, however, the death of the project's primary champion was also observed to be a key factor in the eventual withdrawal.

Implications

Given that escalation occurs in IT projects, it is important to understand why it occurs and how it can be avoided. Though the findings reported here are based on a single case study, they have significant implications for practice.

Implications for IT Managers

For IT managers, the knowledge that escalation can occur in IT projects underscores the important role that psychological, social, and organizational factors can play in the successful management and control of IT projects. In the past, IT managers have relied upon traditional project management techniques to manage and control IT projects. While the traditional approaches are useful, it should be noted that they are based on a rational approach to project management and thus tend to ignore some of the other dimensions that seem to be associated with project escalation. The research results reported here suggest the need for a broader view of project management and control that encompasses both the rational approach for controlling projects and a more psychological or behavioral perspective.

To avoid the escalation trap, IT managers can take actions as individuals to minimize their own risk of becoming overcommitted, and they can also institute organizational policies and practices to reduce their organization's exposure to escalation. The first step in avoiding IT project escalation is for managers to recognize that there is a natural tendency to escalate when one becomes too committed to a course of action. Although there is often a fine line between "an optimistic, can-do attitude and overcommitment," there are several questions managers can ask themselves to help determine whether they have crossed the line (Staw and Ross, 1987b, p. 72):

◆ Am I unable to clearly define what would constitute failure for this project? Has my definition of what would constitute success or failure changed as the project has evolved?

◆ Do I have trouble hearing other people's concerns about the project?

◆ Am I more concerned about the welfare of this project than I am about the organization as a whole?

If the answer to one or more of these questions is "yes," then the manager is probably too committed to the project and needs to reevaluate the project before committing any additional resources. Managers can also take steps to avoid becoming overcommitted to a project in the first place. One approach is to periodically evaluate the project from an outsider's perspective. A good question to ask oneself is: "If I took over this job for the first time today and found this project going on, would I support it or get rid of it" (Staw and Ross, 1987b, p. 72)? Another approach is to always consider alternative courses of action in deciding whether to abandon or continue a prior course of action (Keil, et al., 1995b; Northcraft and Neale, 1986). In the case of CONFIG, this approach might have prompted the managers and developers to consider either alternative solutions to the configuration problem or alternative development projects more worthy of resources.

Implications for Organizations

While individuals play an important role in the escalation process, "much of what causes escalation is in the nature of organizations, not people" (Staw and Ross, 1987b, p. 72). Without the right structures and incentives it is naive to expect that all managers will be motivated to ask the above questions. There are several steps, however, that organizations can take to create an environment in which managers are forced to raise the kind of questions that can avoid project escalation. The prescriptions that follow are meant to be suggestive of the types of actions that organizations can take, alone or in combination, to help minimize the risk of project escalation.

Know the Stage of the Project and Manage It Accordingly

Organizations should create systems to insure that project *management* is appropriately matched to the stage of the project. Projects that are initiated to explore applications involving new information technologies need to be managed very differently once they are moved from research mode into full-scale development.

One of the problems with the CONFIG project was that it was regarded as an R&D project even after it had been fully developed and implemented. To avoid this problem, companies should create a tracking system that gives senior management a full accounting of all IT projects and their current stages. Clear guidelines should be established to mark the point at which projects move from one stage to another. In the case of CONFIG, this would have prevented its supporters from using available "discretionary funds" to continue their so-called "R&D project" at the company's expense.

Assess Risks Early (and Often) During the Development Process

As in the case of industrial research and development, IT projects typically progress through a number of defined stages (e.g., analysis, design, development, implementation) between initiation and "commercialization." At the earliest possible stages of this process, managers need to begin asking whether there are any "red flags" or serious exposures they will face in continuing to pursue a project.

Unfortunately, for most IT projects, risk assessments are usually conducted on an infrequent and informal basis if they are even conducted at all (Ropponen and Lyytinen, 1993). However, since most organizations follow some type of software development methodology, it would be a relatively easy matter to include a formal and periodic risk assessment as part of the overall methodology for developing systems. While the precise implementation of such an approach will vary from company to company, the two critical areas that should be included in any risk assessment are: (1) the probability of technical success, and (2) the probability of customer acceptance (Balachandra and Raelin, 1980).

In assessing the probability of technical success it is important to consider both the current state of the technology (i.e., how mature it is) and the prior experience of the project team in dealing with the technology (McFarlan, 1981). Given the pace of change in information technology and the constant evolution of new hardware and software platforms, technical success should never be taken for granted. This is particularly true in the case of large, cutting-edge, projects. That being said, the more significant risk often lies in the area of customer acceptance. In assessing this risk, it is important to ask whether there is sufficient "demand" for a software application *before* investing huge sums of money to fully develop it. Like good marketers, IT managers need to conduct market research in the form of focus groups, surveys, and observational studies. While such research is costly, it is necessary to insure that the system design concept is appropriate. As part of the overall evaluation process, IT managers must also consider whether the right organizational incentives exist for people to *want to use* a proposed system. In the case of CONFIG, this type of analysis would have highlighted the exposures that the project team would later face when they found out that the design concept was flawed and that sales representatives had no incentive to use the system. Finding out about these problems early in the process might have avoided project escalation by allowing the project to be terminated or redirected at an earlier stage.

Conduct Serious Project Audits

No development methodology—even one that includes risk assessment—will prevent escalation unless managers are motivated to follow the methodology. Therefore, to provide the proper incentives, every major IT project should be subjected to a periodic audit process led by someone who is appointed to serve as the organization's devil's advocate. This individual should be charged with protecting the interests of the organization as a whole and should not have a stake in the projects that are being audited. The devil's advocate should be someone who is not only experienced in the area of project management, but who has been trained to ask tough questions and to recognize escalation situations. To insure that his/her recommendations will carry clout and to avoid recrimination, the devil's advocate should report directly to senior management (preferably the CEO).

The devil's advocate would be responsible for assembling a review board. The board should consist of six to eight individuals; some of the members should be selected on a project by project basis, while others should be appointed to serve the board for a fixed number of years. Three or four individuals representing the company's accounting, IS, and human resource management areas should be appointed to serve on the board for three-year terms that could be staggered to provide some continuity. In reviewing projects, this group would then be responsible for including representation from those areas of the business that will be most affected by the system under review.

The review board should normally meet to review projects on a quarterly basis, although the exact review interval will vary with the size and importance of the project. The review itself should be focused on whether or not the project has achieved specific and measurable goals that are tied to system use and business value. Continued support for the project should be withheld if the goals are not specific or if they are specific but are not being achieved. The review should also involve a careful examination of project risks and exposures. Any significant deterioration in the risk profile of the project should trigger a re-examination of the project to determine if support should be withdrawn. In the case of CONFIG, the approach outlined above would have insured that the project was not subject to "haphazard reviews" and might have led decisions makers to question their continued commitment to the project at a much earlier stage. In addition, it would have prevented the Manufacturing organization from continuing to fund a sales support tool that the Sales organization did not want and refused to use.

Reduce the Need for Self-Justification

In order to reduce the psychological need for self-justification, organizations can separate initial and subsequent decision-making concerning a particular course of action (Staw and Ross, 1987a). Subsequent funding decisions should not be made by those who have vested interests in justifying the initial course of action. A more radical approach is to rotate managers in and out of projects to insure that those who initiated the project are periodically replaced by individuals who have more objectivity. In the case of CONFIG, either of these techniques would probably have caused the project to be terminated much earlier.

Another way of reducing the need for self-justification is to reduce the consequences associated with failure (Brockner and Rubin, 1985). In many organizations, key mistakes can have an adverse effect on one's career or lead to job termination. Such a climate is likely to heighten the need for self-justification. Organizations that are more tolerant of failure, however, are less likely to experience project escalation (Staw and Ross, 1987a). It is important, however, to create an appropriate balance. An environment of infinite tolerance could prove to be just as prone to escalation.

Conclusion

This research has shown that escalation can occur in an IT project and has highlighted some of the factors that may contribute to the problem. A company that continues to "throw good money after bad" on an IT project is making a very bad business investment for three reasons. First, the infusion of additional dollars is not solving the business problem for which the system was intended. Second, escalation means that the company is continuing to waste valuable resources. Third, there is an opportunity cost because the company is missing the benefits from alternative uses of these resources. Thus, preventing IT project escalation can be critical in determining whether firms are obtaining real value from their investments in information technology (Markus and Keil, 1994). For researchers and practitioners alike, escalation offers a new perspective on software project management that holds the promise of improving our ability to successfully manage IT projects.

ENDNOTES

1. An earlier version of this paper was presented at the 1995 Academy of Management Conference and published in its proceedings (Keil, 1995a). An earlier formulation of some of the ideas presented here also appeared in Keil (1995b).

2. Escalation does not necessarily imply an increasing rate of investment over time, but rather, refers to a growth in the cumulative amount of resources invested over time. Thus, escalation can be thought of as continued commitment.

3. Staw and Ross (1987a) initially used the term "structural determinants," which they subsequently relabeled as "organizational determinants" (Ross and Staw, 1993).

4. One of the reasons for choosing this particular project was that the history of CONFIG has been well documented and could be studied by reviewing a variety of historical material. The author is particularly indebted to Dorothy Leonard-Barton for sharing data that she collected on the CONFIG project from 1984–1987.

5. The company name, project names, and the names of the individuals involved have all been disguised to provide anonymity.

6. By the early 1980s, CompuSys managers had determined that roughly 25 percent of the orders coming out of Sales exhibited some type of configuration error.

7. Because the two systems were based on the same underlying knowledge base, it is difficult to separate out the resources that went into CONFIG versus the resources that were directed toward VERIFIER. From 1981 to 1991, the size of the development group in which the two projects were housed grew from 21 people to 115 people. By 1991, the group's annual operating budget had reached approximately $45 million. By this point, approximately $15–20 million was being spent annually on maintaining VERIFIER and CONFIG, with an estimated 40–50 percent of these funds being spent on CONFIG.

8. The history and analysis presented here focuses on Jones and Smith because they were identified by many individuals within

CompuSys as being the primary decision makers responsible for the escalation of the CONFIG project.

9. It should be noted that the UDT was not a decision-making body in the sense that it was not vested with the authority to decide whether to continue funding the CONFIG project. However, the UDT meeting minutes did contain critical information concerning the status and ultimate viability of the project. In many cases the decision makers who had the authority to abandon or continue the project were in attendance at these UDT meetings and in all cases, the minutes were widely distributed and available to the key decision makers.

REFERENCES

Allen, T. J. and Marquis, D. G. "Positive and Negative Biasing Sets: The Effects of Prior Experience on Research Performance," *IEEE Transactions on Engineering Management* (11:4), December 1964, pp. 158–161.

Alter, S. and Ginzberg, M. "Managing Uncertainty in MIS Implementation," *Sloan Management Review* (20:1), Fall 1978, pp. 23–31.

Balachandra, R. and Raelin, J. A. "How to Decide When to Abandon a Project," *Research Management* (23:4), July 1980, pp. 24–29.

Betts, M. "Feds Debate Handling of Failing IS Projects," *Computerworld*, November 2, 1992, p. 103.

Boehm, B. W. *Software Engineering Economics,* Prentice Hall, Englewood Cliffs, NJ, 1981.

Brockner, J. "The Escalation of Commitment to a Failing Course of Action: Toward Theoretical Progress," *Academy of Management Review* (17:1), January 1992, pp. 39–61.

Brockner, J. and Rubin, J. Z. *Entrapment in Escalating Conflicts: A Social Psychological Analysis,* Springer-Verlag, New York, NY, 1985.

Brooks, F. P. *The Mythical Man-Month: Essays on Software Engineering,* Addison-Wesley, Reading, MA, 1975.

Cohen, J. "A Coefficient of Agreement for Nominal Scales," *Educational and Psychological Measurement* (20:1), Spring 1960, pp. 37–46.

Cringely, R. X. "When Disaster Strikes IS," *Forbes ASAP,* August 29, 1994, pp. 60–64.

Ellis, V. "Audit Says DMV Ignored Warning," *Los Angeles Times,* August 18, 1994, pp. A3, A24.

Ewusi-Mensah, K. and Przasnyski, Z. H. "On Information Systems Project Abandonment: An Exploratory Study of Organizational Practices," *MIS Quarterly* (15:1), March 1991, pp. 67–85.

Garland, H. "Throwing Good Money After Bad: The Effect of Sunk Costs on the Decision to Escalate Commitment to an Ongoing Project," *Journal of Applied Psychology* (75:6), December 1990, pp. 728–731.

Garland, H., Sandefur, C. A., and Rogers, A. C. "De-Escalation of Commitment in Oil Exploration: When Sunk Costs and Negative Feedback Coincide," *Journal of Applied Psychology* (75:6), December 1990, pp. 721–727.

Gibbs, W. W. "Software's Chronic Crisis," *Scientific American* (271:3), September 1994, pp. 86–95.

Ginzberg, M. J. "Early Diagnosis of MIS Implementation Failure: Promising Results and Unanswered Questions," *Management Science* (27:4), April 1981, pp. 459–478.

Gladden, G. R. "Stop the Life-Cycle, I Want to Get Off," *ACM SIG-SOFT Software Engineering Notes* (7:2), April 1982, pp. 35–39.

Hastorf, A. H. and Cantril, H. "They Saw a Game: A Case Study," *Journal of Abnormal and Social Psychology* (49:1), January 1954, pp. 129–134.

Hogarth, R. M. *Judgement and Choice: The Psychology of Decision,* John Wiley & Sons, New York, 1979.

Johnson, J. "Chaos: The Dollar Drain of IT Project Failures," *Application Development Trends* (2:1), January 1995, pp. 41–47.

Kahneman, D. and Tversky, A. "The Psychology of Preferences," *Scientific American* (246:1), January 1982, pp. 160–173.

Keider, S. P. "Why Projects Fail," *Datamation* (20:12), December 1974, pp. 53–55.

Keil, M. "Escalation of Commitment in Information Systems Development: A Comparison of Three Theories," *Academy of Management Best Papers Proceedings,* 55th Annual Meeting, Vancouver, British Columbia, August 4–8, 1995a, pp. 348–352.

Keil, M. "Identifying and Preventing Runaway Systems Project," *American Programmer* (8:3), March 1995b, pp. 16–22.

Keil, M., Beranek, P. M., and Konsynski, B. R. "Usefulness and Ease of Use: Field Study Evidence Regarding Task Considerations," *Decision Support Systems* (13:1), January 1995a, pp. 75–91.

Keil, M., Mixon, R., Saarinen, T., and Tuunainen, V. "Understanding Runaway Information Technology Projects: Results from an International Research Program Based on Escalation Theory," *Journal of Management Information Systems* (11:3), Winter 1995b, pp. 67–87.

Kemerer, C. F. "An Empirical Validation of Software Cost Estimation Models," *Communications of the ACM* (30:5), May 1987, pp. 416–429.

Kindel, S. "The Computer That Ate the Company," *Financial World* (161:7), March 31, 1992, pp. 96–98.

Kull, D. "Anatomy of a 4GL Disaster," *Computer Decisions,* February 11, 1986, pp. 58–65.

Landis, J. R. and Koch, G. G. "The Measurement of Observer Agreement for Categorical Data," *Biometrics* (33:1), March 1977, pp. 159–174.

Lyytinen, K. and Hirschheim, R. "Information Systems Failures—A Survey and Classification of the Empirical Literature," in *Oxford Surveys in Information Technology* (4), P. I. Zorkoczy (ed.), Oxford University Press, Oxford, 1987, pp. 257–309.

Markus, M. L. and Keil, M. "If We Build It, They Will Come: Designing Information Systems That Users Want to Use," *Sloan Management Review* (35:4), Summer 1994, pp. 11–25.

McFarlan, F. W. "Portfolio Approach to Information Systems," *Harvard Business Review* (59:5), September–October 1981, pp. 142–150.

McPartlin, J. P. "The Collapse of Confirm," *Information Week,* October 19, 1992, p. 12–19.

Mehler, M. "Reining in Runaways," *Information Week,* December 16, 1991, pp. 20–24.

Meredith, J. "Project Monitoring For Early Termination," *Project Management Journal* (19:5), November 1988, pp. 31–38.

Neuman, M. and Robey, D. "A Social Process Model of User-Analyst Relationships," *MIS Quarterly* (16:2), June 1992, pp. 249–266.

Neumann, P. G. and Hoffman, R. "Risks to the Public in Computers and Related Systems: Details of BofA's Costly Computer Foul-up," *Software Engineering Notes* (13:2), April 1988, pp. 6–7.

Newman, M. and Sabherwal, R. "Determinants of Commitment to Information System Development: A Longitudinal Investigation," *MIS Quarterly,* 1996.

Northcraft, G. B. and Neale, M. A. "Opportunity Costs and the Framing of Resource Allocation Decisions," *Organizational Behavior and Human Decision Processes* (37:3), June 1986, pp. 348–356.

Ropponen, J. and Lyytinen, K. "How Software Risk Management Can Improve System Development: An Explorative Study," working paper, University of Jyvaskyla, Jyvaskyla, Finland, 1993.

Ross, J. and Staw, B. M. "Expo86: An Escalation Prototype," *Administrative Science Quarterly* (31:2), June 1986, pp. 274–297.

Ross, J. and Staw, B. M. "Organizational Escalation and Exit: Lessons From the Shoreham Nuclear Power Plant," *Academy of Management Journal* (36:4), August 1993, pp. 701–732.

Rothfeder, J. "It's Large, Costly, Incompetent—But Try Firing a Computer System," *Business Week,* November 7, 1988, pp. 164–165.

Staw, B. M. and Ross, J. "Commitment to a Policy Decision: A Multi-Theoretical Perspective," *Administrative Science Quarterly* (23:1), March 1978, pp. 40–64.

Staw, B. M. and Ross, J. "Behavior in Escalation Situations: Antecedents, Prototypes, and Solutions," in *Research in Organizational Behavior* (9),

B. M. Staw and L. L. Cummings (eds.), JAI Press Inc., Greenwich, CT, 1987a, pp. 39–78.

Staw, B. M. and Ross, J. "Knowing When to Pull the Plug," *Harvard Business Review* (65:2), March–April 1987b, pp. 68–74.

Yin, R. K. *Case Study Research: Design and Methods,* Sage, Beverly Hills, CA, 1984.

4.4 IT JUST WASN'T MEANT TO BE

If you thought the loss of a decade of development time and tens of millions of dollars in the preceding story represents a colossal calamity, prepare for another such story!

This one took six years, cost $200 million, and resulted in nothing. Further, during the course of the project a mess was made of the various relationships of the company in question with its business partners.

Perhaps the strangest thing about this story is that it is about the grocery industry, but the key player in the story is a bank! Perhaps the second strangest thing about the story is that many people still don't see why this project wasn't a good idea, one to be pursued anew at another time. (Warning: These people may in fact be right!)

The subject of this story is a "Point-of-Sale" (POS) system, one whose job is to capture and/or provide certain information automatically when a sale occurs at someplace like a retail store. The retail store in question, as we mentioned earlier, would be a grocery store. The POS system was to capture information on buying trends, by customer, and sell that information to interested manufacturers of products related to what the grocery customer has just purchased.

Now there's a funny thing about POS, one that I really don't understand very well. I've been collecting computing failure stories now for more than three decades, and POS failures have frequently popped up in those stories during that time. (One or more of my earlier books on computing failure contain POS failure stories!) I'm not sure what it is about POS that seems to spawn failure, but it certainly does.

The ending of this particular story is an interesting case in point. Most failure stories kind of end with a hand-wringing final analysis of what went wrong. But in this story, that final word is relatively positive—". . . other direct marketers will save millions of dollars in being able to see [from this story] where Citicorp (the bank in question) went wrong."

But what are the lessons learned here? Is it that the project leader "thought big, and spent big"? Is it that the project focused on rapid growth instead of on bug corrections in the systems already released and in place? Is it that the leader of the project "didn't want to hear bad news"?

Without a clear answer to these questions, I suppose I must look forward to yet another POS failure story in the next book on computing failure that I put together!

CITICORP'S FOLLY? How a Terrific Idea for Grocery Marketing Missed the Targets

by Fred R. Bleakley

It seemed like a marvelous idea at the time: Grocery shoppers would use an ID card that, combined with the electronic scanners at the checkout line, would tell marketers exactly who bought what.

Maxwell House would have the name and address of coffee-drinkers who bought Folgers. People magazine could send a discount offer to everyone who bought People at the grocery store. Gerber would know who was loading up on baby food.

Not only that, but the effort was the work of the deep-pocketed executives of Citicorp, the big banking company with plenty of talent, experience and patience.

But six years later, the effort looks as if it could turn out to be one of Citicorp's biggest follies. The POS (for point-of-sale) Information Services unit has spent about $200 million, generated just $20 million at best in revenue and made a mess of relationships with many grocery chains and consumer goods producers. Citicorp is hitting the brakes. In November, it abruptly canceled its most ambitious program, fired 174 staffers and shunted aside a gung-ho chief executive it had brought in 2 1/2 years earlier to run the program.

A Futuristic Goal

Citicorp says it still believes in the program and looks for a turnaround. But it has quietly set a deadline for real progress. And many industry observers believe the time for Citicorp's plan has come and gone.

I'm probably more guilty than anyone," says the former POS chief executive, Gerald Saltzgaber—and many observers agree with him. But, he adds, "you cannot talk about this without overpromising. It's such a dynamite concept."

At first glance, this seems an odd business for Citicorp, which last year had $14.6 billion in revenue, mostly from banking. Information

Originally published by the Wall Street Journal, *April 5, 1991. Reprinted by permission,* © *1991 Dow Jones & Co., Inc. All rights reserved worldwide.*

gathering, though, was part of a futuristic goal laid out by former Chairman Walter Wriston in 1984 and put into action by his successor, John Reed, after a mountain of consultants' reports.

The skunk works POS operation, begun in 1985 to mine data from grocery stores, was one such venture. Initially, it was going to help supermarkets electronically keep track of and get reimbursement for all the paper coupons turned in by shoppers. Then it hit on the idea of collecting the names of shoppers and selling those lists to consumer goods companies. "This was absolutely breakthrough stuff," says Barry Shereck, one of the group's first executives. Manufacturers would pay dearly to know the heavy users of rival brands, he and others at Citicorp figured.

To get those prized names, Citicorp would offer merchandise, cash rebates, check cashing or bank-account debiting so shoppers would present a scannable store card. Citicorp's ambitious goal was a data base of 40 million active grocer shoppers. "It was a marketer's nirvana," says Wes Bray, managing partner of Market Growth Resources in Wilton, Conn., a consumer goods marketing consultant.

When coupons are mass distributed, already-loyal customers take advantage and much of the rebated money is wasted. But a manufacturer could offer two or three times the normal coupon rebate with much greater success if it could target just buyers of a rival brand.

That could take target marketing to new heights. Targeting was already moving to replace mass marketing because, with so many products competing over to many channels of communication, tailored promotion messages needed to be aimed at particular audiences.

Citicorp's first shot at name gathering, a program called Coupon Bank, promised a whole new way for coupons to work. Instead of clipping coupons in the newspaper, shoppers could receive cash after the scanner electronically tabulated any purchases eligible for coupons. Besides giving manufacturers a more efficient way to spend the billions that go into paper coupons, electronic couponing could save hundreds of millions of dollars in mistakes by store clerks who redeem coupons that are out of date or don't accompany a purchase.

Big Spender

Electronic couponing and other shopper ID programs were still in the development stages when, in 1988, Richard Braddock, then head of consumer banking and now Citicorp's president, asked Mr. Saltzgaber, then a consultant in Chicago, to write up a business plan for the fledgling unit. The two had been friends at General Foods Corp., where Mr. Saltzgaber, now 54, had been a marketing executive.

Impressed with the proposal, Mr. Braddock hired Mr. Saltzgaber in 1988 to take over the 40 staffers headquartered in Stamford, Conn. Mr. Saltzgaber thought big—and spent big. According to people familiar with POS, the unit's budget was $10 million in 1987 and $17 million in 1988, but then jumped to $40 million in 1989 and $125 million in 1990. Mr. Saltzgaber had originally asked for $200 million in 1990. (Citicorp officials decline comment.)

The money went into larger and larger quarters, dozens of salespeople, more than 100 computer programmers, liberal expense accounts, bonuses and tens of millions of dollars worth of computers and workstations. High salaries—$100,000 to $150,000—were paid to middle managers. Mr. Saltzgaber drew a $250,000 salary and $150,000 bonus in 1989, according to one former executive. (He'll say only that his salary was less than $250,000, declining to comment on the bonus figure.)

Citicorp was spending big because it believed the POS unit could be a huge moneymaker. Not everyone agreed. "I had trouble seeing where there would ever be more than $150 million a year in revenues," Mr. Shereck says. "Yet presentations were being made saying it was a billion dollar a year business. I never saw a detailed plan on how it would get there."

'Reward America'

When Mr. Saltzgaber joined POS, it was already working with customer identification programs at supermarkets in Los Angeles, Dallas, Chicago, Denver and Richmond. He quickly championed a new program called Reward America. By awarding cash rebates monthly to customers buying a certain number of specific products, it had the advantage of combining the concept of electronic coupons with a frequent-shopper program, presumably strong incentives for shoppers to ID themselves. In addition, the cost of running Reward America was borne by the participating manufacturers, thus encouraging the likelihood, Citicorp thought, that more stores would get behind the program.

Reward America had been proposed before. Mr. Shereck, now a consultant to troubled companies, says he had rejected it because there wasn't enough in it for everyone, especially the retailers.

Mr. Shereck, who was the senior operating executive of the POS unit in 1987 and much of 1988, recalls disagreements he had with Mr. Saltzgaber over the pace of growth. "Jerry thought the business could be grown faster by spending more money. He said he had approval from Rick Braddock to spend $150 million over three years," says Mr. Shereck. (Mr. Saltzgaber denies saying that or having such authority, and says he had strict performance and budget reviews with Mr. Braddock every six months.)

"I said that was wrong. I didn't think spending vast amounts of money was the answer," Mr. Shereck recalls. "Better to keep a low profile and work out problems quietly." He added that the sign-up of stores and shoppers, as well as management of the data, for the unit's other programs were not going as well as had been expected even then.

Reward America and other POS unit programs had some basic flaws. Grocers didn't sign up in the numbers expected, and some that did join were lukewarm in promoting it to customers. Many didn't want to see manufacturers gain access to shopper names because that would surrender more control over promotions, a long-standing tussle. In addition, if the data were going to be sold, the grocers wanted the revenue. Citicorp insisted on owning exclusive marketing rights, so some big chains, like Super Valu Stores, opted out.

Nice Offices

Worse, Citicorp made grocers pay for the use of data generated from their own stores. Mr. Saltzgaber says Citicorp paid stores to share customer purchase information, but doesn't dispute that Citicorp also charged them for its use.

Bart Foreman, president of Group 111 Marketing in Wayzata, Minn., says grocers also didn't like Reward America because by rewarding shoppers for buying specific brands, it "generates incremental sales for some brands, but the retailer nets out with very little. Yoplait yogurt might do well, but it's at the expense of Dannon, for instance."

Then too, there was what one grocer calls a "We're Citicorp" attitude that smacked of arrogance. Part of that perception stemmed from the contrast between free-spending big-city bankers and the penny-pinching regional grocers. Some retailers were shocked by the large, well-furnished offices of the POS executives when they visited Stamford. "Remember, these were guys who were working out of 10-by-10 space that still had furniture from the '30s," says one marketing consultant.

Without strong store support, shopper participation in Reward America also was disappointing. Most of those who signed up lost interest. Each month they were told what they had bought and how many more of each item they wold need to buy to receive a cash rebate of, say, a few dollars. "It was too complex. They wanted instant gratification," says James McConnell, an executive with Donnelley Marketing.

Rather than spotting these problems early, Citicorp POS, after the pilot program of 27 stores that began in October 1989, quickly launched successive Reward America phases that included first 90 stores and then a total of more than 200.

Technology Overload

Although the Reward America activity was less than had been projected, it sent the POS unit's technology into overload. It couldn't write enough software or handle all the data that flowed in from scanners recording tens of thousands of shopping carts full of groceries daily. "It became their Achilles' heel," says Mr. McConnell. "If they ever get up to the levels they are shooting for, they will dim the lights in the city where they are processing."

Mr. Saltzgaber wishes he had stayed with the initial 27-store pilot before proceeding so quickly. "We would be in better shape if I had not pushed Reward America so fast," he says. "The data was pouring in. I misjudged how difficult it would be to come up the learning curve."

That miscalculation doomed Reward America. "Their marketing and sales teams were out selling before they had the technology in place," says Mr. Bray, the consultant." Citicorp offered tantalizing capabilities and did not deliver."

Shoppers were refusing to provide much demographic data about themselves, for one thing. There weren't enough of them, for another.

And, because so many were dropping out along the way, there was little continuity of purchase patterns by household name. Even worse, the POS unit had not lined up "control" stores without the program, so manufacturers could see what difference Reward America was making.

Clients soon were complaining. The data were late and the promised national data base nowhere in sight. A POS client survey showed that companies like Scott Paper Co., Campbell Soup Co., and Reynolds Metals Co. weren't getting what they had expected. Colgate-Palmolive Corp. vowed it would "never again do business" with the Citicorp unit, according to the study. "What Colgate said they experienced was total disorganization and bad service," the study reported.

Mr. Saltzgaber maintains that manufacturers were happy with Citicorp's programs and on average posted 8% gains in sales at the stores that participated. Still, he knew there were problems. He took his staff to task in January 1989 at a conference in Ryebrook, N.Y. There, quoting a line from what he said was his "favorite 'Nam movie," "Full Metal Jacket," he said, "You've got to walk the walk, not talk the talk."

The hiring juggernaut continued nonetheless. During the first three months of last year, the POS staff, which had already jumped from 40 to 294 people under Mr. Saltzgaber, leapt to 444, a 50% increase. POS had become "exponentially overstaffed for its market potential," says Joseph Fenton, an executive with Computerized Marketing Technologies, Hicksville, N.Y. Suddenly, Mr. Saltzgaber admitted he had overexpanded. In a March 26, 1990, memo to his staff, he said, "Earlier this year, the management of POS received the clear message from you (and ourselves) that we were trying to do too much. . . . We should have taken more action—slowed down the hiring."

But retrenchment was not in the air even then. In mid-May, the unit signed an 11-year lease on 136,000 square feet of space covering five of the seven floors in a new luxury Stamford office building. It took an option, good until Dec. 1, for the other two floors.

Despite all the new spending, largely for Reward America, the POS unit fell well short of its goals. Mr. Foreman of Group 111 Marketing says he had seen Citicorp projections that envisioned the entire POS group ending 1990 counting purchases at 4.8 million households from 800 stores. Instead, the count, including Reward America, was slightly more than half that.

The writing was already on the wall when the headquarters staff assembled last July for the "State of the Business Review." The group was told that the company had picked up only $2 million in revenue for the first six months, which made it highly unlikely it would reach its $29 million goal for the year. "When I heard they had projected $29 million, I knew they were dreaming. It was like someone went crazy on a Lotus spreadsheet and hit the exponential key," says one staffer.

At the same meeting, the results of an employee survey showed that only 54% of them were happy with their jobs, and half felt "the pace of change is becoming too difficult to manage." Mr. Saltzgaber's optimism causes him to have blind spots, say some line managers who reported to him. One says, "He didn't want to hear bad news." As a result, says another, "Everyone was trying to please Jerry: they weren't solving problems or surfacing the reactions from clients." (Mr. Saltzgaber says he can understand the criticism because he does tend to look on the bright side.)

That mood persisted despite Mr. Saltzgaber's casual dress code, which gave the Stamford office the air of a California software firm. Although Mr. Saltzgaber usually wore jeans, a collarless shirt and ankle-high boots, there was still a lot of tension about him, former staffers say. One described that combination as "sort of like PLO chic."

What was missing at POS, say several former executives, was the creative, problem-solving give-and-take that should exist in an entrepreneurial operation.

Back on Track?

Last November, Citicorp pulled the plug on Reward America. Mr. Saltzgaber was replaced in day-to-day control of POS by Bert Einloth, also from General Foods. Mr. Saltzgaber remains chairman, concentrating on "long-range planning." The budget was cut to $65 million this year.

Citicorp officials maintain POS now is on the right track. James Bailey, who oversees the unit and also heads Citicorp's enormously profitable credit-card business, says the POS unit still has the edge over competitors because of the lessons it has learned, the systems it has in place and ongoing programs at supermarkets in six cities that will be expanded.

The unit already has made progress getting purchase data into the hands of clients sooner, says Mr. Einloth. "We now can turn around data in a few weeks," he says. "A year ago it took a few months, and our goal is a few days." Current clients say they like what they see so far.

But even Mr. Saltzgaber concedes that to be effective, POS must build a data base of at least 10 million households, nearly five times what it now has. And the amount of money the current crop of clients is spending is a fraction of what will be needed to support the business and pay back the investment Citicorp has made.

"We are learning a lot from testing with Citicorp, but the results do not indicate we will do something big next year," says Jim Spector, director of consumer promotions for Philip Morris Cos. "It depends on how effective other vehicles are." Besides other forms of electronic target marketing, he says, "a lot is going on in telemarketing and selective magazine bundling."

The clock is ticking on POS, indicating that a make-or-break date has been set. Mr. Bailey says that "at the end of 1992 if all goes as we expect, and we believe it will, this thing will continue."

The irony is that many competitors are finding that targeting marketing really *is* a marvelous idea—and are building businesses by learning from Citicorp's mistakes. Supermarkets now are setting up their own, similar programs. So are big consumer-goods companies. Helping them is a bevy of large and small marketing companies. Catalina Marketing Corp. of Anaheim, Calif., for one, is already entrenched in 3,500 supermarkets with an electronic checkout coupon program.

One thing all have in common: They work with the supermarkets and don't charge them for information, making cooperation much more likely. Other direct marketers, says one former POS executive, "saved millions of dollars in being able to see where Citicorp went wrong."

The Taming of the Shrewd: Stories of Failures of the Best and Brightest

It would be easy to get the impression from the industry stories that preceded this section of this book that computing failure is a uniquely industrial experience. Nothing could be further from the truth.

It is important, in the telling of these stories, to keep in mind the youth of the computing field. As we go to press with this book, the computing and software fields are somewhat more than 40 years old. Oh, of course the history of the field goes back further than that, but the hard, practical realities are that not much happened in the field until the mid-1950s, when such companies as IBM and Sperry Rand began selling computers into a marketplace that seemed reluctant to buy the ephemeral promises those early machines offered. The prospect of computer sales running into double digits, which some computing contemporaries predicted back then, seems laughable today, but back then even the most forward-thinking computing gurus could not envision the tremendous growth that has come about since those early days.

In what remains a somewhat primitive computing culture, then, it should not be surprising that there have been more kinds of computing calamities than industrial project failures. Research projects have formed and failed. Academic institutions have began computing educational programs, only to severely modify or close them. It remains a time of trial and error, and although tremendous progress has been made in moving the field forward, there have been catastrophic failures along the way as well.

In this section we dwell specifically on the failures of the best and brightest of the field. In the first story, we discuss a research institute that began its life with tremendous hope, only to close its software-related project amidst claims that nothing had been accomplished. In the second, we cross the ocean to Japan to explore yet another research project, one which met an ending disturbingly similar to that told in the first story. And in the third, we look at the story of an entire academic institution that had to close its doors when the realities of the business marketplace undermined its lofty goals.

5.1   THE SUCCESSFUL RESEARCH CENTER
THAT FAiLED

In the early 1980s, as progress in the computing field began to accelerate and yet problems in using the field's products persisted, it
became obvious that some kind of infrastructure was needed to help
support the field. At that point in time, there had been successful
computing companies and projects for 25+ years, computing academic programs for 15+ years, and research support from both academic institutions and industry for perhaps 40+ years. But in that relatively short period of time, computing in industry had gone one
direction, and academe and research had gone another. The two rarely
spoke to each other, and when they did it seemed impossible to find
common ground on which to seek agreement. One contemporary
computing spokesman of the time spoke of a "communication chasm"
between industry and academe, a chasm that seemed to be increasing
with the passage of time.

At almost the same moment in time, three different thrusts began
whose goal was to provide this infrastructure, to overcome this chasm.
Two were industry-driven—the Microelectronics and Computing Consortium (MCC) was formed in Austin, TX to use communal industry
funding to explore basic computing issues, and the Software Technology Consortium (STC) was formed just outside of Washington DC to
focus in a similar fashion on software issues. The third thrust was gov-
ernment-driven. The U.S. Department of Defense, seeing clearly that
the future of weaponry lay in computer control, formed the Software
Engineering Institute (SEI) and placed it at Carnegie Mellon University
in Pittsburgh.

In this section, we tell the story of the MCC's software thrust, its
Software Technology Program. As you will see, it started with high
spirits and hopes, only to dissolve into nothing an all-too-short seven
years later. But before we go further with the story of the MCC STP,
let's answer the obvious question of what happened to the other two
thrusts, the STC and the SEI.

The STC exists today, continuing to focus its industry member support funding on software solutions to their problems. Some would

express disappointment at the amount the STC has achieved, in that it is difficult to point to significant achievements that one could attribute to STC efforts, but nevertheless it is important to acknowledge that the STC has succeeded where the STP failed.

The SEI also exists today, and is best known for its Capability Maturity Model (CMM) of the process steps that projects use to build software. Its five process levels (ranging from "chaotic" to "optimized") are fodder for important and ongoing discussions of the best ways to build software, and it easy to say that the SEI succeeded in ways that its founders probably never anticipated.

But what about the MCC STP? Here, the story is considerably more sad.

The author of the story to follow, Les Belady, was in charge of the STP. He tells us of "the most exciting period" of his professional life, and documents the reasons for the failure of the program in a way that only a story insider can. But before we begin his story, I would like to add a few STP recollections of my own.

Probably the most significant achievements of the STP lay, as Belady himself will tell us in his story, in the area of software design. Noted researchers, relying on studies of real designers in real industry settings, carved out an understanding of the inherent processes that designers use to create a design. Having identified those processes, the researchers hoped, they would be able to translate them into design support components of the "Leonardo" tools environment that was the overriding goal of the STP.

Those hopes were to be dashed. The most significant components of the design process, as they discovered in their research, lay in (a) trial and error, and (b) immediacy. Designers quickly formed and expanded design solutions, they learned, in a process that involved enormously fast iterations, beginning with an inadequately small solution evolved into a comprehensive, problem-encompassing one. The goal of this research project was to envision and construct tools to support what turned out to be this iterative, cognitive process. It couldn't be done. Design must be performed at mind speed. And no matter how well we think through the interface a design support tool must have, it will of necessity function at sensory (e.g., fingers on a keyboard) speed, not mind speed.

In other words, the findings of the design-focused research project itself doomed the goals of the overriding research project, the construction of tools to support the process. There was simply no way—not then, not now, perhaps not ever—to provide tools support for the most problem-solving, intimate moments of the designer at work. Research is, in some ways, a cruel endeavor. In this case, that was certainly true. The findings of the project negated its goals.

Now let's step away from the details of the MCC STP a bit, moving upward to the vice-presidential view. Les Belady, tell us what went wrong—as seen from the top—on the MCC STP.

THE 7 YEARS OF MCC'S INNOVATIVE SOFTWARE TECHNOLOGY PROGRAM

by Laszlo A. Belady

In October 1991, fragments of MCC's Software Technology Program (STP) were distributed into the reorganized hierarchy of the consortium, putting an end to perhaps the most coherent and innovative of all major software technology efforts. This article summarizes the history of the program and speculates about the reasons for its relatively early and unsatisfactory termination.[1] (As the author was the leader of the program for its entire life, minus the last four and one-half months, this account cannot be considered entirely unbiased.)

The First Year: Mission, Focus, Vision, Strategy, and Staffing

On September 10, 1984, the Software Technology Program had a secretary and six technical employees: five liaisons—representing DEC, CDC, Rockwell, RCA, and Harris—and a researcher hired by STP's program director just one day before his own arrival. STP was one of the seven programs[2] created by the founding fathers of MCC, which started under the direction of Adm. Bobby Ray Inman, Ret., as president. The spirit in the consortium was high, and everybody—from the Austin community to the shareholders (at that time, there were 18 of them)—was upbeat and friendly.

The small STP staff turned quickly to work. After a full-day meeting with shareholder technical representatives[3] on September 21, it was clear that the main problems with industrial programming lie in the development (and maintenance) of large, software-intensive systems. Since both MCC management and the participating companies offered little and sometimes contradictory advice—except for something like "fix the software problem"—it became obvious that MCC, and in particular STP, would have to take the initiative for the direction of the programs.

This was a tall order, quite unusual for someone coming from IBM where every new idea or direction must be presented to, and approved by, numerous organizations, experts, and executives before anything can happen. How refreshing was Admiral Inman's inspired leadership,

Originally published in American Programmer, *January 1992. Used with permission.*

with significant decisions delegated to the program directors and bureaucracy held to a delightful minimum!

This freedom of choice, offered by both "customer" and MCC management, was of course a mixed blessing. While we received an immense amount of advice—from academia and elsewhere—as to what to do for software research, we quickly realized that we could not do everything and that we should not mimic an academic computer science department. We should certainly rely on good academic research, for instance in theoretical areas for which the university environment is more nurturing, but we should exploit our real advantages: potentially more intimate involvement with the ultimate customer, namely, the industrial software developer, and the capability of establishing a set of coherent projects, sharing a vision and feeding on each other's results. This led to STP's sustained belief in *problem-driven* research that is *focused* on an emerging and increasingly important area.

By the end of 1984, our direction evolved along the following lines: given our mission, namely, to improve programming, productivity and the quality of the resulting product significantly, we would attack the large-scale (if you like, organizational) programming process, leaving the problem of small programs written by individuals or by informal teams for others. We must aid the professional, systems-oriented software engineer.

To focus further, we selected requirements formation and systems design as the "upstream" phases of the standard software process,[4] the phases that ultimately lead to more formal specifications. Specifications then form the basis for trained programmers of the "downstream" to construct machine interpretable programs. So we started talking more and more about *design,* specifically early systems design, which we thought included decisions about hardware. Indeed, the names of the first four groups we formed at the end of 1985, once we were large enough, were design environments, design information, design interface, and design process.

We organized a workshop on "interdisciplinary design" in Austin quite early in 1985. This meeting was the first of its kind to which we invited not only software researchers and practitioners, but also, as speakers, design theorists and chief designers of complex (but not necessarily software) projects. Another STP innovation was to launch, again in Austin, the "computer-supported cooperative work" sequence of conferences.

Finally, we thought that computer science was too compartmentalized: for instance, software engineering and distributed systems were studied by researchers separately, without much interaction. We wanted to be in the intersection of these disciplines, and since we thought that distributed systems would be even more challenging to design than serial ones, we launched an effort in this area.

This brief article does not permit the enumeration, not to mention elaboration, of many other important facets of shaping STP during its early phases (which, incidentally, may have been the most exciting period of this author's life). What we did was the forging of a lasting focus[5] based on a shared vision. This vision, in turn, led us to a problem-driven approach, to selecting research areas, to openness for incorporating solutions even if they came from the outside (e.g., universities), to the insight that software design transcends pure programming and that technology developed for its support may also be useful to aid the design of other complex systems.

One issue, however, deserves more attention. This is our process of building the team, almost the only asset a research organization like STP has. Here, unfortunately, we yielded to pressure from both "owners" (shareholders) and MCC management to build up rapidly. This resulted in somewhat lower quality than a slower staffing process might have, but more important, it made later "team building" more difficult. The newcomers were mutual strangers, each looking for something meaningful to do since there were no existing projects to fit the experience of the typical researcher we hired. I had to learn my lesson the hard way.

There was another sign of early impatience: in our sixth month of existence, I was courageous enough to call our first "Program Technical Advisory Board" meeting with our shareholder representatives. In the true tradition of short-term thinking and in a rather massive misunderstanding of our research vision, one delegate stood up and asked: "Where are the deliverables?" We had a hard time answering the question.

The Middle Years

After about two years, the major effects started taking shape. The method with which we achieved this is, I believe, still the best: move deliberately, but push ahead early with some rough ideas. As you move and do, getting your hands dirty, you'll learn from your experiences and find the right way.

We had only one shared "mantra" (as Stu Feldman of Bellcore referred to it), and we called it "Leonardo." The essence of this was that we perform good industrial research toward a comprehensive (software) design environment called Leonardo, which would bring together the required variety of people—programmers, users, customers, managers—via a network of interactive workstations. While we organized ourselves into four groups, spontaneous "activities" based on one or more person's ideas could emerge and eventually become a "project," as long as it was judged to be consistent with Leonardo. (The detailed description of this "activity" versus project dynamics lies outside the scope of this article.)

Several projects emerged. We started building an environment for LISP-based programming that we called DELI. Aided by my 10-year contact with Professor H. Rittel[6] of Berkeley, we imported the "issue-based information system" concept and merged it with Hypertext-oriented graphics, ending up with our own gIBIS technology. We designed and built a "groupware" laboratory and organized history's first "computer-supported cooperative work" workshop to which we invited everybody interested in the subject in 1986. We started work in reusing design, not just code segments. And our Petri net-based language effort gave us the chance to offer a graphic aid to design distributed systems better.

Of course, as in other organizations, communication was a continual problem: first, not the entire staff "bought in" to the Leonardo concept, and many researchers tended to continue their old line of research; second, while program management put lots of energy into keeping all efforts well aligned and synergistic with each other, some individuals spent too little time in understanding and discussing STP research beyond their own efforts and so became influenced by other people's work.

Over the years the original project composition changed, thanks to our dynamic "activity" mechanism. By the end of the 1980s, we had gIBIS, a graphic distributed system building tool called VERDI, a brand-new effort in (human) coordination technology based on our distributed system experience, a design recovery (also reverse engineering)[7] tool built upon our reuse work, a new effort in the practical use of formal methods, and, by transfer from another program, a logic-based database and programming language called LDL.

The Leonardo concept faded away: we had to give up building even an incomplete environment, due to the very difficult problem of technology transfer. The DELI prototype was transferred elsewhere for commercialization, although we kept experimenting with "systems integration technology."

The Last Two Years

The last two years were characterized by a reduction of funds. For instance, while STP peaked in 1986 with 10 shareholders (Bellcore and Motorola joined the original 8), by 1989 only 6 remained. We lost RCA and Sperry because of mergers and acquisitions, while Lockheed and Harris lost patience with the sluggish absorption of technology. The remaining shareholders changed their funding policies in different ways. The end result was a drop in the budget available for the program.

By then we understood and practiced the transfer of technology much better. It is sad that the founding fathers did not foresee the efforts needed back in the shareholder organizations to work with MCC and to prepare for the absorption of novel technology. By the time this need became clear, the money to support it was simply not there.

It is worth mentioning that the six core shareholders—at least their regular visiting representatives—were on our side; they kept saying how satisfied they were with the program's direction and approach, and they encouraged us to "market" more aggressively (i.e., go after other companies to join in).

This was a new task for the entire staff. We did not anticipate the huge amount of time, travel, and effort this marketing venture would require. It became a continuous crescendo, culminating in a sizable professional marketing staff and a huge load on all the senior people: almost daily travel and presentations.

Yet it was not successful. Most prospects believed they should be able to join for just a couple thousand dollars; they compared us to universities with regard to funding. When we created individually supported projects out of the program, the complexity of marketing increased, and we ended up with meager results.

Why did STP, along with MCC's CAD-VLSI program, have such a short life and so little direct impact on the software industry? The answer is complex, and the brief history I have given offers a glimpse at some of the pieces, among them underestimating the time scale of a new research effort, leading to shareholder impatience; an insufficient budget for the cost of absorbing the technology back home at the participating companies, resulting in a "gap" between research results and finished software tool usable in the trenches; delayed discovery of the marketing necessary to secure sufficient, and patient, funding; shareholder company mergers and acquisitions; and other changes in management resulting in decision makers unfriendly to MCC and the concept of consortia in general.

Other possible reasons for failure are the following:

♦ STP was embedded into an essentially "microelectronics" research environment. On the surface this looked very progressive and promised interdisciplinary work, but in reality it provided a hardware-flavored management with reduced understanding of and sympathy for software.

♦ During the second half of the 1980s the CASE industry started flexing its muscles, offering packaged and sometimes turnkey tools to support selected phases of the software process. These tools were attractive because they were closer to "industrial strength"—difficult to reach with research-only funds—and thus competed well with STP's output.

♦ Many participants had their own research or at least their own advanced development groups in software technology. These people were not friendly to STP. Instead, they lobbied to channel funds intended for MCC into their own organizations. And all this in the face of shrinking funds available for any longer term research at all!

♦ As a result of the "what have you done for me this week" atmosphere of the late 1980s, we lost many good people who were not willing to spend their creative energies for presentations and salesmanship. They went to larger, more stable organizations.

♦ We did not build up a sufficient network of university contacts to tap academic talent via joint efforts and intensive exchange of ideas. While we believed, from the beginning, that this would be important, the implementation failed.

♦ Finally, in spite of all our efforts, we could not build a bridge to our *real* customers; we did not even find them in the maze of the large organizational bureaucracies of our participants.

There were shareholder technical committee members on our side, but their influence—indeed their experience—was rarely on a par with that of a powerful software development "line" executive. When we occasionally succeeded in finding such a champion, we were well respected and had "broad bandwidth" relations with the respective company.

Summary

Given the lack of patient funding and time, perhaps we were too ambitious. Instead of attacking the design of complex systems—a huge and persistent *problem*—perhaps we should have joined others and continued research along established lines of *technologies,* such as programming languages, object orientation, testing, and the like. I learned from this experience. I hope that with this article, others will too.

NOTES

1. Editor's note: MCC, Microelectronics and Computer Technology Corporation, was chartered in 1983 and based in Austin, Texas. The May 1989 issue of *American Programmer* contains an article by Ed Yourdon describing the organization.

2. Four of the seven programs—parallel processing, database, human interface, and artificial intelligence—were collectively referred to as advanced computer architecture (ACA) and were later merged into a single program called advanced computing technology (ACT), resulting in only four major programs in MCC.

3. Each shareholder was free to support any number of programs but had to support at least one. By the end of 1984, STP had CDC, DEC, Harris, Lockheed, RCA, Rockwell, Sperry, and NCR as "participants."

4. While the author had been quite active since the early 1970s in making software maintenance an accepted research topic, in STP we chose not to go into this area directly but rather to keep the focus sharp and hope that well-designed systems would be more maintainable. As we will see, this rule was slightly violated five years later.

5. It is interesting that the chosen focus (upstream of large-scale systems development, etc.) remained unchallenged during the entire life of STP.

6. Also the originator of "wicked problems."

7. This was clearly in support of maintenance.

5.2   THE FAILED RESEARCH PROJECT THAT
SOME CALLED A SUCCESS

Let's hold the clock still here for a moment. We've just stepped away from a failed MCC Software Technology Program, sobered by the massive "unsatisfactory termination" of the work of a bunch of really bright people who were seeking a better way to build software.

Across the Pacific Ocean in Japan a mighty eastern culture is beginning to focus its sights on software, as well. If establishing an infrastructure to support computing and software is important to U.S. business and government interests, it is at least as important to the Japanese. This was, after all, the era in which Japanese industrial might was seen as ready to take over the world. Several computing research thrusts began there at about the same time as the STP, STC, and SEI were getting well underway here in the United States.

Perhaps the most visible of those Japanese computing research thrusts was the Fifth Generation Computing project. I well remember sitting in a meeting room at the top of a tall skyscraper in Tokyo in about 1983, listening to a presentation on that research project to be, during which the Japanese researchers presented their proposed achievements. The reaction of the audience was mixed. Some Americans looked on with alarm, concerned that if the Japanese succeeded in what they proposed, they would take the lead in the rapid race to lead the computing field. But others of us had a more quizzical look on our faces. Those Japanese researchers, we realized, were proposing—in the course of their research project—to solve some of the leading unsolved computing research problems of the time. We had quizzical looks on our faces because most of us believed that there was a reason why those computing research problems were unsolved, and that reason was that they were unsolvable!

If those who looked on with alarm were correct, of course, the resulting Japanese research results would indeed vault them into global superiority in the computing field. But if those of us with quizzical looks on our faces were right, on the other hand, then the Japanese were about to embark on one of the greatest financial boondoggles in the history of the computing field!

For better or for worse, we quizzical-look people were right. The Fifth Generation Project struggled on for several years, never solving any of the unsolvable problems it needed to solve in order to produce results, wasting gazzilions of yen along the way, eventually dying with a whimper. I would love to bring you the story of that failure here in this book, because it is perhaps the Mother of all computing research failure stories, but I am not aware that it has ever been told in any cohesive fashion anywhere.

So we'll settle for next-best here. A few years after the Fifth Generation Project got underway (but before it crashed and burned), the Japanese embarked on an important but less ambitious parallel research project. This was to be the Sigma project, which involved (as, interestingly, did the MCC STP) the goal of constructing better tools to assist software developers. In the acronym-based spirit of the time, these tools were called "CASE" (computer-assisted software engineering) tools. The research goals were much less ambitious and more realistic than the Fifth Generation project, and many of us—even those of us with occasional quizzical looks on our faces—suspected that on this project, the Japanese would succeed. However, even success would not lead to global domination of any part of the computing field—there were many vendors of marketplace CASE tools (largely in the U.S.) already, and IBM was at the same time embarking on its (equally ill-fated) AD/Cycle integrated CASE tools project. In short, even if Sigma had succeeded, the face of the computing field would probably have been little changed.

For that reason, the failure of the Sigma research project was more surprising than the failure of the more visible and exciting Fifth Generation Project. Why did Sigma fail? In the story to follow, Ed Yourdon, one of the best and brightest of computing's gurus, has just returned from a trip to Japan to check on progress in the computing field there. It is 1991, and rumors that the research project is a disaster have just begun to hit the computing press. At that point in time, Sigma might still have turned out to be a success (note that Yourdon referred to it as a "public success, but a private failure"). What Ed Yourdon did not know then, but which we all know now with magnificent hindsight, is that the whole CASE tools industry was to be a disaster. Too much had been promised, and too little was to be delivered.

Like the design tools envisioned by the MCC STP research people, it was simply not possible to build tools to accomplish what too many CASE hypesters had promised. It is not that CASE tools were a failure per se. Used appropriately, most CASE tools were (and are) helpful, probably reducing the cost of software development by 10–20%, a modest but worthwhile achievement. But not the "order of magnitude" (10 times better) promises that too many had forecast.

Sigma, like most other CASE tool efforts, was to founder on the horns of the dilemma that it could not possibly deliver on all the promises that had been made for it. So, Ed Yourdon, tell us the Sigma story, circa 1991.

SIGMA: Public Success, Private Failure

by Ed Yourdon

Those of us with an interest in international software developments have watched the Sigma project with a great deal of fascination over the last five years. For those who have never heard of Sigma, it's Japan's $200 million CASE initiative.

In February 1990, *Nikkei Computer* published an article entitled "Sigma: The $200 Million Disaster." Rumors about the article began circulating through the software community at the ICSE conference in Nice last March, but they were difficult to confirm since the majority of us couldn't read Japanese, and nobody could find a translation. Rumors and reports have continued to circulate, so it was with some anticipation that I visited the offices of Sigma System, Inc., this trip.

The bottom line is, in public, the project is being declared a success, and the original five-year research project has now been spun off into a self-sustaining corporation. In private, though, nearly everyone I spoke with (except for the people I met at Sigma System) agreed that the overall project was indeed a failure. However, nobody wanted to go on record with such a statement because

♦ many of the knowledgeable people in the Japanese software industry work for companies that funded the original project and are still investors in the current spin-off.

♦ nobody wants to go on record criticizing a project that was the brainchild of MITI (Sigma's original director, Kouichi Kishida, did offer some public criticisms and subsequently left the project).

♦ it is not part of the normal Japanese culture to offer harsh criticism or to dissent in public.

This is hardly a foreign concept. How many American CASE vendors would go on record today stating that AD/Cycle is a disaster and that it will fail if it continues in its current direction? What sort of awful penalties would result from such a public castigation of IBM?

In private, the knowledgeable software engineers from Hitachi, Toshiba, NEC, Fujitsu, and other companies with whom I spoke offered the following explanations of the Sigma failure:

Originally Published as part of "Japan Update," in American Programmer, *February 1991. Used with permission.*

1. *Mainframe orientation of the Sigma sponsors.* An enormous number of hardware and software companies were members of the Sigma project, but the large mainframe vendors—Fujitsu, NEC, Hitachi, Toshiba—dominated. As we have seen in the United States, mainframe vendors tend to be biased toward mainframe CASE tools and have often been slow to move to workstation-based tools. And mainframe vendors, because of their history and orientation, often emphasize lower-CASE tools such as source code libraries and text editors ("You can edit COBOL programs and FORTRAN programs with the same editor!" Wow!) rather than the upper-CASE tools that provide automated support for analysis and design.

2. *Emphasis on developing a specialized UNIX-based Sigma operating system.* American CASE tool vendors seem to understand instinctively that they have enough work to do building tools on top of standard operating systems. While they may bitch and moan about the limitations of MS-DOS or OS/2 or UNIX, they surely aren't going to waste any time trying to get into the business of building their own operating systems.

   Germany's Softlab, on the other hand, is quite proud of the effort it has invested in its own window manager and multitasking software for Maestro II; it sits on top of MS-DOS, and, while it may be the most elegant 68K bytes ever written, it nevertheless represents a distraction from the vendor's *real* business of building tools.

   Sigma apparently decided to take this a step further by defining its own operating system as an extension of UNIX. The problem is that there isn't any one standard version of UNIX yet, and the major dialects continue to evolve, with the majority of new releases and features coming out of the United States. Hence Sigma spent some of its time and energy simply trying to keep up with UNIX, when it could have been spending its time building tools.

3. *Schedule and budget problems.* The original Sigma project began in 1985 and was scheduled to be converted into a commercial enterprise in April 1990. I haven't seen a detailed schedule or budget for the original research effort, but I have been told that only two years and $50 million were devoted to the actual

building of tools. This may not seem like a problem until you realize that Sigma's original concept involved some 70 tools. Ask any CASE vendor how much it would cost to build a full-spectrum suite of CASE tools, and you're likely to hear numbers closer to $100 million and schedules closer to five years than two years.

In any case, the budget and schedule pressures apparently led to a decision simply to convert a number of existing tools (lower-CASE tools, for the most part) into the Sigma format and architecture. (The official Sigma statement is that budget and schedule limitations led to a decision to build "better" tools rather than "more" tools.)

But wait. How can you retrofit existing tools into a modern repository-centered CASE environment without problems? Aha! Therein lies another dilemma: the original Sigma project didn't include a repository (more about that later).

4. *Politics.* Joint ventures and consortium efforts invariably involve political issues, whether they take place in the United States, Europe, or Japan. If you're a contributor to a project like Sigma, do you contribute your best people? Your best tools? Your best ideas? How do you reach compromises on technical issues that may put your own company's hardware and software products at a disadvantage?

In addition to all the normal problems one could expect in this area, Sigma ran into another problem based on its objective of creating a national repository of reusable software components. Who would own the components? Who would hold the copyrights? How would royalties be paid? Who would be liable if there were software defects in the components? And on and on and on. Companies in the United States have enormous difficulty dealing with these questions at the corporate level, so it's not surprising that the Japanese should have problems resolving these issues at the national level.

In spite of problems, Sigma had indeed passed into its second phase and does exist as a stand-alone, revenue-generating organization. And while it may have its share of problems, its very existence suggests that it was not a complete disaster. As Fujino of Fuji Xerox Information Systems commented to me, Sigma may have been at least a partial success by focusing attention on the need for standardized workstations (a problem that the U.S. CASE industry seems to have avoided entirely by simply accepting the de facto IBM PC "standard" for the majority of its products and tools).

Sigma's Yukio Sugahara made a presentation of the current Sigma status and plans during my visit. Among other things, he described the organization of the Sigma Members Association, which consists of some 102 companies. I won't bother listing the 50-odd tools in the current Sigma inventory; you can get more information by contacting the Sigma office (see Sources).

After listening to the Sigma presentation, I was left with the following impressions:

◆ The lack of a repository is a major technical flaw in the current Sigma architecture, and it does not appear that the problem will be fixed soon. I was told that the Sigma project began "prior to the repository concept," an arguable point. While it may be true that in 1985 no CASE vendors included the word "repository" in their marketing literature, it was certainly clear by 1987 or 1988 that tool integration was going to be important and that it could only be achieved through some kind of common storage mechanism. In any case, the fact that Sigma didn't include the repository in its 1985 plans is not the issue; the issue is that Sigma *still* doesn't have a repository. When I asked whether Sigma plans to interface with AD/Cycle, the answer was that there are "no plans today for AD/Cycle." What about IRDS and PCTE? Well, they're looking at them and studying them, and they will listen to their members to see what they think.

◆ There don't seem to be any current plans to interface Sigma with existing third-party (non-Japanese) CASE tools. I was told that a committee has been established to look into this possibility. Meanwhile, Excelerator, KnowledgeWare, Cadre's Teamwork, and IDE's Software Through Pictures are making important inroads into Japanese MIS organizations. How are those going to fit together with Sigma?

◆ With no repository and therefore no real-world *experience* with repositories, I didn't sense a great appreciation for the repository technology issues with which major American CASE vendors are grappling. Must the repository reside on a mainframe host, or should the user have the freedom to place the repository on a PC or file server? Must the repository be centralized, or should there be a capability for a distributed repository? And should the repository *implementation* be cased on a disk-based relational DBMS technology, or should it be based on an optical-storage OODBMS technology?

My hosts at Sigma said they are thinking about these issues but have not reached a conclusion. However, there did appear to be some consensus that a distributed repository would be a necessity for the future, reflecting the trend in Japan toward physically distributed software development organizations.

◆ Reverse engineering is not yet a big part of Sigma. There are some tools that will produce design-level structure charts from source code but nothing on the level of sophistication of Bachman Information System's data-oriented reverse engineering tools or any of the other forms of reverse engineering tools that are beginning to pop up in the United States and Europe. This certainly doesn't mean that Japan is oblivious to the problem or ignorant in the technology, as illustrated by the fine work that Horiuchi's group is doing at Hitachi. But it does not appear to be a high priority at Sigma.

So much for my opinions of Sigma. They probably don't matter much since I'm not likely to be a customer of Sigma CASE tools, no matter how good they might be. What really matters is what the Japanese marketplace thinks. When I asked for estimates of the number of Sigma tools being used—for example, how many copies? How many seats? How many software engineers are actually using them?— I was told there were no estimates. Whatever the number, it's apparently fairly small. It remains to be seen whether the number will increase over the next couple of years now that Sigma is in a position where it needs to generate revenues to justify its continued existence.

SOURCES

Terunobu Fujino
Manager, Planning Department
Fuji Xerox Information Systems Co., Ltd.
16-6 Nishishinjuku 3-chome
Shinjuku-ku, Tokyo 160
JAPAN
fax: +81-33-378-6244

Hajime Horiuchi
Manager
Hitachi Ltd.
Computer Division
6-27-18, Minamiohi
Shinagawa-ku, Tokyo 140
JAPAN
fax: +81-33-700-2589

Yukio Sugahara
Senior Staff
Advanced System & Technology Division
Sigma System, Inc.
Akihabara Sanwa Toyo Building 6F
16-8, 3-chome, Sotokanda,
Chiyoda-ku, Tokyo 101
JAPAN
fax: +81-33-255-0437

5.3   BLIGHT COMES TO THE IVY-COVERED WALLS

Academic institutions, it is easy to imagine, last forever. Those hallowed halls of Cambridge or Oxford or Harvard or Yale have been around now for centuries, and they show little sign of going away.

So it will probably surprise you to learn of one academic institution that totally failed. And it will probably surprise you even more to learn that the major thrust of that institution was in the computing field. Isn't it a giant irony that, in the computing era, a significant academic institution focused on computing joined the computing calamities that we have discussed in this book?

The name of the school was the Wang Institute, and its focus was on the software field. Let's step back to the beginning, the better to understand the failure story to follow.

Wang Labs was an early powerhouse in the computing field. That was a long time ago, of course, and we have already seen (earlier in this book) the story of its demise. But it is important to remember, for the sake of this story, that An Wang—the founder of that powerhouse company—was an early mover and shaker in the computing field.

In the midst of Wang's success, he performed one of the most generous public service efforts of any computing professional I know of. He took some of his money and started up an academic institution. Wang Institute, it was called, and it was designed to produce graduates in that new field called "software engineering." In Wang's vision, and in the minds of many of us who agreed with him, there was a gap between the too-theoretical computer science field, and the too-business-application focused information systems academic field, and as a result of that gap few students were emerging from the halls of academe with any practical background in the construction of software for fields other than information systems. Software engineering was to be the academic field to fill that gap.

Ever the innovator, Wang took over an old but dignified religious complex, converting its buildings into his Institute. I remember the magnificent chapel of the institution, an architectural marvel, where some of the classes were taught. It was a wonderful mix of the best of antiquity (if anything American can be called "antiquity") and the best of "today."

Unfortunately, as we will see in the story to follow, Wang Institute succeeded only for a short while, and then disappeared from the academic scene. Fortunately, however, the academic field of software engineering that his institute pioneered persisted, and there remain several thriving software engineering programs (largely in graduate schools) today. I am proud, for example, of my own faculty affiliation with the similar program at Seattle University, which is still pumping out MSE (Master of Software Engineering) graduates to this day.

Before you read this contemporary account of the demise of Wang Institute, it is important to share one more piece of hindsight insight. What killed Wang Institute, more than its own internal failings (discussed in the story that follows), was the slowly growing demise of Wang Labs itself. What started out as a generous contribution to the software engineering field became a terrible drain on the resources of that dying company.

And now, on to Galen Gruman's account of the demise of Wang Institute.

NEW SE PROGRAMS PLAN TO AVOID
WANG INSTITUTE'S MISTAKES

by Galen Gruman

Beset by huge financial shortfalls, the Wang Institute of Graduate Studies in Tyngsboro, Mass., closed Aug. 17 after founder and primary benefactor An Wang discontinued funding.

Wang's closing prompted the Computer Society's Technical Committee on Software Engineering to express concern about the potential effects on software engineering as an academic discipline, fearing the closure of the highly praised institute could make the start-up of similar programs elsewhere more difficult. "The Wang program was being used as a model. It's really the momentum that was being established [that concerns us]. And they had a lot of weight," explained committee chair Lorraine Duvall, a consultant in Rome, N.Y.

But Wang's closure has not prevented several other software-engineering programs that have geared up in the past year. These programs may benefit from the lessons learned from Wang's failure, lessons that may prevent similar shutdowns in the future, according to those involved in the new efforts at the Rochester Institute of Technology and George Mason University.

High Costs Blamed

Wang's biggest problem was its costs, according to several people interviewed. "It was too expensive to run. It was nowhere near break-even," said J. Joseph Meng, Boston University's vice president for external programs. Boston University bought Wang Institute's physical plant and will use it as an extension campus.

Wang had asked several universities to continue the software-engineering program, but none would because of its high cost, Meng said. "They were hurting for an academic institution to take on the [software-engineering] degree," he explained, but "we've all concluded that the way it's set up, it couldn't have been run on a financially sound basis."

Originally published in IEEE Software, *September, 1987. Used with permission.*

The institute spent more than $100,000 per student but only received a $10,000 return, largely because of its five-to-one faculty–student ratio and small number of students, said James Palmer, director of the new Center for Software Systems Engineering at George Mason University. Wang's losses are estimated in the tens of millions of dollars. Wang Institute would not confirm the amounts, but the estimates were made by Meng, Palmer, and others.

Despite its costs, the software-engineering program did not cause Wang Institute's closure, said Susan Gerhart, a researcher at the MCC Software Technology Program in Austin, Texas, and a former Wang Institute professor. The program "was not set up to ben autonomous entity. If you separate it [from the rest of the institute], it's no more expensive than any other academic program," she said.

Once An Wang decided to stop funding the institute, it had no way to make up the lost income, Meng said. "They lost their sugar daddy," said Wiley McKinzie, chairman of the Rochester Institute of Technology's Computer Science and Technology School.

Before it closed, Wang Institute had 11 professors, 34 staff members, 28 full-time students, and 27 part-time students, a press release announcing the closure said. About 170 students have attended the institute since it was founded in 1981, the release said.

(Wang Institute officials did not return several phone calls to discuss the closure, and spokesmen for Wang Corp., a separate firm headed by An Wang, said they could not speak for the institute.)

Summary: Now Remind Me— What's So Great About Failure?

The directions were fairly clear. Take this bumpy, dusty, gravel cum dirt back country road about 40 miles into the Sierra Nevada wilderness. At the end of the road, you'll find . . . Hold on a minute; we're getting ahead of the story here.

I turn off the main highway, head the car up into the hills, not sure I really want to subject my non-SUV to a roadway that is deliberately unkind to a softly-sprung, highway-designed car. Billows of dust blow up behind the car, as I accelerate to a scary 40 miles per hour, a nearly-unsafe speed on this rutted and twisty road. There's nothing commercial or residential along the way; the roadway is lined with precisely nothing. Well, perhaps a Ponderosa or Jack pine or two, and a rattler that serenades us off in the distance. We're heading toward the ends of the earth.

Time seems to stand still. The heat bounces off everything around us, turns the car into an oven. The low humidity whisks every ounce of moisture off our skin before we even know it is there. I turn on the windshield washers to clean the front window; the water evaporates before the wiper can swipe it. With no water source along the road, we're going to have to peer through splattered bug juice for another hour or more.

One more turn, and a flat plain opens ahead of us. There, off in the distance, is what we have come for. The ghost town of Bodie, on the Nevada-California border. A leftover relic of the silver and gold mining rushes of over 100 years ago.

It is surprisingly intact for a town that has had no substantial habitation in well over 100 years. The same dryness that has parched our throats and left the bugs on our windshield has preserved the buildings. There are 100 or so wooden homes still standing here. Their doors front on streets that haven't seen residents walking down them in longer than we can imagine.

The wind whistles through the streets, picking up tumble weeds and rolling them along as if propelled by little boys. Doors swing idly, moved by the unseeable hands of the wind. Curtains rustle at the windows of the homes.

Curtains? After all this time there are still curtains? They are torn and faded, ragged impostors, but they still billow in the windows, as if inviting the former residents to return. "I'm just as livable as ever," the house seems to be saying through its curtains.

But no one will be coming back.

There is a wide place in the road, a turnoff, a lane leading toward our destination. A sign ahead tells us we are there—"Parking $10." $10? Here, high in the Cascade Mountains of Washington state, with nothing apparently around but a faded restaurant? Why would anyone expect to get $10 from people wanting to park in this Godforsaken place?

Well, there is a reason. This parking lot is where you leave your car if you want to see the remains of Cascade, a ghost town from about the same era as Bodie, but as unlike it as night and day.

We ease the car into its parking place, noting that no one else is there. Outside, a steady mist enswirls us as we get out of the car. We turn, following the signs to the remains of Cascade. The mist turns into a drizzle. Our feet paddle in puddles as we take the trail into the overgrown greenery that apparently surrounds Cascade.

Moving stalwartly along the trail, we fight the overgrown trees and bushes that brush water against us as we move into the ghost town. There is greenery everywhere. There are houses nowhere. Where, oh where, has Cascade gone?

There, in the overgrowth three feet off to the left, is a small sign. Moving closer, we read it. It tells the story of a particular building that occupies this site. Looking closely, pushing the bushes aside, we see a ruined foundation, rotted logs, a decayed roof now resting on the ground. I take back "occupies this site." "Occupied this site" is more accurate.

Moving further on the trail, pushing the all-too-wet bushes and trees aside, the story is repeated over and over again. A sign tells us of a building that occupied the side. Nothing but ruins remain. The drizzle and the state of disrepair tells us that very little of Cascade is going to be here in another few years.

The silver mining ghost town of Cascade is nearly gone, now. No well-preserved wooden buildings; no curtains rustling in the windows; nothing but the signs and the $10 parking lot to tell us that something important once happened here.

The concept of a ghost town is the same, whether we are in the dry Sierras or the moist Cascades, we begin to see. But the reality of those ghost towns is vastly different.

Computing is the gold and silver rush of the last half of the 20th century.

As with any mineral rush, there are some who get rich quick, being in the right place at the right time, carrying away riches beyond belief. And there are those who toil just as hard, but come away with virtually nothing. This book has been about the latter.

The residue of the gold and silver rush is the ghost town. People came, lived and laughed and loved, and moved away when the minerals played out. There was nothing about the site to cause others to come in their places. Whatever the miners left behind remains, ravaged by time and the elements, but still there.

Computing, on the other hand, is largely about concepts. When a computing company fails, it leaves behind no tailings, no environmental damage, no houses, no towns. What it leaves, instead, are memories. And those memories are as different from one another as Bodie is from Cascade.

The people of the late 21st century will not be able to get in their cars and drive to the middle of nowhere to see what remains of the exciting computing rush that captivated nearly everyone a century before. It is difficult to imagine that Silicon Valley or Silicon Forest or the Boston Beltway will be left as ghost towns in the same way that Bodie and Cascade were. It is difficult, in fact, to imagine that the computing rush will ever end. Even those people caught up in the failure stories we have included in this book have gathered themselves up, by now, shaken off the patina of failure, and moved on with their computing lives.

Early in this book I gave you several reasons why I wanted to share failure stories with you, my reader. I told you there that failure was a learning experience; that it was fun; that success was, by contrast, transient; and that failure never quits happening.

There is another reason why I write about failure. It is time to share it with you here.

Failure is poignant. It is captivatingly sad. The sadness is in some ways exquisite. Humans have striven in these stories. They have failed, of course. But, like the miners of a century and a half ago, they have chosen to be caught up in the most powerful movement of their time. The failures these stories tell us are far more exciting than the equivalent stories of those who did not choose to get caught up in the computing rush.

It is important to me, in capturing these stories, to make sure that the memories of the computing rush live on. After all, there are unlikely to be ghost towns. It is these words on these pages that commemorate what happened here . . .

. . . in the Computing Rush that characterized and consumed the last half of the 20th century!

Index

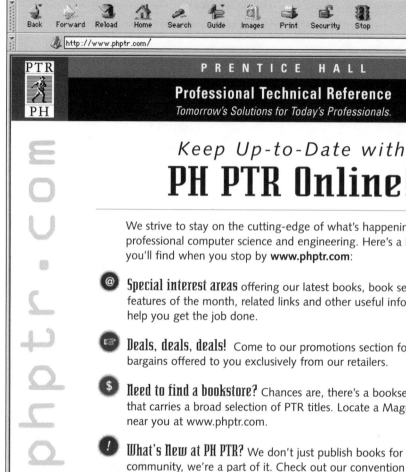